A JOURNEY
WITH
JESUS

Biblical Reflection on God, Faith,
Ministry, And Tradition

A JOURNEY
WITH

Biblical Reflection on God, Faith, Ministry, And Tradition

Richard Gribble, CSC

ARPress
ILLUMINATING IDEAS
EMPOWERING VOICES

ARPress
45 Dan Road Suite 5
Canton, MA 02021

Hotline: 1(888) 821-0229
Fax: 1(508) 545-7580

Ordering Information:
Quantity sales. Special discounts are available on quantity purchases by corporations,associations, and others. For details, contact the publisher at the address above.

Printed in the United States of America.

ISBN-13:	Softcover	979-8-89330-247-9
	eBook	979-8-89330-246-2

Library of Congress Control Number: 2024901764

TABLE OF CONTENTS

DEDICATION

The Christian journey of faith is never traversed alone. On the contrary, while our relationship with the Lord Jesus is personal, we walk with fellow travelers toward the common goal of eternal life with the Lord. I have been privileged to have many excellent "mentors," people who through their words and actions have been models in living a faithful and purposeful Christian life. Among the many for whom I am grateful, none rank higher than my parents, Richard and Dorothy Gribble, both of whom some time ago completed their journey and now rest with the Lord. It is appropriate, therefore, that this monograph be dedicated to them. May the road they showed me to walk be a model to others as well through the reflections in this book.

INTRODUCTION

The constitutions of the Congregation of Holy Cross, my religious community begin: "Come, follow me. It was the Lord Jesus calling us." These words were inspired by those of the gospel evangelist who quoted Jesus in his initial call to the apostles: "Come follow me and I will make you fishers of men." (Matthew 4:19) We recall that Peter and his brother Andrew, James and his brother John "immediately" left family and livelihood and accepted the invitation of Jesus. Quite obviously, the call of the Lord must have been powerful and his personality truly charismatic for these men to change their lives immediately and become the disciples of a man who was basically a stranger. Their acceptance of the invitation of Jesus initiated for them a journey. Initially they walked alongside Jesus, listened to his words of instruction, challenge, and compassion, and witnessed his numerous acts of kindness. Some invitations were miraculous, others somewhat routine, but all oriented toward a new way of thinking and acting. Certainly, these first followers of Jesus Christ had no idea what their acceptance of his invitation would entail. Not only were they leaving behind everything they knew, but their response to Jesus' call also led them to journey to foreign lands through their newfound responsibilities to preach the Lord's gospel message. Eventually, their response led to martyrdom. Remarkably, they were able and willing to answer the call and to initiate a lifelong journey with Jesus Christ.

Since the time of Jesus, Christians have been making a similar commitment to journey with the Lord. While few of us recall the event, on the day of our baptism we gained the privilege to walk with Christ throughout our lives. This commitment was, of course, made for us by our parents and godparents, but hopefully that message was communicated to us as we grew from youth into adulthood, not only by those who spoke for us on the day we entered the Church, but through education, the example of others, and our own determination to meet the various commitments of life. As we have learned along the journey of life. Every endeavor that brings privilege incurs significant responsibility. Thus, while we didn't realize it at the time of our baptism, nonetheless, we were commissioned that very day to journey with Jesus, by living a life of commitment to the ideas and principles he taught in his public ministry. We agreed to walk with Christ and do what we can, based on the talents and opportunities provided in life, to build the Kingdom of God in our world. That was the initial call of the apostles; it is the same invitation we accepted.

The journey we undertake with the Lord is not one that can be adequately negotiated without proper preparation and sustenance along the way. Our initial preparation was given us through our parents in their role to be the primary educators of their children in every aspect of life, including the faith. Their fidelity to each other, their family, responsibilities in life, and most especially to God, placed us on the proper path. Additionally, during the years of our youth, we had the privilege of education to enhance the foundation given to us at home. There came a time, however, when we needed more. Possibly we had forgotten some of the foundational principles, or maybe we somehow got off the proper path and needed fraternal correction. In other cases, we simply needed to update and reanimate the ideals enshrined in our initial Christian commitment to God.

The reflections in this volume seek to assist Christians to re-energize and possibly reawaken the basic principles upon which the Christian faith is founded. Additionally, the essays that follow can inspire us to fulfill our Christian responsibilities more fully and faithfully. To meet this goal, one must follow a basic pattern. First, Christians must consider and demonstrate gratitude for the God who gave us life and provides for our daily sustenance. Thus, Part I of this volume presents reflections on the goodness of our God. Next, realizing that God is with us every step of the way, it is essential that we reflect upon various challenges that the Christian life entails. Therefore, Part II provides reflections that address the many challenges of being followers of Jesus Christ. Reminding ourselves of the goodness of God and the challenges the Christian life presents, leads us directly to the basic Christian vocation to minister, to do what we can to build the Kingdom of God in our world. Thus, Part III, "The Challenges of Ministry," presents essays that address this basic Christian responsibility. Ministry is a general requirement for those who follow Jesus, but this is not an easy proposition. Thus, assistance to meet this goal is important. Part IV, "Teachings and Traditions," presents a "refresher course" for many of the basic Church teachings, those derived from Scripture and Sacred Tradition. Lastly, Part V "Saints: Past and Present," illustrates the lives of men and women who can serve as exceptional examples of Christians who took up the mantle to journey with Jesus, understanding the privileges and meeting the responsibilities as contemporary disciples of the Lord. Readers are encouraged to read and reflect upon one or two of the short essays at each siting, rather than read a series of reflections. Such a method will provide an avenue for daily or periodic spiritual reading.

It is my hope that these reflections will be a source of inspiration, as well as instructive, helping all who bear the name of Jesus Christ to walk more faithfully and completely on their journey with him. What a privilege we have been given to be disciples of Jesus Christ. Realizing that privilege, may we be inspired to meet our responsibilities in our daily walk, our daily journey with the Lord.

Richard Gribble, CSC

PART I: THE GOODNESS OF GOD

INTRODUCTION

Christianity teaches that God is omnipotent, omniscient, all loving and full of compassion. If we did not believe this, there would be little reason, other than fear, to follow an inanimate being whom we cannot physically sense. Sometimes, however, the busyness and vicissitudes of the world, along with the reality of much suffering and apparent injustice, prompts us to question our basic assumptions of God. The classic question of theodicy, "Why do bad things happen to good people?" challenges the idea of an all-loving God who wants nothing but good for humanity. While the dynamism of the natural world that God created can explain the reality of earthquakes, hurricanes, cyclones, and similar natural disasters, we still ask why God allows such things to happen? Similarly, we wonder why innocent people suffer and die for no apparent reason. Again, humanity's poor use of the great gift of free will can explain the inhumanity we perpetrate against each other. Still, the question of God's apparent inaction to prevent such horrific acts, prompts people to ponder and question the awesomeness and goodness of God.

The reality that people do suffer unjustly and the apparent truth that God has distanced himself from humanity, must be countered by the truth that God walks with us, present in both our daily triumphs and our defeats. The popular poem "Footprints," reminds us that when we believe the Lord has abandoned us, and we are walking

1

through life alone, it is at these precise times of difficulty that the Lord is carrying us, helping us to get through to the other side, to see the light at the end of the tunnel.

The reflections in Part I: "The Goodness of God" help us to straighten out our, at times, battered image of God, and realize what God does for us daily. God's generosity is found in his acceptance of all people, his setting out a plan for our lives, and seeking to transform them, placing us on the proper track and in the correct direction that leads to eternal life. The journey is long and difficult, but our good and gracious God is always present, if we have the eyes of faith necessary to find him.

ACCEPTING THE UNACCEPTABLE

Today people throughout the world refer to the Hawaiian Islands as "paradise." Visitors come to enjoy the plush beaches, the warm weather, and the friendly atmosphere that have become trademarks of the islands. In the mid-nineteenth century, however, Hawaii, especially the island of Molokai, was not so inviting. The northwest section of this little island was home to victims of Hansen's Disease, commonly known as leprosy. People from throughout the world were ferried to this spot by ships that were more like prisons than vessels of transportation. Because lepers were believed to be highly contagious, the ship did not dock. Ship captains maneuvered sufficiently close to shore so that the unlucky passengers had at least a chance to make it to land. Passengers were thrown over the side. Those who could swim made it to shore, but many drowned.

A small settlement, Kalapapa, was started on the island by the lepers themselves. Their daily existence was one of true misery as they slowly, day-by-day and one-by-one succumbed to the debilitating and disfiguring effects of their common affliction. The outside world cared little for the plight of these people. Molokai's isolated location was a perfect spot, it was thought, to keep these people away from society.

There was one man who cared, one person who was willing to demonstrate that God cared for all, including those with leprosy.

3

Joseph de Veuster, a Belgian missionary priest who took the religious name Damien, came to Molokai in the early 1870s to minister to those who had been abandoned by society. Damien was not only the priest of the settlement, but he was also the doctor, social worker, and possibly most importantly the friend of all in the Kalapapa settlement. Daily Father Damien attended to the needs of his brothers and sisters. He dressed their wounds, dried their tears, listened to their stories, and prayed with them and for them. Each Sunday in his sermon Father Damien began, "You the lepers of Kalapapa... ." His message spoke to the people of how the power of God was with them in their time of trial. God would always remain faithful for he could act in no other way.

One day, after many years of labor among the lepers of Molokai, Father Damien mounted the pulpit to address his congregation. His usual opening contained a subtle but very important difference. He began, "We the lepers of Kalapapa ... ." Father Damien had become one with the people he served in every way. Damien de Veuster died in April 1889, a victim of the very disease that had claimed so many to whom he ministered faithfully. He was canonized by Pope Benedict XVI on October 11, 2009.

Father Damien was a minister of God who accepted people for who they were. He was not concerned that they were sick or had been judged by society to be unworthy of care. He realized that all who seek God, listen to his voice, and do their best to carry out the Lord's commands are members of God's family. All can be brothers and sisters to the Lord.

The life and ministry of St. Damien is a good example of God's work as we hear related in the Scriptures. In the Gospel of St. Luke (15:1-10) we hear of the compassion and patience of the Lord. Jesus tells us that the mercy of God is like the shepherd with 100 sheep. If one sheep goes astray it seems illogical to leave the 99 and go in search of the one. It seems foolish to jeopardize the whole for only one. But God defies the logic of humans. God goes after the one so that as Scripture says, "None will be lost." God created us to be with him forever; thus, God never tires in his endless pursuit of our souls. And, lest we forget, God rejoices over the lost one who returns. In the same Gospel passage Jesus gives another analogy of God's mercy with the woman and her lost coin. A celebration in heaven occurs each time the lost is found. God will never give up on us!

Salvation history many times describes how God's people turned away from the Lord, yet God is always there to welcome us back. The Hebrew Scriptures are filled with episodes of unfaithfulness to God. One fine example is when the Israelites forgot all that Yahweh had done for them in their deliverance from Pharaoh and worshiped the golden calf (Exodus 32:1-20). Although God was very angry with the people, he forgave their great sin; he would never abandon them.

We might ask how God can accept what others reject? How can God continually say yes to us, as individuals and as community, when society says no? The answer, of course, is that God is full of mercy and compassion. We might ask, why are we worthy of such treatment? What did we do to deserve such an honor to be in God's presence? The answer quite simply is that we have done nothing to earn such beneficent treatment. God accepts us the way we are today, with our faults, our problems, our hang-ups, and our sin. St. Paul is the perfect example of how God cares for and guides us. He was a zealous and well-educated Jew who did everything he could to wipe out the New Way of Jesus and his followers. Yet, God had plans for Paul, after his conversion, Paul, who did not feel worthy for his mission because of his actions against the fledgling Christian community, nevertheless became the great apostle to the Gentiles. God did not count his sin against him; rather the Lord forgave Paul and used him as the primary vehicle to bring Christianity to the Eastern Mediterranean world.

God accepts us as he accepted the Israelites, the lost sheep and coin, as he accepted Paul. We are acceptable as we are, without reservation. There is nothing, absolutely nothing that can keep us from God's love. As Paul wrote to the Romans, neither height nor depth, neither angels nor principalities, not even death can separate us from the love of God manifested in Jesus. (Romans 8:38-39) We might think ourselves unworthy, that God could never accept us, but God accepts the unacceptable.

Since God accepts us, should we not be more accepting of others? Should not the parent accept the son or daughter who goes astray but returns? It is true that correction may be required; change may be necessary. But we still need to accept one another, no matter what has happened. Young people should be more accepting of one another. Rather than keeping people at a distance and only associating with those who think and act as we do, we need to reach out and say welcome in word and deed to those who may be different than us. Spouses must be accepting of the foibles of each other. We need to be more accepting of differences in our society. We are different by race, ethnicity, social status, and religious preference, but we need to find acceptance, not division. We need to welcome others so that as Jesus has said, "That they may all be one. As you, Father, are in me and I am in you, may they also be in us." (John 17:21).

God the ever merciful and compassionate one stands ready for our return. God accepts us as imperfect as we are. God does not seek perfection in us. God asks that we strive each day to be better and, thus, approach the perfection which is God's alone. Yes, God accepts the unacceptable. The question remains, are we willing to do the same? Each of us must answer!

THE AMAZING POWER OF GOD

ower is a concept which can be experienced in two different ways. The power of physical things is readily visible, measurable, and limited. Anyone who has been on a ship at sea, especially during a storm, knows that the ocean possesses great power. Ships of great tonnage are tossed about like plastic toy boats in a bathtub. Rockets send satellites and humans into space; planes, trains, and automobiles carry us to and from work, recreation, and church. The ocean and these vehicles each possess a measurable and limited amount of power which can be harnessed for the betterment of humankind.

There are forms of power, however, which are subtle, defy measure and limit, and yet many times possess greater strength than physical sources. Think of the power of suggestion. How is it that the mere presence of tobacco, alcohol or drugs to the addict presents such a temptation? Ideas planted as seeds in the minds of people can be very powerful and influential as well. Infamous twentieth-century dictators such as Josef Stalin and Adolph Hitler began their reigns of terror by promoting ideas that attracted a following. The power of words, both aural and written, defies measure and limit. Martin Luther King, Jr. stirred the hearts of African Americans when he proclaimed at the end of his famous, "I Have a Dream" speech at the foot of the Lincoln Memorial during the August 1963 March on Washington,

"Free at last, free at last, thank God Almighty, we are free at last!" Less than three years earlier, John F. Kennedy had challenged the American people to act in his inaugural address stating, "Ask not what your country can do for you, ask what you can do for your country." It was the words of Abraham Lincoln, written on the back of an envelope and delivered in a quick five-minute address when dedicating the Gettysburg National Cemetery in November 1863 that have become for many the foundation of American democracy, "That government of the people, by the people, and for the people shall not perish from the earth."

Power can be confined and measured, or it may defy any quantifiable bounds, but power in all its forms moves us, in mind, soul, or physical body from one point in life to another. It is the operative power of God, which possesses no limits, and can be felt and experienced, but at the same time can be so subtle that it does not appear to be present. Yet, this power controls our world through creation, redemption, and sanctification. It is God's action in the world, the powerful and subtle, which if understood and heeded can bring our world greater wholeness and unity in imitation of the oneness of God.

God's power was first seen in creation. The Lord's work in creating the world was not an isolated action that happened at one time and then ended. Rather, the creation story of Genesis recurs daily as the world renews itself. The changing of the seasons, the daily weather patterns, and the dynamic nature of our earth all demonstrate how God's creative power continues to operate in our world. God's power in creation is readily visible in the beauty which surrounds us; it is a gift made for the enjoyment, care, and use of God's greatest creation, humanity.

God's power and action was next seen in the redemptive life of Jesus Christ. In his life as teacher, miracle worker, and reconciler, Jesus taught us how to live, to love, and to grow in God's grace and providence. Through the paschal mystery, the passion, death, and resurrection, Jesus showed us that it is only through death that we can find eternal life. Jesus' total self-sacrifice was the model we need to imitate in our relationships with each other. This example of God's power is nearly invisible and is totally unmeasurable, yet it is the essential action of our Christian call to discipleship and to the paradox of the cross. Dietrich Bonhoeffer, the famous Lutheran theologian and pastor, put it well in *The Cost of Discipleship* when he said that when God calls one, he calls that one to die. Jesus made his teaching crystal clear, "Unless a grain of wheat falls to the ground and dies it remains just a grain of wheat, but if it dies it produces much life." (John 12:24)

The third manifestation of God's power in our world is the work of sanctification in the person of the Holy Spirit. After the resurrection Jesus commissioned his apostles, "As the Father has sent me, so I send you." (John 20:21) It was only later, on the day of Pentecost, however, that the Apostles understood what the commission meant, for it was on that day that the Holy Spirit, God's Spirit present in the world, came in a special and powerful way to lead and guide, to enlighten, and to strengthen us for the daily tasks of our lives. It is the Spirit of God acting each day which brings light to God's creation and renewal to the faith planted like a seed by Jesus, which must be watered and nurtured.

God's power is all about us--it can be seen, felt, and experienced. God's creative, redemptive, and sanctifying action in the world eludes bounds and measurement; it is a gift provided by our loving Father to his greatest creation. Yet, unlike all physical manifestations of power, both those in nature and those with human origins, God's power is not thrust upon us in a way that gives us no choice. Like all God's gifts, we can accept or reject God's power. We can abuse God's creation and destroy its potential for future generations. We need not be saved; we can ignore Jesus' teaching and example. God does not place us in a strait jacket and demand compliance, rather God always gives us a choice; the decision is ours to accept or reject God's grace.

In a similar way God's Spirit of direction can be ignored and the opposite path taken. God may suggest one road, but we may find that journey too much for us today. God does not give up, however. Francis Thompson's immortal poem, "The Hound of Heaven," says we can flee, but God is always with us:

I fled Him, down the nights and down the days;

I fled Him, down the arches of the years;

I fled Him down the labyrinthine ways

Of my mind; and in the midst of tears

I hid from Him, and under running laughter.

God is relentless in his pursuit of us. If we ignore the direction or call today, God will knock again tomorrow. But the burden to respond is upon us. As the Book of Revelation (3:20-21) states, "Here I stand, knocking at the door. If anyone hears me calling and opens the door, I will enter his house and have supper with him, and he with me. I will give the victor the right to sit with me on my throne, as I myself won the victory and took my seat beside my Father on his throne." God knocks on the door to our heart; it is our responsibility to answer.

The power of God in all its forms stands ready to embrace us and provide our daily sustenance. All God asks for these abundant gifts is trust and the patience to believe in their possibility. It was the physical power of propulsion which created our "it's a small world" syndrome by making travel swift and simple. It was the power of words that challenged us to overcome oppression, contribute to our nation, and promote the democratic rights of life, liberty, and the pursuit of happiness. It is the power of God, however, with its actions of creation, redemption, and sanctification that has given us our world, taught us how to live, and guides our every action. May we respond to God's power and action in the world. Let us live the faith given us by Jesus, and guided by the Holy Spirit, proclaim in our words and actions the power of God in our lives.

GENEROSITY: THE HEART OF GOD

Mayor Fiorello LaGuardia of New York, who served during the years of the Great Depression and the whole of World War II was one of the most colorful characters in the city's history. People called him "the Little Flower," due to his short five feet four-inch frame and his custom of always placing a carnation in his lapel. He did all sorts of "crazy" things that endeared him to the people of the city. He often rode on fire trucks to emergencies and accompanied the police when they raided speakeasies. He was known especially for his generosity. He often took entire orphanages to baseball games and when the New York newspapers went on strike he took to the radio waves and read the Sunday comic strips to children.

One incident provides an excellent illustration of how he cared and demonstrated generosity best. One bitterly cold night in January 1935 LaGuardia showed up at the night court in one of the city's poorest wards. The mayor dismissed the judge for the evening and took his place on the bench. Within a few minutes a women, tattered, dirty, and obviously desperately poor, was brought before him, charged with stealing a loaf of bread. She told the mayor that her grown daughter's husband had deserted the family, her daughter was sick, and her grandchildren were starving. The story did not impress the shopkeeper who refused to drop the charge. He told LaGuardia,

"It is a bad neighborhood, your Honor. She must be punished to teach others a lesson."

The mayor sighed and said to the woman, "I must punish you. The law makes no exceptions. Ten dollars or ten days in jail." Even as he announced the sentence, the mayor was drawing from his pocket a $10 bill that he tossed into his hat and began to pass through the court room. "Here is the ten dollars fine which I now remit. Furthermore, I am going to fine everyone in this court room fifty cents for living in a city where a person must steal bread in order that her grandchildren can eat. Bailiff, collect the fines and give them to the defendant."

The following day the New York newspapers reported the $47.50 was turned over to a bewildered woman who had stolen a loaf of bread to feed her starving grandchildren, fifty cents of the amount being contributed by the red-faced grocery shop owner who pressed charges. Some ninety petty thieves and New York police officers, all of whom also paid their fifty cents, gave the mayor a standing ovation.

Mayor LaGuardia was a generous man who taught others the need to be generous toward their sisters and brothers. God is ever generous, providing all that we need in all circumstances, to do what needs to be done and to continue the Lord's work in our world. Scripture provides ample examples of how God's generosity is overflowing since it lies at the heart of God's presence in the world.

The generosity of God is manifested strongly in the Exodus story, which is most assuredly one of the most significant events in Jewish history. In this realm, God's generosity began by raising up Moses to be the great deliverer of the Israelites. He was drawn from the water and raised in the family of Pharaoh as if he were his son. When Moses began his effort to free the Israelites, God sent a series of ten plagues, including the death of the firstborn, both humans and animals, so that Pharaoh would get the message, "Let my people go!" God opened the Red Sea to allow the people to escape; he sent a cloud by day and a pillar of fire by night to guide the people to their promised home. Moreover, God provided physical sustenance, water, quail, and manna, so the people could continue their journey back home. God's generosity continued to be manifested throughout the historical periods of Israel and Judah, sending prophet after prophet with a general message of the displeasure of God concerning much of what the religious elite was doing.

Clearly, the greatest example of God's generosity was his willingness to send his Son, divine, but human like us in all things but sin, into the world. During his public ministry Jesus generously shared everything with those who walked in his footsteps, heard his words, and followed his lead. His generosity was manifested in restoring life and health to some, providing food to those who are hungry, forgiveness and reconciliation to those who had sinned, and hope to those who had little or nothing. God's manifest generosity was experienced by each action he performed and word he spoke, even when he challenged others to transform their lives and believe in the Good News that he brought. The apex of Christ's generosity was the gift of himself in the Eucharist. As he says, "He who feeds on my flesh and drinks my blood has eternal life and I will raise him up on the last day." (John 6:54)

The generosity of God, the Father, Son, and Holy Spirit, demonstrated in Scripture challenges us to act similarly in our day-to-day activities with one another. To imitate the generosity of God and make it a central virtue of our lives, there are a couple of prerequisites. First, we must develop a generous and caring attitude that says we are no more important than any of our sisters or brothers. This is certainly true in the eyes of God, and it should be the same for all of us. Next, we must realize that we all have the responsibility to practice the generosity of Christ. Our baptismal call requires us to act. If we don't take our responsibility seriously to be generous and give, then we fail in our responsibility and the needs of others are not satisfied. These were the lessons that Mayor LaGuardia taught to those present in that

New York City court room. He taught the shopkeeper that he was no better than the woman. He realized generosity was the responsibility of all, and thus everyone present paid a fine. The lesson taught by Fiorello LaGuardia is the same presented in Scripture. God has been totally generous with us; we must be generous with others.

Generosity requires us to be converted, transformed in mind, heart, and action. St. Paul in writing to the Ephesians (4:23) put it this way: "Lay aside old ways and acquire a fresh spiritual way of thinking." Let us, therefore, seek the transformation we need in our lives to truly be generous and not merely symbolically.

The message of God's generosity and our need to follow the one who first loved us is depicted in a simple but profound tale. Once there was a beautiful tree that was situated at the main entrance to a city located in the desert. This tree had truly been touched by the hand of God, for no matter what time of year or the weather, the tree was always laden with delicious fruit. People entering and leaving the city always nourished themselves with the magnificent fruit the tree produced. Then one day a rather miserly man purchased the land around the tree. Still, people continued to refresh themselves with the tree's fruit, but this angered the man. He said, "This is my tree, on my land, purchased with my money." To prevent people from using the tree he built a wall around it. The local people complained but to no avail. Then one day, quite suddenly the tree died. The man was confused, but not the people. They told him, "When you give freely you have life; when you stop giving you die." Let us learn a lesson, be willing to give, and find life today and eternal life tomorrow.

GOD HAS A PLAN

Why do bad things happen to good people? This question passes through our minds periodically as we observe the world around us. Why, we might ask, are so many innocent people the victims of random violence; why do people who seem to be so positive and great contributors to society fall victim to accidents, sudden-death, or numerous other tragic scenarios? At times we might even ask ourselves, "Does God know what he is doing?"

It might not always be clear in our finite and limited understanding of life, but God does know what he is doing, and he has a plan that cannot be frustrated. His overall plan for the world is known as salvation history, the great story of how God chose the Hebrew people to be special, to be unique among all the peoples of the world. It was to the Hebrews that God revealed the initial message of salvation. This story finds its apex and climax in the life and work of Jesus Christ. We are inheritors of that great promise and thus God's great plan. Scripture must be a source not only of inspiration, but also a great consolation, for it clearly describes how God's plan for the world has been manifest from the time of Moses to the time of Christ. The challenge for us is to be transformed, moving away from the wisdom of this age and seeking the wisdom which only God can provide.

God's plan to save his people began with the great patriarch Abraham, but the Book of Exodus most clearly demonstrates that God had a preferential option for the Israelites who suffered as slaves under the rule of Pharaoh. The Israelites had enjoyed freedom and prosperity under Joseph and his immediate successors as rulers in Egypt, but we are told that the prolific nature of God's people was such a concern to the ruling Pharaoh that the people were oppressed and placed into slavery. Thus, God devised a plan, centered about Moses, but it necessitated the cooperation of the people. Pharaoh thought he could snuff out the Israelites by his order to kill all male children, but God's plan could not be frustrated. When Pharaoh ordered all male children to be killed, the midwives responded: "The Hebrew women are not like the Egyptian women; for they are vigorous and give birth before the midwife comes to them." (Exodus 1:19) Moreover, God's plan contained significant irony in the life of Moses. Not only does the great deliverer survive the scourge of Pharaoh, but he is discovered and raised as a member of the ruler's immediate family. Even more dramatic is that Pharaoh's daughter asks Moses' own mother to nurse the child in his infancy. God's plan to rescue the Hebrews from their oppression in Egypt could not be frustrated, even within the family of Pharaoh.

This theme of the maintenance of God's plan is clear in Psalm 124 as well. The psalmist writes that if God had not been on our side our enemies would have swallowed us. We read: "Blessed be the Lord, who has not given us as prey to their teeth. We have escaped like a bird from the snare of the fowlers; the snare is broken, and we have escaped." (Psalm 124:6-7)

God's plan for the world continued into the time of Jesus. The Lord chose his select twelve apostles and instructed them in many ways. Jesus came to the world to bring hope, love, and to demonstrate the presence of God all around us. Yet, central to his presence and message was the need for people to recognize who he was. Thus, he challenged his apostles, "Who do people say that the Son of Man is?" After receiving the basic response that people see him as a contemporary manifestation of the prophets of old, he says directly, "But who do you say that I am?" Peter's response, "You are the Messiah, the Son of the living God," (Matthew 16:16) demonstrates how God's plan for the world continued to move forward. God will not allow ignorance, inability, or the evil intentions of people to frustrate his plan of salvation for all.

For us to appreciate and fully participate in God's plan, we need to get on board. But this is not an easy proposition, especially in our twenty-first century first-world Western society where self-autonomy, individualism, secularism, and apathy vie for our attention continuously. St. Paul gives us the challenge we must accept to fully appreciate God's plan. He writes, "Do not be conformed to this world, but be transformed by the renewing of your minds, so that you may discern what is the will of God--what is good and acceptable and perfect." (Romans 12:2) Today's society claims that God's plan is antiquated and generally not applicable to our world but, quite obviously, this is completely contradictory to Christian thinking. How can we, the creation of God, think that our plans are better, clearer, and more important than those of God? On the surface we readily answer that God's plan is the proper one, but too often our words and our actions betray this reality. We think we know better than God; we become frustrated and even angry when things do not work out as we anticipate or hope. Sometimes we even think that God is no longer on our side, that the Lord has abandoned us. Such ideas are clearly misguided; Scripture makes this clear. Isaiah (49:15) proclaimed, "Can a woman forget her nursing child, or show no compassion for the child of her womb? Even these may forget, yet I will not forget you."

Yes, God has a plan, and it cannot be frustrated. While we might neither understand nor have the capacity to see beyond our finite limits, God's wisdom and power have been guiding the world from the outset and will continue to do so throughout all history. St. Paul

(Romans 12:33-34) had it right when he wrote, "O the depth of the riches and wisdom and knowledge of God! How unsearchable are his judgments and how inscrutable his ways! Or who has known the mind of the Lord? Or who has been his counselor?" We must trust that God truly knows what he is doing. There is a plan, God's plan, and each and every day of our lives it is manifest in our world.

The main problem is that too often we think we possess more wisdom than God. We fervently ask God for guidance and advice and then when God speaks, we refuse to listen. What God says, whether it comes in the voice of family and friends, events, or a deep-seated feeling, is often too challenging and we choose another route to walk. God gave us freedom to make our own choices, but too often we seek the easy path, the one of least resistance. However, Jesus suggests that the narrow, more difficult, and less traveled path is the only one that leads to life (Matthew 7:13-14).

We must develop more trust in God. Trust and confidence in God are not easy in a world which seeks quick answers to all questions and problems. We become impatient and too often wait in anticipation of the answer we want, not necessarily what God wants for us. Possibly the wisdom of the author of the Book of Proverbs (3:5) can help us: "Trust in the Lord with all your heart, and do not rely on your own insight." God truly does know what he is doing.

It is true; at times it is very difficult to understand our world. Things seem out of control on many occasions. However, upon reflection we often find the reason is that we are not in control of ourselves; God always has control. Let us be transformed by the renewal of our minds to a deeper and more profound trust in the abiding presence of God. Let us truly believe that God has a plan that cannot be frustrated. Yes, God truly does know what he is doing!

GRATITUDE TO GOD

"I need to speak to Father." From the periphery I heard this comment at the end of a class session. The one who spoke, Charlie, maneuvered his motorized wheelchair around a couple of desks so that he could speak with me. Charlie was a victim of cerebral palsy which rendered him a paraplegic, with limited hand and arm dexterity. "Do you want to speak to me privately or about something in class," I responded. "We can talk here; this is fine," was his reply. He went on to say, "I cannot believe how blessed I am and yet I have not responded as I should. You know, Father, how life with all its busyness, opportunities, and activities often takes us away from the basic foundations of our life. I love sports; I am really into it. Yet, I know there are things of higher priority. God has given me so much, yet my response has not been what it should be, especially recently. I want to thank you for helping me to return to the basics. The passion in your method of teaching has helped me to realize my need for God. I want to thank you for that."

Charlie's words struck me to the heart in two diverse ways. First, I was very happy that he was enjoying the class and that in some way what had occurred to date was beneficial for his faith journey. More importantly, however, I was powerfully and even shamefully made aware of my failure to adequately thank God for the abundant blessings in my life. Before me sat a young man in a wheelchair, a victim of a debilitating disease. Yet, despite his perceived handicap (he never viewed his condition in this way), which prevented him from physically doing many things that he enjoyed, especially athletics, he nevertheless was able to give thanks to God. He realized his faith was probably the greatest of those gifts and one that needed his attention.

My encounter with Charlie was providential for it prompted me, even forced me, to look seriously at how I demonstrate gratitude to God. It is a question that needs to be addressed by all Christians. In our daily prayer we often voice our needs and concerns to the Lord, asking his assistance to meet the needs or desires before us. But how often do we pray simply in gratitude for all that we have been given. The majority, who have all their faculties and can physically and mentally function in normal ways of society, often forget to recognize, appreciate, and give thanks to God who has provided the needs, and many times the desires, for all his children.

Gratitude is certainly a significant virtue that is addressed in various ways in the Scriptures, with thanksgiving to God being most prominent. The prayerful verses of the Psalms are filled with examples of gratitude expressed to God. Psalm 30:13 reads, "O Lord, my God, I will give thanks to you forever." Psalm 57:9 expresses a similar sentiment, "I will give thanks to you, O Lord, among the peoples." The power and beauty of Psalm 103:1-2, succinctly captures the idea of gratitude: "Bless the Lord, O my soul, and all that is within me, bless his holy name. Bless the Lord, O my soul, and do not forget all his benefits." Thanksgiving for God's wondrous deeds is expressed by the Psalmist in 75:1: "We give thanks to you, O God; we give thanks." Exclamations of praise to God are also found in the Psalms. We read in 147:7, "Sing to the Lord with Thanksgiving; make melody to our God on the lyre."

The expressive prayer of thanksgiving in the Psalms is presented in a more dramatic way in the New Testament. For many the most powerful story of Thanksgiving is found in Luke 17:11-19. While traveling between Samaria and Galilee ten lepers approached Jesus as he prepared to enter a small village. Collectively they call out, "Jesus, Master, have mercy on us!" Jesus responds by telling them to go and show themselves to the priests. While all ten are cured of their infirmity, only one, a Samaritan, returns to give thanks. In what must have been an exasperated tone, Jesus declares, "Were not ten made clean? But the other nine, where are they; was none of them found to return and give praise to God except this foreigner?" (Luke 17:17-18) While certain details of Luke's account are not provided, presumably the other nine were Jews. Thus, the one who stood most outside the purview of Israel, the one who probably was most persecuted and marginalized, was the only one who returned to give thanks.

My encounter with Charlie and the story of Jesus' cure of the ten lepers presents a consistent message with respect to thanksgiving. In both cases those, those from the perspective of society who are most afflicted, those who it would seem have the least for which to be thankful, are the ones who manifest thanksgiving the most. This should be a powerful message in a world where we presume far too much and make insufficient effort to express our thanks. For those who do not struggle in any overt way, it is easy to place life on "cruise control" and fail to acknowledge with gratitude what we have been given. The basic tools that make life as we know it "normal," functioning senses, intellectual reason and acumen, as well as basic physical mobility, are so much taken for granted that it seldom crosses our mind to express gratitude for them. The well-worn adage is true, "Familiarity breeds contempt." However, as soon as we find ourselves not able to do something we once did, due to physical impairment, age, or lack of opportunity, or intellectually express our thoughts and desires because of illness or the reality of time, then we begin to give thanks.

Gratitude to God as expressed through daily prayer, and equally importantly service toward our brothers and sisters, the Body of Christ on earth, must be our daily mantra. Expressing our thanks for the grander and more explicit things we receive is generally easily done. Such actions are normative for many. However, how frequently and how well do we express our thanks for the ordinary things, people, and opportunities of life that we enjoy each day? From the dawn of creation God has showered humanity with daily blessings, some magnificent and obvious, others small and subtle. Yet, have we even noticed many of God's gifts, let alone expressed in word and deed our gratitude for them? What has been our response to the love and generosity which daily rains down on the world, inspiring humanity to maximize its potential?

Jesus says in the Scriptures (Mark 2:17), "Those who are well have no need of a physician, but those who are sick; I have come to call not the righteous but sinners." Thus, Jesus reaches out; he awaits our response. The Lord stands with arms outstretched on the cross seeking only our movement toward him. We need God, the redemption of his Son, Jesus Christ, and the sanctification of their Holy Spirit. Hopefully, the realization that we are the sick, sinners, in other words those in need of God, will prompt us to be thankful, for the grand and powerful as well as the insignificant and subtle. Let us not be shamed into expressing our thanksgiving by those who, from the perspective of society have so little, but rather use their grateful actions and attitudes as the model for living a life of gratitude in every word and action of our lives. The Lord does not ask much from us, but he does provide everything we need. May our lives mirror his through the gratitude we demonstrate to God and to our brothers and sisters with whom we walk the road, the redemptive path that Jesus trod, today and to life eternal.

INSIGNIFICANT TO GOD?
– IMPOSSIBLE

A few years back a military jet was on final approach to land at an Air Force Base in California. The pilot had successfully completed his checklist and it was now time to lower the wheels and nose gear for landing. Pushing the button for the nose gear to deploy, he was shocked to see that it did not respond. He radioed the control tower requesting a flyby so that he could hopefully repair the problem. After some troubleshooting, he discovered that an electric relay was malfunctioning, necessitating that the device be bypassed for the nose gear to deploy. Looking about he saw some papers in the cockpit held together with a paperclip. He thought, "Maybe this paperclip will do the job." He straightened the paperclip and then bent it in such a way to bypass the faulty relay, allowing the nose gear to deploy. In the end the plane landed safely.

This incident, which clearly demonstrated the ingenuity and knowledge of the pilot as well as an ability to stave off fear, presents an additional theme present in our everyday lives. Contemporary society exalts the beautiful, powerful, wealthy, intelligent, and prestigious, that is the "jet planes" that fly above all others. We may be in one of these categories, but most of us are like the paperclip, people who might seem insignificant, but can play vital roles in our world. No one is insignificant.

In a similar way, Scripture demonstrates the reality that nothing is insignificant in God's sight. We are all broken vessels that regardless of our fractured nature still manage, with God's grace, to accomplish great things. In the Book of Judges, we read of the call of Gideon. When God commanded his servant to go forward and deliver Israel from the hand of Midian he responded, "But sir, how can I deliver Israel? My clan is the weakest in Manasseh, and I am the least in my family." (Judges 6:15) God assured Gideon that he was with him. Still, Gideon was unsure and felt unworthy. Not until a fire consumed the meat and unleavened cakes which Gideon had prepared for the angel of God did he begin to believe in his personal merit.

Some of the prophets as well perceived themselves to be of no account and thus unworthy for their ministry. Amos, who proclaimed God's word to the Northern Kingdom of Israel, once exclaimed, "I am no prophet, nor a prophet's son; but I am a herdsman and a dresser of sycamore trees, and the Lord took me from following the flock, and the Lord said to me, 'Go, prophesy to my people Israel.'" (Amos 8:14-15) Jeremiah, who prophesied to the Southern Kingdom of Judah just prior to the infamous Babylonian Exile, complained to God about his call, stating, "Ah, Lord God! Truly I do not know how to speak, for I am only a boy." But God responded, "Do not say, 'I am only a boy'; for you shall go to all to whom I send you, and you shall speak whatever I command you. Do not be afraid of them, for I am with you to deliver you." (Jeremiah 1:7-8) Isaiah, who also proclaimed God's message to Judah, lamented, "Woe is me! I am lost, for I am a man of unclean lips, and I live among a people of unclean lips." (Isaiah 6:5a) Despite their feelings of unworthiness, their belief that God could never use them for his purposes, all eventually did their duty; they came to realize that no one is insignificant to God.

The New Testament gives ample evidence of this same reality. The Roman Centurion who came to Jesus seeking a cure for his paralyzed servant did not feel worthy of Christ's presence in his home, proclaiming "Lord, I am not worthy to have you come under my roof; but only speak the word, and my servant will be healed." (Matthew 8:8) Even Peter, Jesus' chosen leader, felt inadequate before God. In his first encounter with the Lord, Peter is so amazed at the great catch of fish that he exclaims, "Go away from me, Lord, for I am a sinful man!" But Jesus assured him, "Do not be afraid, from now on you will be catching people." (Luke 5:8b, 10b)

A feeling of inadequacy or unworthiness before God is certainly understandable and helps us maintain our perspective and proper priorities, but too often our feelings paralyze us; we cannot properly move forward to accomplish what God expects of us. Poor self-image and past experiences of being "put down," cajoled or "written off" by others might lead us to despair, believing that as the world thinks of us so too God. But examples abound of how the Lord takes seemingly weak and unimportant people to accomplish his great work in our world. This is clear evidence that there is nothing insignificant with God. Yes, it is true; few of us will make the newspaper headlines as major players in contemporary society. We may consider who we are and what we do to be of little significance to others, including God. But we must be reminded of Jesus' own words when speaking about his care for us: "Are not two sparrows sold for a penny? Yet not one of them will fall to the ground apart from your Father. And even the hairs of your head are all counted. So do not be afraid; you are of more value than many sparrows." (Matthew 10:29-30) Truly in God's sight everyone is of inestimable value.

Contemporary society demands much of us. Many people feel like a small fish in a big pond; they are only one small cog in the machine of life. But we must remember the value of both the few players with names and the many that make the efforts of those more prominent people possible. Take the back off a typical wristwatch and look at all the various gears and moving parts. When telling time, we only see the face and the hands for the hour, minute, and possibly seconds. We never see all the small parts, without which, the watch cannot function. So, let us be satisfied to be only a paperclip or a small gear in a watch, for God can use us in ways only the Lord knows to achieve the ends and the purpose for which we were sent into this world. Let us rejoice that we have done our part in God's wondrous plan of salvation!

Jesus the Transformer
of Our Lives

One day a middle-aged woman entered a small antique shop to browse. As she walked through the aisles, she noticed an exquisite and beautiful vase. She thought to herself, "This will indeed beautify my home." She was pleasantly surprised that the vase was reasonably priced and, therefore, she purchased it. The proprietor wrapped the beautiful ceramic for safety and the woman returned home with great joy. She placed the vase on the coffee table in the middle of her living room. She noticed immediately that the vase, while indeed beautiful, did not go with the room as it was presently accented. Thus, she decided to "spruce up" the room. First, noticing that the walls were rather drab, she bought some paint and brightened the room with a livelier color. The windows in the room were a bit pitted and some were so dirty that they could not be properly cleaned, so she decided to have new windows installed. Then she installed clean new draperies, with a valance, to accent the windows even more. Since the chairs and sofa in the room were old and dilapidated, she replaced them as well. Finally, she stripped the beautiful wood floors, waxed them, and then purchased two throw rugs to place in appropriate places. She then looked about and exclaimed, "The whole room has now been transformed; the old has been cast out and the new has replaced it--all because of the beauty of the vase." The vase was indeed exquisite, but the woman discovered that the room was inconsistent with its great beauty. Thus, she transformed the room, making it as beautiful as the vase.

The story provides some important insight into our need to transform our lives around the beauty of Jesus. For those who profess the name Christian, Jesus, quite obviously, is the beautiful center, but too often the uniqueness and beauty that he brings is surrounded by an ugly veneer. John the Baptist certainly understood the beauty of Jesus and the necessity for those who would be his followers to transform their lives, to cast out the ugliness of our lives, that which was inconsistent with Christ's beauty and replace it with what was beautiful and consistent with his teaching. John proclaimed, "You brood of vipers! Who warned you to flee from the wrath to come? Bear fruits worthy of repentance. ... Even now the ax is lying at the root of the trees; every tree therefore that does not bear good fruit is cut down and thrown into the fire." (Luke 3:7b, 8a, 9) St. Luke tells us that tax collectors and soldiers asked John specifically what they needed to do to transform their lives and he responded with appropriate advice. (Luke 3: 10-14) Peter, who was transformed by the power of the resurrection, challenged the Jews to reform their lives: "And now, friends, I know that you acted in ignorance, as did also your rulers. In this way God fulfilled what he had foretold through all the prophets, that his Messiah would suffer. Repent, therefore, and turn to God so that your sins may be wiped out, so that the times of refreshing may come from the presence of the Lord." (Acts 3: 17-20a) Jesus himself taught the need for personal transformation. In a powerful scene, Jesus challenged the woman caught in adultery to transform her life. Christ had entered, and thus it was now necessary for her to transform her life to be consistent with the beauty she had received. He told her: "'Has no one condemned you?' She said, 'No one, Sir.' And Jesus said, 'Neither do I condemn you. Go your way, and from now on do not sin again.'" (John 8:11)

St. Paul observed this situation in his travels and warned the new Christian communities that he founded that there was a need to transform their lives, to cast out that which was ugly and inconsistent with Christ and replace it with virtues consistent with Jesus' teaching. He told the Colossians, "Seek the things that are above, where Christ is seated at the right hand of God. Set your minds on things that are above, not on things that are on earth, for you have died, and your life is hidden with Christ in God. He continued, "Put to death, therefore, whatever in you is earthly: fornication, impurity, passion, evil desire, and greed (which is idolatry)." (Colossians 3: 1-3) Additionally, he told them, "You must get rid of all such things—anger, wrath, malice, slander, and abusive language from your mouth." (Colossians 3:8) In other words, Paul told these new Christians that because the beauty of Jesus had come to them, they must transform their lives. The old must be cast out; it must be replaced by the new and beautiful things of Christ.

We, the contemporary disciples of Jesus, must learn to better appreciate the beauty that Christ brings to our lives and remove those things that negate or deny the loveliness that he brings. In our relationships with others, too often we are arrogant, extremely judgmental, or unaccepting of differences. All of these are forms of ugliness that tarnish the magnificence of Christ's presence in our life. At times as well, we feel superior to others, are convinced that our way of accomplishing tasks is the only possible way, or are unbending, completely inflexible in our opinions, attitudes and at times prejudices. These attitudes clutter our lives, making it difficult for the wonder of Christ to shine forth. Thus, we need to take stock of our lives, conduct an internal "house cleaning" and remove those actions, attitudes, or even failures to act from our lives. Taking this spiritual inventory of our relationship with God can at times be a perilous journey, but if we are to truly appreciate the beauty of Christ and all that he brings to us, our lives cannot be mired in things, people, and ideas that draw us away from the source of our salvation.

The vase transformed the woman's house, prompting her to spruce up the room, to appreciate the beauty of her new purchase. Similarly, through baptism and our Christian heritage and faith, we have the beauty of Christ, who walks with us each step of our daily lives. Let us, therefore, root out that which darkens our world, those things which might cause us to stumble and fall, and replace them with things of light that direct us toward Christ and eternal life. The daily journey may not be easy, but our goal of eternal life is worth every ounce of our effort.

FOLLOWING THE LEAD
OF THE SPIRIT

A group of young students was sailing from the mainland of Nicaragua to the island of Utila, some 40 miles to the northwest of that Central American nation. The students had never been there and when the trip began, they could not see the island. One young man asked if he could steer the boat. The captain of the vessel agreed telling him, "Just keep the needle of the heading at 335°." The young man was a bit wary, blindly going in a direction with no ability to see the destination. However, in a few hours they saw the island directly ahead of them. How did the student steer the vessel to the correct location without being able to see the destination? The answer is simple, he simply followed the directions that were given him. It's not always easy, but our life of discipleship is ultimately following the direction given by the Holy Spirit. We cannot see the destination, but we believe it is there. Following the direction provided by the Spirit will eventually bring us home to God.

Praise and worship of God must always be our highest daily priority, but most must admit that the direction of their prayer, quite naturally, is directed to Jesus, the Son of God and second person of the Blessed Trinity. After all Jesus became incarnate, lived among us, and provided a message that is presented in the Gospels and amplified throughout the New Testament. Our faith, Christianity,

31

bears his name. At times we invoke the Father, especially in our common recitation of the Lord's Prayer. Unfortunately, short shrift is often given to the Holy Spirit. Yet, it is God's Spirit, present from the beginning of time, but even more present now after the Pentecost event, who sanctifies our world as the presence of God.

The presence of the Holy Spirit in our world, while too often taken for granted, provided the guidance necessary for the nascent Church to coalesce, gain converts, and to spread throughout the then known Western world. After Christ's Ascension, the apostles and other disciples of Jesus were basically lost. Their teacher, mentor, and friend, the one upon whom they all counted, was no longer physically present. But Jesus promised to send the Spirit. Recall the conversation between Jesus and his apostles when he informed them about his forthcoming death, resurrection, and ascension. He told them, "For if I do not go, the Advocate will not come." (John 16:7) Surely the apostles were confused as to what precisely Jesus meant, but he kept his promise. On Pentecost, the Holy Spirit entered the lives of those first followers of "The Way," providing them with special gifts and making a significant impression upon the many visitors from various parts of the world who found themselves in Jerusalem at that time. The Spirit came to guide and to sanctify, but God's Spirit offered more. The Spirit came to direct our lives, placing us on the proper road that will lead to Christ and the Father, and eventually to eternal life.

Scriptural Themes of the Spirit

Scripture offers four major actions of the Holy Spirit in our world. The Spirit is clearly the presence of God in our world. The Pentecost event is most illustrative. Acts 2:1-13 describes how the Spirit was sent by God in a magnificent and powerful way, allowing un-learned people to speak in languages with which they were not familiar. The Spirit's presence is one of power and the bestowal of gifts, not only tongues, but many others as St. Paul describes in I Corinthians 12:4-11. The gifts of the Spirit include expressions of wisdom and knowledge, faith, healing, prophecy, discernment, languages, and the interpretation of those languages. We are told that "[T]he same Spirit produces all of these, distributing them individually to each person as he wishes." (I Corinthians 12:11) Acts 2:33 tells us that the Holy Spirit comes from the Father and is poured forth upon us.

The Holy Spirit is one who provides instruction and information. Wisdom 1:7 reads, "For the Spirit of the Lord fills the world, is all embracing, and knows what man says." The Spirit instructed Peter to follow three men sent to him from Caesarea. The Spirit brought the good news of the annunciation to Mary (Luke 1:26-38) and informed her of her cousin Elizabeth's pregnancy with the future John the Baptist. Jesus spoke to Peter, James, John, and Andrew about the end times and how persecution would be their lot. But he went on to say that they should not fear what they might say at that hour, for they will not be speaking, but rather the Holy Spirit will speak for them. (Mark 13:11b)

God's Spirit is also a source of great wisdom. Isaiah writes to the Hebrews after their return from exile stating, "The spirit of the Lord is upon me, because the Lord has anointed me; he has sent me to bring glad tidings to the lowly, to heal the brokenhearted, to proclaim liberty to the captives and release to prisoners, to announce a year of favor from the Lord and a day of vindication by our God, to comfort all who mourn." (Isaiah 61:1) God provided Isaiah with the knowledge he needed to carry on his ministry of prophecy. The Lord knew that the Hebrews needed a positive message, one that would help them as they returned to their homeland to rebuild their lives, institutions, and society in general. The Holy Spirit is described by Jesus as the manifestation of wisdom. Speaking to the disciples about prayer, Jesus says, "If you then, who are wicked, know how to give good gifts to your children, how much more will the Father in heaven give the Holy Spirit to those who ask him?" (Luke 11:13)

The Holy Spirit manifests the power of God. The famous "dry bones" passage of Ezekiel 37:1-14 is a good example. The prophet speaks metaphorically of the Hebrews in exile as dry bones in the desert that, through the power of the Spirit, will be joined, augmented by flesh and muscle, and eventually brought back to life. The prophet proclaims, "I prophesied as he told me and the Spirit came into them [the dry bones]; they came alive and stood upright, a vast army." (Ezekiel 37:10) Again, the annunciation story in both Matthew (1:18) and Luke (1:35) speaks of the power of God to make Jesus, the Word, the second person of the Blessed Trinity, incarnate in the womb of Mary. It was the power of the Holy Spirit, as Paul reminds us, that raised Jesus Christ from the dead (Romans 8:11). Additionally, the authoritarian power of the Spirit is described by Paul: "For God did not call us to impurity but to holiness. Therefore, whoever disregards this, disregards not a human being but God, who [also] gives this Holy Spirit to you." (I Thessalonians 4:7)

Following the Lead of the Spirit

The Holy Spirit's four-fold action presents both an opportunity and a challenge to all the faithful to follow his lead. Being present to others is a fundamental ministry for those who bear the name Christian. Today, the busyness of our world often pulls us away from this basic attribute of the Spirit and Christian action. We may think that presence is marked in quantity of time. Certainly, taking the time to be with people is extremely important, but quality rather than quantity is what is necessary. People generally do not ask for huge blocks of time, but rather for us simply to be present at important moments. This may mean visiting someone who is sick, down on his or her luck, in need of counsel or correction, or celebrating a triumph in life. However, presence can be as simple as listening to a person for five minutes. Generally, people do not expect remarkable answers, but simply hope we can slow down long enough to listen.

A wise priest once told me, "Ninety percent of community is just showing up." We must be present to others in imitation of the Spirit.

We are all called to provide instruction and information to others. This may be through institutional ways such as the classroom and preaching or formal ways such as public speaking and writing. Again, however, often the best lessons we have learned in life have come simply through example. Mother Teresa of Calcutta was not a great scholar, and did not teach in institutional ways, but her example provided both instruction and information internationally. How could one not learn from observing what she and her religious community collective have done through their ministry for the poor and destitute of the world. People are not neutral in their observations of us; they are either drawn closer to Christ or pushed further from him by what they hear and observe in us. The example we set is critically important and serves as a basic way to manifest the Holy Spirit's action of instruction.

How can we manifest the Spirit's gift of wisdom? It is true, I believe, that wisdom often comes with age; it is not a product of "book" learning but rather experiential. All people who have reached the age of maturity have had many experiences that have taught them important lessons. These lessons, some that are great and highly significant, others minor but nonetheless important, should be shared with others. We have certainly learned many important lessons from both the triumphs and failures of our family members as well as former teachers and mentors of various sorts. Sharing the wisdom that we have gained from our experiences in life can assist others to avoid certain pitfalls, learn how to properly negotiate various hurdles, and help others to travel a more direct path to Christ.

Exercising the Spirit's gift of power in our lives is an important action in judgment and prudence. All people have some power and authority, but priests and religious, because of their position in the Church, may have more than most Christians. Right judgment and prudent utilization of the power and authority they possess are critically important. These people have been placed in positions of authority and given certain "power" to build the Kingdom of God in our world. Unfortunately, there are far too many examples where authority and power have been utilized to dominate individuals or groups or to preferentially aid one at the expense of the whole. Thus, to utilize the power of the Spirit means to choose wisely in utilizing the authority and power we have, gifts that differ depending on position, opportunity, and judgment. The proper utilization of authority and power can bring much good to the Church and our world. It is necessary, however, to consider how we have used power and authority in the past, correct our mistakes as necessary, and continue forward in ways that will benefit the common good.

Conclusion

What does it mean to be guided by the Spirit? It is certainly true that we cannot see the Spirit and rarely, I suspect, are people granted the privilege of such direct contact, but we can look at Scripture and have a good idea of what it means to follow the Spirit's lead. We are called to be present to one another in positive ways, to instruct our brothers and sisters, especially through example, to teach others and provide wisdom from our own experience, and to properly exercise authority and power as it has been bestowed upon us. While it is understandable that our prayer is generally directed towards Christ, or in some cases to the Father, we must not forget the Holy Spirit, the sanctifier, who was sent by the Lord into our world to be God's presence. Following the lead of the Spirit will bring us home to God's promise of eternal life. St. Paul has described well, "What eye has not seen, and ear has not heard, and what has not entered the human heart, what God has prepared for those who love him." (I Corinthians 2:9)

Part II: The Challenges of Contemporary Christian Life

Introduction

Contemporary life is anything but simple and easy. Rather, with time things seem to be increasingly more complex. We never seem to have fewer things to do, only more. While technology appears to make tasks simpler and more rapid in their accomplishment, the expectation of others, especially employers and people who "want something" of us only seems greater. Today we are asked to be more productive, complete our tasks more swiftly, and be available, as the common dictum today says, 24 /7.

As with the world in general, the Christian journey is not easy, but then, Jesus never claimed it would be. On the contrary, he very clearly stated it would be a challenge: "If a man wishes to come after me. He must deny his very self, take up his cross, and follow in my steps." (Mark 8:34) The basic Christian commitment to journey with Christ has always been a great challenge, but today the trials are heightened. The expectations of society to conform to contemporary "norms," the abundance of options and opportunities that many possess, combined with the presence of an increasingly more secular-oriented society, present a challenging combination to the Christian life. Families are busy from sunrise to sunset. Children go to school, participate in sports, musical activities, and more. Most families find mom and dad both working outside the home to provide not only necessities, but the style of life to which many today have become accustomed. The loss of the concept of the sacred with the consequent rise of the secular is palpable; the reality is all about us. The rapidity with which these challenges have increased over the last half-century or so only exacerbates the daily challenge Christians face in our twenty-first century world.

Part II, "The Challenges of Contemporary Christian Life," presents reflections that address many of the challenges contemporary disciples of Jesus face. Rather than adopting the world and its fascinations, we are asked to adopt God's plan. Do we find our sustenance in the wisdom of the world or in God? Are the goals we set simply for the world we experience or for the eternal life that God has promised to those who believe? Do we understand our basic call to evangelize the nations by being disciples of Jesus Christ? These and similar questions are addressed herein. Hopefully, the challenges we face will never deter us, but rather serve as a catalyst to work that much harder to achieve the one and only goal that we need, a return to the God from whom we came. May the challenges of the Christian life today spur us on to greater accomplishments in our daily journey with the Lord.

ADAPTING TO GOD'S PLAN

It wasn't easy but adapting to life's circumstances allowed Golda Meir to achieve greatness. We remember her as the Prime Minister of Israel, who led her country during a period of great tension with the Arab world. From the time of her youth, Golda was not blessed, at least from the world's perspective, with physical beauty. As a young woman this was certainly a trial; she realized the need to develop aspects and virtues of her life that were more important than physical beauty. Thus, she developed her intellectual brilliance, political savvy, and mental toughness, which allowed her to stand as a star on the world stage, taking her place among the most prominent of world leaders of the 20th century. If she had "swept a man off his feet" by her physical beauty as a youth and gone in a different direction, the world would have lost a true political giant. Her ability to overcome what society might have termed an obstacle and adapt to the situation she found in life, allowed her to lead her nation and bring the world to a greater sense of peace.

Golda Meir's story can be applied in many aspects of life. Often, we observe situations where people with handicaps, such as being blind, deaf, or physically impaired have excelled because they were able to adapt and develop to a much higher extent than might be originally thought, certain skills, talents, and other aspects of the human condition that only compensated for the handicap, but more importantly allowed the individual to blossom in ways that made our world a better place. The famous composer Ludwig van Beethoven was completely deaf when he composed his famous ninth (chorale) symphony, arguably the most famous piece of classical music ever written. After contracting a childhood disease, Helen Keller was struck blind, deaf, and mute. Yet, not only did she graduate from prestigious Radcliffe College before many of her peers her age but became an international spokeswoman for those with handicaps. President Franklin Delano Roosevelt was in a wheelchair due to polio, yet he was the only person to serve in the White House for more than two terms, and successfully led the United States through the Great Depression and World War II

Adapting to new situations in life is described throughout the Scriptures. Noah was asked by God to drop what he was doing and build an ark, a massive undertaking to say the least, and to gather a male and female species of all God's creation to save them from the peril of the forthcoming flood. Abram was called by a God he did not know to leave his native land of Ur and travel with his family to a new land with the promise that he would be the father of a great nation. Many judges and prophets were asked to adapt to new situations to fulfill God's plan for their lives. Gideon perceived himself to be the least person in his family. Similarly, Isaiah felt unworthy of his call. Amos was a shepherd, yet he was called to be a prophet; Jeremiah had to negotiate out of a plot hatched to kill him.

The New Testament provides additional examples. Mary, I am sure, saw her future life as a wife and mother in the small village of Nazareth, but the Lord's invitation through the angel Gabriel to be the mother of God forced her to adapt. The first apostles, Peter, Andrew, James, and John were all fishermen and, most probably, were content with their lot in life. However, Jesus' call prompted them to adapt, go in a different direction, leading to the foundation of Christianity. St. Paul was making his mark with the Pharisaic Jewish community, doing all he could to wipe out the "New Way," but Jesus appeared to him on the road to Damascus, cajoling him to go in a different direction (Acts 9:1-9). What would the Christian world be today without the ministry of St. Paul, especially his letters and the basic theological principles they articulate? In all these cases, when the situation required the individual to adapt, great things were accomplished. Quite obviously, with faith in God and our own ability to adapt to the vicissitudes of life, all things are possible.

Life in general and ministry in the Church more specifically often requires us to adapt to the situation. In many cases we are initially caught off guard and may reject the new direction that our life has taken. We might become angry at God for what happens to us or blame our supervisor at work for decisions made that we consider wrong or detrimental. As with all decisions in life, we have two options. We can remain angry and disappointed, feeling that we have been wronged and wallow in our own pool of pity. We can cry out, complaining of the injustices in the world, especially those perpetrated on us specifically. However, there is another response, the response of Golda Meir, others in history, and that of the men and women about whom we read in the Bible, who were similarly challenged to adapt. The first option is, for the Christian, not truly operative. This is the position of surrender and defeat. The true Christian must, when circumstances require, be resilient enough to adapt to the situation, trusting that all we need, especially those things we perceive we lack, will indeed be provided. Recall the words of the author of the Book of Proverbs (3:5): "Trust in the Lord with all your heart, on your own intelligence rely not."

The contemporary situation, both in the world generally and the Church specifically, necessitates that we adapt to many different circumstances. Unfortunately, today many of our long-held work environments have changed due to technology; the recent Covid-19 pandemic transformed business in massive ways. In the Church ministries, whether they be parishes, schools, retreat centers, or other institutions are either closing or experiencing significant changes.

The loss of the Church's vitality within contemporary society forces those of us who remain active to adapt to the present need.

Adapting to the new path that the Lord provides is not easy. Most of us will not have to adapt as did Beethoven or Roosevelt; the change required generally will be more subtle. Nevertheless, for some adapting to the present reality, in the world and the Church will require patience and endurance.

The inspiring story of Heather Abbott, a survivor of the Boston Marathon bombing of 2013, can be illustrative of what is possible for those who believe and have the courage to continue to move forward despite the situation. For a few years Abbott and some of her friends had participated in a Boston tradition, Patriots Day. This group of friends attended the early start Boston Red Sox game at Fenway Park and, as the game was winding down, walked the relatively short distance to the finish line of the Boston Marathon, two of the annual events held on this Massachusetts holiday. On April 15, 2013, however, Abbott and scores of others were forced to adapt their lives in ways they never could have imagined. In the bombing Abbott lost part of her left leg. While one can only imagine the devastation in her life, she did not allow the situation to defeat her. In a graduation speech presented in May 2019 she provided from her own experience some excellent advice on the need to adapt. She described a threefold approach to transitions that are necessary to successfully adapt. First, she suggested that we need to realize that we cannot control everything that happens to us. Health issues arise and other events happen, oftentimes without warning. Understanding that we have no control over such occurrences in our life is essential. Second, Abbott advised that it was important to accept the reality that there will be times in our lives when we need to depend on others. Generally, we all like our independence; we want to help others. However, times will come when we must allow others to serve us. Lastly, she advocated the need to "pay it forward." If we need to adapt to continue as in the past, then we must use our time and energy to assist others who may be in the same position we once faced.

The Boston bombing in April 2013 forced Heather Abbott to move in a new direction. Eventually she formed the Heather Abbott Foundation, a donation-based organization that provides customized prostheses for those who have lost limbs. She would never have considered such work had she not been forced to adapt and move in a new direction. Certainly, many individuals will be assisted and brought to a greater sense of wholeness because Abbott was forced to follow another path.

Our journey to eternal life is certainly not in a straight line. We experience great triumphs and exhilaration, and the depths of despair and defeat. We are forced to negotiate some barriers and hurdles and at times must take detours that we never considered when we first set out on our trek. Adapting to the situation, while challenging and for many not desired, can bring the opportunity to fulfill part of God's plan of building the kingdom, but in a way we didn't anticipate. Let us, therefore, not run away from but rather engage the new directions that come our way. We can bring light and hope to others while simultaneously fulfilling God's plan in our lives.

OUR AVAILABILITY TO GOD

What is the greatest gift or talent a Christian can possess? Is it to exhibit compassion, be a good listener, teacher, or speaker? Is the answer to be a person of service in outreach to the poor and marginalized in our society? Is the greatest gift to possess significant faith? Certainly, all these answers at different times could be more than satisfactory, but the one gift that is essential and lies at the base of all of the aforementioned, and many others, is the gift of availability. If we are not available, then any gift we possess cannot be utilized. In fact, any great talent without availability in essence becomes a liability. God's availability to all of us has been demonstrated throughout salvation history and continues to be manifested each day. The question is, how available are we to God and God's people?

God's availability stands at the heart of the Scriptures. God is present to lead and direct, to guide and protect, to teach, and when necessary to correct. God's magnificent gifts, shared with humanity in every conceivable way, are only beneficial, however, because the Lord is available to us. God never hides from us; he is never absent. Rather, he is available as contemporary parlance says, 24/7. When the Hebrew people cried out to God, the Lord responded, sending great leaders and prophets to rescue the people from distress or to guide them back to the correct path. When in bondage in Egypt, the

Israelites cried out, and the Lord responded by sending the great deliverer, Moses, who led the people to the door of the Promised Land. When rival forces plagued the people with oppressing armies, God sent judges, such as Gideon, Deborah, and Samson, to restore order and bring victory to Israel. When the Hebrews needed good leadership to solidify their nation, God raised up David and then his son, Solomon, making Israel a light to the nations. Even when the Kings of Israel and Judah continually disobeyed God, even to the point of idol worship and oppression of the poor, God was available and sent numerous prophets who proclaimed God's message of both righteous anger and correct direction. Even after the infamous Babylonian Exile, God remained available by softening the heart of King Cyrus of Persia (Ezra 1:1-4), who mandated the return of the Hebrews to their homeland.

God's availability, manifested through Jesus Christ, is equally apparent. Jesus was present to all, reaching out to the poor and marginalized, and challenging the rich and the famous. When lepers, a hemorrhaging woman or Legion, a man possessed with many evil spirits, sought healing, Jesus was available. When the Samaritan woman needed someone with whom to discuss her life, Jesus was there (John 4:4-42). When justice needed to be served in the confrontation between the woman caught in adultery and Jewish religious leaders, once again Jesus was available to correct an injustice. When Jairus, the Roman centurion (Mark 5:21-24), Martha and Mary (John 11:1-43), or the widow of Naim (Luke 7:11-17) needed a physical cure, Jesus was available to grant their requests. Jesus was equally available to provide spiritual healing, granting Peter the opportunity to express three times his love for the Lord to atone for his three denials (John 21:15-19).

God's availability to humanity is compassionate, constant, and always positive, even when correction is necessary. God is available to correct our mistakes and place us on the proper path; he is equally present to soothe our pain and pick us up from our failures and, thereby, help us to overcome adversity. We recall Jesus' words, "Come to me, all you that are weary and are carrying heavy burdens, and I will give you rest. Take my yoke upon you, and learn from me; for I am gentle and humble in heart, and you will find rest for your souls. For my yoke is easy, and my burden is light." (Matthew 11:28-30)

God's availability to us cannot be questioned, but the reverse scenario provides a great challenge for us. How available are we to God and God's people? The Acts of the Apostles provide one of the most famous and significant examples of one's complete transformation to a total availability to God. Saul of Tarsus was a great persecutor of Christians; he was zealous in his desire and action to destroy the New Way followed by Jesus' disciples. Yet, when knocked to the ground and temporarily blinded by a great light from the sky, Saul (later Paul) heeded the challenge and completely transformed his life. It was a complete *volte-face*, a 180-degree shift in attitude and action. Paul instantaneously became totally available to God, leading eventually to his three great missionary journeys, his establishment of nascent Christian communities, and the composition of his famous letters, which serve as the foundation of Christian theology.

The Gospels also provide some important examples of people who were available to God. The evangelists report that when Jesus called the apostles, they "immediately" left their past life, as fishermen or tax collector, as well as their families (certainly in the case of Peter). They were available to the Lord. The woman with the hemorrhage, Bartimaeus, the blind beggar and even Legion made themselves available to Christ through faith. Each placed great faith in Jesus; they believed his words and in his power. It was their availability, their openness to Jesus, that brought the cure they desired. Stories abound of the sick and the marginalized who made themselves available to Jesus. Even the curious, such as Nicodemus, a member of the Jewish Sanhedrin, engaged Jesus in a conversation, an encounter that would have been impossible had the former not been open, that is available to Jesus.

God's availability to us and the clear evidence of how numerous people during the time of Jesus were available to him challenges us to ask how available are we to God? Our busy lives, which only grow more complex and diverse with time, present a major obstacle to our availability. We are so caught up with personal accomplishment or working for the "company" that we are not sufficiently available to God. What part of our day can God claim? Do we give God five minutes; do we give the Lord a full hour? Are we available to family members, friends, colleagues at work or neighbors down the street? We can become so consumed by our own agenda, one that is often driven by the competitive world in which we live, that availability to others, including God, is something difficult to fit into our schedule. Yet, if the gifts we possess are liabilities if not available to others, then what benefit have we brought to ourselves or the world? We must correctly set our priorities; availability must be at the top of our list. If we are not available and open, we will never be able to utilize properly the gifts God daily bestows upon each of us.

It might seem odd, but clearly the most important gift we possess is availability. And one thing totally unique about this gift is that all possess an equal amount of it. Surely our specific vocation, personality, time, and a host of other factors influence our availability. However, availability begins as an attitude and then is manifested in our words and actions. All have the common opportunity to be available to others; some because of their situation have more actual time or opportunities to manifest their availability. God is available to any of us at any moment; we are asked in reply to be open to God and to God's people. If we are courageous enough to take up the challenge and thereby demonstrate our availability, most assuredly our Christian journey will be enhanced and more importantly our reward in heaven will be great.

BAPTISM: THE CALL TO DISCIPLESHIP

" Jesus came forward and addressed them in these words: 'Full authority has been given to me both in heaven and on earth; go, therefore, and make disciples of all nations. Baptize them in the name of the Father, and of the Son, and of the Holy Spirit. Teach them to carry out everything I have commanded you. And know that I am with you always, until the end of the world!'" (Matthew 28:18-20) Jesus' words echo with a command, a privilege, and a challenge. The Lord has challenged us to go forward as disciples and share his message with others. As God's children through baptism, we are privileged to share his life, but this privilege does not come without the consequent command to go forward. Baptism, the sacrament which unites all Christians in one family also unites us in the common call to discipleship.

The concept of baptism as a rite is rather straight forward, but the responsibilities that come with this sacrament are more complex. We all know that baptism makes us children of God and all the privileges that come with this elect position. Most people are not equally knowledgeable, however, about what baptism requires, or possibly we refuse to accept the responsibility that comes with the privilege. Baptism is a call to discipleship - but what exactly is discipleship?

Discipleship may be defined in many ways, but I would like to suggest three principal aspects that are crucial. To be a disciple first means to be a follower. Through baptism we become followers of Jesus and the Church. Baptism next calls us to ministry, the work of a disciple. Lastly, discipleship requires that we become evangelists in response to Jesus' command to go and make disciples of all nations.

The process of being a follower of Jesus necessitates our total dedication to his principles and message. We cannot be a follower some days and one who goes it alone on others. Our mind must be fixed on the Lord. St. Peter puts it well, "This baptism is no removal of physical stain, but the pledge to God of an irreproachable conscience through the resurrection of Jesus Christ." (I Peter 3:21b) Baptism is more than an act; it is a promise. Whether we knew it or not our baptism bound us to Christ and the Church. Thus, our attitude must be such as to seek union, with God and God's people.

Following Jesus is not easy; nobody said it would be. St. Paul expressed this idea when he wrote, "In baptism you were not only buried with him but raised to life with him because you believed in the power of God who raised him from the dead." (Colossians 2:12)

Discipleship requires us to minister to God's people. The tendency for many is to think that only certain people are called to ministry; one must have a vocation for such work. All the baptized, however, are called to work in the vineyard of the Lord. As Scripture states, "The harvest is rich, but the workers are few; therefore, ask the harvest master to send workers to his harvest." (Luke 10:2) We are the workers; we are the Body of Christ. We are members of the priesthood of believers. Whatever our vocation, the single life, marriage and family, or religious life, we are all one through baptism. Again St. Paul has written, "It is one Spirit that all of us, whether Jew or Greek, slave or free, were baptized into one body."(I Corinthians 12:13a). As members of the one body, as brothers and sisters in the Lord, our ministry is a service to God and God's people.

Within the Body of Christ, we minister in specialized ways. Marriage places emphasis on ministry to spouse and children. Professionals can transform their daily work to ministry by an attitude of service to others. Single people also demonstrate ministry in their association with people around them. The ordained priesthood, a special invitation to discipleship, is a vehicle to minister in ways, if done well, which can touch many people. Priests, through the sacraments and preaching, minister to all God's people and provide a special face to the presence of God in our world. This is the essential work of discipleship.

Evangelization is another important aspect of discipleship. Jesus commands us to be evangelists, to go forth and spread his message. When we think of evangelization the image of the street-corner preacher comes to mind. Sermons of Hellfire and brimstone and selling the faith door-to-door are other popular images. Evangelization is practiced in these ways, but there are less overt and more common ways in which we bring others closer to God, which is the essential ministry of the evangelist.

Evangelization is practiced in the active life of the minister. As mentioned above, ministry and service are not optional works for the Christian; all are called to work in God's vineyard. How many of us have been touched by the works and service of others? When we see someone who reaches out to another, as Mother Teresa famously did, we are challenged to go the extra mile for those who need our assistance. The actions of others force us to act; their service becomes an instance of evangelization. Active ministry and service to others is something in which we can participate each day. There are formal ministries in the Church and the community, but more commonly service is performed in everyday events which few think is of any significance. Courtesy in our manner of life, calmness in a time of strife, using conciliation over argumentation in time of conflict are all ways of demonstrating service to others and ministry in God's Kingdom on earth.

Another important method of evangelization is the process of reconciliation. The ability to admit one's brokenness, especially before another, is an act of evangelization. How many times have we been inspired and had our hearts lifted by seeing another turn away from evil and begin a new path which leads to God? Baptism is a rebirth into the life of repentance. Scripture states that John the Baptist came as a precursor of the Lord to provide a baptism of repentance for the forgiveness of sins (Mark 1:4; Like 3:3, Acts 13:24). When one turns away from sin and begins anew, the value of such an act is incalculable. Repentance and reconciliation require courage and provide a challenge for others to seek a similar road in their lives.

Reconciliation as a means of evangelization and discipleship is most strongly seen in the Sacrament of Penance. The courage to honestly face one's human brokenness, imperfection, and sinfulness is of incalculable witness value to others. Like the reaction of the forgiving father in the parable of the prodigal son (Luke 15:11-32), we are moved in emotion and brought closer to God by the humility of a fellow human. Moreover, the sacrament itself, which celebrates God's forgiveness and our reconciliation with God's people, the Body of Christ, empowers us through a renewed spirit to bring God's message of love to all. Thus, reconciliation becomes a vehicle for evangelization.

Baptism as a call to discipleship is an active sacrament; it is anything but passive. This first sacrament calls us to be followers, ministers, and evangelists. We must live the vocation of holiness to which we have all been called. Our call is to be members with all the privileges which come with being part of God's family. Our membership gives us responsibility as well. We must go forth in an active manner to do God's work in our world. Baptism is the original call to a life which seeks to bring others closer to God. May the baptism which we all share, our common denominator in the faith, allow us to be disciples and show the face of God to others.

BE NOT AFRAID: LIVING IN A COUNTERCULTURAL WORLD

O n October 16, 1978, the date of his election as the 264th Supreme Pontiff, Pope St. John Paul II proclaimed to the world from the balcony of St. Peter's Basilica, "Do not be afraid; open wide the doors to Christ." For the next almost 27 years, Pope St. John Paul lived these words by demonstrating to all that we must never live in fear, but rather by embracing Christ we must find the courage to live in a world that often embraces values, principles, and ideas which are counter, even antithetical to those professed by Christ and his Church. All privileged to bear the name Christian have the obligation to fight secularism and the prevailing tendency to relativize all Christian teaching to a common denominator acceptable to society. The challenge that Pope St. John Paul II proclaimed and lived is indeed one that requires constant effort and daily vigilance. We are called to cast out fear, and to trust Christ to live as countercultural people in our contemporary world.

Evidence of Scripture

The Hebrew Scriptures provide numerous examples of people of faith who were asked to and successfully lived a life that was countercultural to their contemporary society. Although most people of his day transgressed God's law, Noah was faithful. Thus, God asked him to do a crazy thing, to build a huge ark and to house in it one male and female of each animal species. Imagine being asked to do such an irrational task; to say the least it would be difficult to carry out. But Noah was willing to accept the insulting words and possibly physical actions of those who saw his effort as ludicrous. He was willing to do something that no one else had done, to be completely countercultural, because the Lord had spoken to him personally. Even if there had been no one to ridicule him, still Noah's task was immense, certainly not one for the fainthearted or those who were not completely dedicated. Noah's ability to follow the command of God allowed creation to survive the great flood. (Genesis 7:1-8:22) Later, God came to Abram with a message and a command. He was asked to follow the instructions of an unknown God and move with his family to a new land. He was asked in essence to completely trust with no specific guarantees other than the promise that he would be the father of a great nation. But like Noah before him, Abram was able to take the crazy route, follow the countercultural path. In the process he became the first great patriarch of the Hebrew people and indeed became the father of a great nation. (Genesis 15:1-21)

The work and the message of the Hebrew prophets was equally countercultural. While people today, when considering the concept of prophecy, think of future predictions and forecasting, the basic message of the Hebrew prophets centered around the ongoing problems in society and the need to find solutions. Amos was a prophet to the Northern Kingdom of Israel some 700 years before Christ. He challenged the ruling elite of his day to fulfill the responsibilities they had been given by God to lead the people. Rather than assisting the people to find the common good, and following God's law, many of the Jewish rulers ingratiated themselves fulfilling their own perceived needs and desires. Thus, Amos was forced to "buck the system" of his day and to speak God's word boldly. Speaking to the elite of Israel, he proclaimed, "Thus says the Lord: For three transgressions of Israel, and for four, I will not revoke the punishments; because they sell the righteous for silver and the needy for a pair of sandals—they who trample the head of the poor into the dust of the earth, and push the afflicted out-of-the-way; father and son go to the same girl, so that my holy name is profaned; they lay themselves down beside every altar on garments taken in pledge and in the house of their God they drink wine bought with fines they imposed." (Amos 2:6-7)

The message of social justice proclaimed by Amos to the rulers and citizens of Israel was matched by his contemporary, Hosea, who chastised the elite for their idolatry. Rather than worshiping Yahweh, who had rescued them from Egypt, brought them into the Promised Land, and established their nation, the leaders chose to worship false gods of the people in the region. Like Amos, Hosea was forced to speak boldly, but he did so in a straightforward way, even though he realized his message would probably not be well received. For example, he proclaimed, "My people consult a piece of wood, and their divining rod gives them oracles. For a spirit of boredom has led them astray, and they have played the poor, forsaking their God. They sacrifice on the tops of the mountains, and make offerings upon the hills, under oak, poplar, and terebinth, because their shade is good." (Hosea 4:12-13)

Being a prophet in ancient Israel placed one in harm's way. Amos, Isaiah, and Jeremiah all felt unqualified for their common prophetic role, yet each answered the call of the Lord, even though the cost was high. Hearing the verbal abuse and ridicule of those in contemporary society seemed to embolden them, making them that much more able to speak the truth, even when facing death, such as Jeremiah. (Jeremiah 37:11-38:13) They proclaimed their countercultural message without fear, confident that God was with them every step of the way.

The New Testament is equally full of examples of those who were countercultural in their pursuit of Jesus and his message. John the Baptist, living on wild honey and locusts, proclaimed a message of repentance. People needed to reform their lives and prepare themselves for the coming of the Lord. John said what needed to be said, even when he knew his words would cause him great personal distress. He spoke directly against Herod and his lifestyle, an act which landed him in prison and eventually cost him his life. (Mark 6:14-29) But John was not afraid; he possessed an inner strength that prompted him to go forward. He lived a countercultural existence. Mary and Joseph showed no fear, but rather with boldness and confidence followed the path mapped out for them. Both violated the norms of their day, but they did so because of God's message and promise delivered by the Angel Gabriel. They stood against the prevailing tide to bring Jesus into our world.

Obviously, the best example of one who lived a countercultural life was Jesus himself. In every conceivable way, the Lord challenged the prevailing system. He violated the precepts of the Sabbath Law on several occasions asking, "Was the Sabbath made for man or man for the Sabbath?" He went even further claiming that he was "Lord of the Sabbath." (Mark 2:28) Jesus was one who in essence turned the norms of society upside down; he reversed the roles. So countercultural was he that he claimed that a Samaritan was a hero and a priest and a Levite, those who were the religious elite, were in error. (Luke 10:25-37) Jesus offered compassion over the Law. What he said and did were so antithetical to the norms of his day that the Jews sought to kill him. Why was Jesus crucified? Yes, he claimed to be a king; yes, he indirectly claimed to be the Messiah. Yes, he associated himself with God, a blasphemous claim for sure. However, Jesus was crucified because he simply didn't fit into the neat categories of the society of his day. He died because he was countercultural.

The Contemporary Situation and Challenge
Clearly our contemporary 21st century environment is in many ways vastly different from biblical times, but Pope St. John Paul II, demonstrating great insight, realized that in many ways today's

world is not that much different from any time in history. Since the dawn of humanity, the three great temptations of power, wealth, and prestige have tantalized society. When Jesus went to the desert and spent 40 days on what one might call his own personal retreat before the inauguration of his public ministry, Satan tempted him with these same ideas— turning stones into bread, desiring the goods of the world, and knowing his angels will save him because of his high status. Like biblical times as well, a popular elitism prevails in contemporary society. Sometimes described as the haves and the have-nots, the ins and the outs, people are defined in society and placed in categories based on educational level, economic means, family heritage, religious preference, as well as race and ethnicity. Those who stand on top tend to dominate those on the lower rungs of society. The hierarchy of society generally defines what happens and how events proceed with a definite favoritism toward those who stand on top. Today as in the past there exists a constant battle between good and evil. Evil seems so much more profitable and enticing; to profess and manifest the good too often seems to be the fate of losers, those who come up one dollar short, one step behind or one minute late.

Still, contemporary society has its own new and unique problems. We have rapidly moved into a permissive society where almost nothing is wrong and almost everything can be found acceptable in some way. This trend has created a slippery slope that threatens to plunge society into a deep pit from which it will be difficult to extricate itself. Natural law, the law of God, has been relegated to the trash bin as outdated and irrelevant for a modern society that claims human domination over every aspect of our environment. Additionally, today we find those who seek to uphold God's law as outsiders, ostracized because we refuse to accept the big picture of a society that claims no limits for human action.

Living as a Christian in the 21st century indeed presents numerous challenges, but in many ways the basic need is to follow the advice articulated by Pope St. John Paul II in his first public words as pontiff: to cast off fear and to bring Christ into every word and action of our society. As described above, such a message is completely countercultural to the rhetoric proclaimed by many in today's world. Thus, the challenge is real and significant. It is not easy to stand against the tide, to take the less traveled road, the more difficult path. It's much easier to take the well-trod way, the less cluttered path. Yet, Jesus, understanding this reality, challenged people of his day and all of us when he proclaimed in his Sermon on the Mount: "Enter through the narrow gate; for the gate is wide and the road is easy that leads to destruction, and there are many who take it. For the gate is narrow and the road is hard that leads to life, and there are few who find it." (Matthew 7:13-14) Jesus' words must serve as a challenge to be countercultural as a primary way to follow in his footsteps.

The whole Christian community bears the responsibility to walk this less traveled and more encumbered road. We must stand tall, be willing to be criticized, even ostracized, and lose friends if we are to faithfully walk the less traveled countercultural path but the only one, as Jesus says, that leads to life. The people of God deserve our good example; they need to be brought to Christ. Jesus challenged the people of his day; we must do the same to those we meet on the journey of life. Let us be bold and faithful in living the life of Christ and assisting others to do likewise.

BEARING THE CROSS WITH JESUS

The great paradox of Christianity was best expressed by Jesus himself: "Whoever would save his life will lose it, but whoever loses his life for my sake will find it." (Matthew 16:25) Like all paradoxes, Jesus' words on first examination seem unbelievable, but closer scrutiny and prayerful reflection show us that not only are the Lord's words true, they ultimately lead his followers to the cross, a reality which Paul declared as, "absurdity to those who are headed for ruin, but to us who are experiencing salvation it is the power of God." (I Corinthians 1:18) The cross continues to mystify Christians 2000 years after the event of calvary, for as strange as it may seem, it is only by bearing the cross with Jesus, with its pain and daily dying, that we find life.

In June 1958 Bishop Fulton Sheen, then at the height of his popularity and fame through his television ministry, public speaking, and numerous books and essays, gave a commencement address which described our need to embrace Jesus' cross. In his speech the bishop spoke about the heightened state of cold war, existent since the end of World War II, between the Soviet Union and the United States. The Soviet Union was characterized by the bishop as a nation under the weight of a cross, but with no Christ to bear it. Sheen referred to the severe plight of Soviet society which continued thirteen years after the end of the War. During the war thirty million people died, almost half were Russians. Besides the great carnage of death and injury wrought on the Soviet people, scars were still present in economic hardship, lack of food, clothing, and shelter, and a totalitarian government which opted entirely for the Communist elite. The Soviet Union was a nation that bore a great cross, but it was done without the aid of Christ, who was a non-entity in the ideology of atheism which the Communist government promoted.

The 1950s in the United States saw a much different picture. Bishop Sheen characterized our nation as a country with Christ but no cross. America, which suffered the least damage to its people and way of life of any of the major belligerents, emerged from the War as the leader of the free world. Economically the country saw a boom period; the American people clearly saw themselves atop the pack in the race for productivity and a higher standard of living. Catholicism in the 1950s also experienced a flood tide of enthusiasm. Despite the anti-Catholic rhetoric of Paul Blanchard's *American Freedom and Catholic Power* (1949), the Church experienced high water marks in several measurable areas. Mass attendance was never greater; more children were attending Catholic schools than ever before. Vocations to the priesthood and religious life reached their apex as well. The United States had Christ, as evidenced by religious practice, but it had no cross.

Bishop Sheen's comparison was used to show, as the words of Jesus indicate, that there is a need for the world to have both the cross and Christ, one without the other results in a state of incompleteness that must be satisfied. The life of Jesus and the message of Scripture tell us that the cross will be part of our lives and that we must embrace it, rather than run away or reject it, to find eternal life. It seems that this is all wrong, backwards, and foolish. But the reality is, as Jesus reminds us, "Unless the grain of wheat falls to the earth and dies, it remains just a grain of wheat. But if it dies, it produces much fruit." (John 12:24)

The primary example of one who embraced the cross was Jesus himself. Unlike the synoptic Gospels which see the great triumph of Jesus in his resurrection, St. John's narrative portrays Jesus' greatest triumph, his highest exaltation, in his crucifixion and painful death. On Good Friday Jesus was not taken to the cross kicking and screaming. Rather, he went voluntarily; he chose to die so that we could have eternal life. If Jesus had not embraced the cross our existence would be meaningless. Jesus knew his future fate and professed it openly. The Gospels tell us that on three different occasions he predicted his ignominious death, yet he continued the journey toward his final fate in Jerusalem. Jesus knew, as the author of Ecclesiastes (3:1-2) tells us, "There is an appointed time for everything, and a time for every affair under the heavens. A time to be born, and a time to die." His death brought life for us, but this great paradox of our faith was not possible without his embrace of the cross.

The apostles, especially Peter, were not ready for Jesus' cross and they ran from it with all due speed and strength. Immediately after the Lord declares Peter to be "rock," the one upon whom the Church would be built, the apostle is unwilling to accept Jesus' first prediction of his future death; he runs from the cross: "May you be spared Master! God forbid that any such thing ever happens to you!" Jesus' response to Peter's rejection of the cross is swift and severe, "Get out of my sight, you Satan! You are trying to make me trip and fall. You are not judging by God's standards but by man's." Jesus provided a general teaching for all his followers, "If a man wishes to come after me, he must deny his very self, take up his cross, and begin to follow in my footsteps. Whoever would save his life will lose it, but whoever loses his life for my sake will find it." (Matthew 16:22-25) Eventually Peter came to understand the need for the cross in human life: "There is a need for rejoicing here. You may for a time have to suffer the distress of many trials: but this is so that your faith, which is more precious than the passing splendor of fire-tried gold, may by its genuineness lead to praise, glory, and honor when Jesus Christ appears." (I Peter 1:6-7).

Mary, the mother of God, was another one who lived her life by embracing the cross. The Church's liturgical calendar is filled with feasts which celebrate the great privileges which Mary was granted in her life, the Immaculate Conception (December 8), her birth (September 8), the Annunciation (March 25), and her Assumption (August 15). Saturdays during ordinary time may be celebrated with the Mass of the Blessed Virgin Mary. Yet, on September 15 the Church honors Mary as Our Lady of Sorrows. The feast commemorates how Mary suffered through her "yes" to God at the invitation of the Angel Gabriel, "I am the servant of the Lord. Let it be done to me as you say." (Luke 1:38)

Mary, like her son, embraced the crosses which entered her life. When Jesus was presented in the temple after his birth Simeon prophesied in speaking to Mary, "This child is destined to be the downfall and the rise of many in Israel, a sign that will be opposed - and you yourself shall be pierced with a sword - so that the thoughts of many may be laid bare." (Luke 2:34-35) Later Mary was forced into exile in Egypt with her husband and new-born son. Still later she was forced to endure the hardship of her son being lost in the city of Jerusalem. The popular movie, "Home Alone," and its sequels, have made mothers think about how they would feel if their child was lost. Although Scripture does not recount the great middle period of Jesus' life in Nazareth with his parents, it most certainly must have been true that Mary endured, as do all parents, several other trials with her son.

Mary's greatest cross came on Good Friday when she witnessed the cruel and ignoble death of Jesus. Certainly, her heart must have cried out that events be changed. Maybe she wanted Jesus to do something, change history, and relieve himself and her of their present misery. But she remained silent and resigned to the need which the sacrifice of her son would satisfy. Mary was able to embrace Jesus' cross and make it her own and because of this she is honored as a spiritual martyr, Our Lady of Sorrows, and in her eventual coronation as queen of heaven.

The examples of Jesus and Mary have been followed by many Christians throughout the centuries. The great saints and martyrs embraced crosses in their lives and used them to triumph over the evil and anti-God forces which threatened them in their task of being disciples of Jesus. The litany of saints and martyrs of Christian history, those who embraced the cross and used it to bring others closer to Christ, continue today with such names as St. Oscar Romero, Dorothy Day, and St. Teresa of Calcutta.

Christianity is not an easy way of life, but then Jesus never said that being a disciple would be simple. The great task of Christians today is to see how victory can be snatched from defeat, how good can come from bad, how wrong can be converted to right. To do nothing, to say, "It is too difficult" or "I cannot be involved; it is too messy" or "I do not have the time" is to run from the cross which we must embrace. The crosses of life will come our way. If we run, then the challenge is not met, and we cannot grow. But if we pick up and carry the cross, if we walk the road that Jesus walked, then we will not only grow, but we will also be found worthy of God and eternal life. The author of the Book of Wisdom (3:4-6) places the cross in perspective, "For if before men, indeed, they be punished, yet is their hope full of immortality; chastised a little, they shall be greatly blessed, because God tried them and found them worthy of himself. As gold in the furnace, he proved them, and as sacrificial offerings he took them to himself."

Christianity as we know is a paradox. It does not make sense that we must die to find life, yet our faith teaches us the truth of this statement. One cannot escape the cross, but if we accept it as did Christ, if we combine the cross with the presence of Jesus, then the difficulties and pain we suffer become means to salvation. We certainly do not look for the cross, but it will find us whether we like it or not. Let us, therefore, embrace the cross and know that its weight when born alongside Jesus will bring us home. May the Good Friday experience be lived each day as we journey toward the Kingdom of God, present today and to eternal life.

Reconciliation: Building Bridges of Relationship

Two brothers who lived on adjoining farms developed a bitter dispute. It was their first serious rift in forty years of farming side-by-side, sharing machinery, and trading labor and goods as necessary. They had never had a quarrel until now. It began with a small misunderstanding but eventually mushroomed into a major difference, and finally exploded into a war of words, followed by separation and silence. One morning there was a knock at the back door of the elder brother's door. He opened the door and found a man standing outside. He was stooped and was holding a carpenter's toolbox. "I am looking for a few days' work," said the itinerant carpenter. "Perhaps you have some small jobs that I can do." "Well, I believe I do," said the older brother. "Look across the creek at that other farm. That is my neighbor, in fact, my brother's property. Last week there was a meadow between our farms, but then he ran a bulldozer through the river levee and now there is a creek between us. I suspect he did that to spite me, but I will do him one better. You see that big pile of lumber. I want you to build a fence, an eight-foot-high fence, between us so that I never have to look at his place again. Can you handle such a job?" The man replied, "I think I understand the situation. Please show me your tool shed and I will do a job that will please you."

The brother was going to town, so he got the carpenter all set up and then left for the day. The carpenter toiled all day, measuring, cutting, sanding, and pounding nails. At sunset the brother returned from town just as the carpenter was finishing. The brother was aghast; there was no fence but rather a bridge across the creek. It was a magnificent piece of workmanship, even including handrails. And to the older brother's surprise he saw his younger brother crossing the bridge with his arms outstretched. "You are quite a craftsman and brother to do this after all that was said between us," cried the younger brother. The two brothers warmly embraced at the center of the bridge. As they turned, they saw the carpenter packing up his tools. "No wait," they said, "Don't leave. We have other projects for you to do." "No thanks," said the carpenter. I must be moving along. I have other bridges that need to be built."

Building Bridges in Scripture

The physical bridge that the itinerant carpenter constructed was made possible when he recognized the need for reconciliation between the two brothers. Scripture provides numerous examples of similar bridge building efforts between God and communities of faith or individuals. The reconciliation that God continually provided to the Israelites during their 40-year sojourn in the desert to the Promised Land serves as an initial example. The great work of God, as seen in the ten plagues that were wrought upon Pharaoh and the Egyptians and the raising up of Moses to be the great deliverer of the people should certainly have been seen by the Israelites as evidence of their favor in the eyes of the Lord. Moreover, the passage of the community through the Red Sea and the destruction of Pharaoh and his army, plus the many examples of how God provided food and water in the desert were additional signs of God's great favor for his people. Yet, we know that, despite all of God's work, the Israelites fell into the great sin of apostasy by their construction of a golden calf and worshiping it (Exodus 32:1-6) Understandably, God was disappointed and angry, and he threatened to destroy the community, but Moses interceded saying:

> O Lord, why does your wrath burn hot against your people, whom you brought out of the land of Egypt with great power and with a mighty hand? Why should Egyptians say, "It was with evil intent that he brought them out to kill them in the mountains, and to consume them from the face of the earth?" Turn your fierce wrath, change your mind and do not bring disaster on your people. Remember Abraham, Isaac, and Israel, your servants, how you swore to them by your own self, saying to them, "I will multiply your descendants like the stars of heaven, and all this land that I have promised I will give to your descendants, and they shall inherit it forever."

We are then told, "And the Lord changed his mind about the disaster that he planned to bring on his people." (Exodus 32:11b-14) Through the encouragement of Moses, God built a bridge of reconciliation between himself and the Israelites.

Similar bridges of reconciliation are found throughout the Hebrew Bible. On an individual level, we recall the great sin of David, who committed adultery with Bathsheba and then even more seriously arranged for her husband, Uriah's, death on the battlefield (II Samuel 11:1-25) Despite this serious sin, Nathan was sent to David to build a bridge of reconciliation. Nathan chastised David, but in the end says, "Now the Lord has put away your sin; you shall not die." (II Samuel 12:13b) The middle chapters (40 to 55) of Isaiah, written during the time of the infamous Babylonian Exile , describe one of the more profound bridges the Lord constructed. The people had been punished for the many collective sins of the ruling elite who had abused the people and, in many cases, worshiped idols.

Numerous prophets had been sent to warn these rulers of impending disaster, but the prophets' words were not heeded. Still, in the master plan of God, it was necessary that the chosen people return home for the Messiah to be sent and proclaim his message of salvation. Thus, God builds a bridge of reconciliation in the words of Isaiah: "Comfort, O comfort my people, says your God. Speak tenderly to Jerusalem and cry out to her that she has served her term, that her penalty is paid, that she has received from the Lord's hand double for all our sins. (Isaiah 40:1-2) The prophet then speaks of a metaphorical highway, with every valley filled, every mountain made low, and every rough stretch made smooth. God will construct a metaphorical "superhighway" so the people may return home. Once again, God builds a bridge of reconciliation.

The New Testament is also filled with many stories of the construction of bridges of reconciliation. One of the most famous is the encounter of Jesus with the adulterous woman (John 8:1-11). John the evangelist tells us that this woman was caught in the act of adultery; there is no indication at all that she is innocent. Nevertheless, Jesus, contradicting the Law of Moses which says that such an offense should lead to death, offers a bridge of reconciliation. He says to the woman, "Has no one condemned you?" Knowing that the men accusing the woman have drifted away and receiving the response from her that no one has condemned her, he continues, "Neither do I condemn you. Go your way, and from now on do not sin again." (John 8:11) Even more powerfully is the bridge of reconciliation that Jesus built between himself, and the thief crucified on his right on Calvary. Rebuking his compatriot and realizing that Jesus is completely innocent, the "good" thief, traditionally known as Crispas, calls out, "Jesus, remember me when you come into your kingdom." In response, Jesus completes the bridge of reconciliation, "Truly, I tell you, today you will be with me in Paradise." (Luke 23:42-43) How can we forget the bridge of reconciliation the Lord constructed between himself and his chosen leader, Peter, after the latter's three great denials (Luke 22:54-62). The three denials are bridged with the three great affirmations of faith (John 21:15-19).

The message of reconciliation and the need to build bridges rather than construct walls between ourselves and others is necessary in many of our relationships. Too often, unfortunately, significant bridges need to be repaired or even reconstructed within families. Specific events, situations, and circumstances often arise in families that strain or even break relationships. Small misunderstandings if not settled can fester and grow into major conflicts, leading to strained and broken relationships. Addictions of all types—drugs, alcohol, aberrative behavior— can also drive a wedge between people. The problem may be between husband and wife, parents and children, angst between siblings or problems with relatives beyond the nuclear family. In all cases, however, bridges of reconciliation need to be built. Reconciliation is often necessary between co-workers in our places of employment. Disagreements over methods of operation, future plans, and certainly perceived or actual favoritism of one person over another can certainly strain or even at times fracture relationships. Once again, the solution is not to build walls that curtail or even stop communication, but rather to build bridges that can lead to reconciliation. We certainly need to build bridges in our relationships with friends and neighbors. Rather minor disappointments and disagreements between friends can, if not settled, grow into major problems. Lack of communication and even, in the busyness of our world, our failure to nurture friendships can prove problematic. We often say, "I will contact Jane our Jim," but the phone call, E-mail, text, or other means of communication never seems to happen. If we want our friendships and relationships to flourish, we must be willing to build bridges.

While our relationships with family, co-workers, and friends are essential parts of our life, the most important bridge that we need to repair and, unfortunately, the one that often receives our least attention, must be between ourselves and God. When things are going well, when we are on a "life high" and things are going smoothly, we too often forget about our relationship with God. When we encounter problems, find roadblocks, or suffer through personal or familial difficulties of any kind, then we pull out God and say, "Lord, help me!" God will always help us, although the response might not be what we want or desire. Our outreach to God, the building of bridges, should not be only when we are in extremis and feel we have no other place to turn. Our relationship with the Lord must be renewed daily. Yes, we live in a busy world, but as we all know there are 24 hours in a day. How we spend that time is completely up to us. Therefore, it is incumbent that we take the necessary time, and make a good effort to daily renew our relationship with God. We do this through prayer, good works, reading the Bible and other spiritual sources, and our participation in the sacraments. If we are not careful, we tend to drift off because God is not immediate; he does not challenge us directly. Rather, God stands on the side waiting for us to respond to his call and invitation.

The itinerant carpenter "understood" the situation between the two brothers and realized that a fence was not the answer to their difficulty. Thus, he built a bridge which led to reconciliation and certainly a renewal of the good relationship the brothers previously enjoyed. In a similar way, we need to build bridges in our life. The message of the Scriptures is clear— God continually builds bridges with us, seeking to be one with us in all things. Let us respond to the Lord's challenge by building bridges within our family, with our coworkers, and friends. Most especially, let us redo and as necessary re-build our relationship with God. The prize of eternal life is worth every ounce of our effort.

THE CONSEQUENCES OF DISCIPLESHIP

In his book *Awareness*, Jesuit Father Anthony de Mello tells the following short story. One day a man went to his son's room and knocked on the door. "John, wake up, it is time for you to go to school!" From inside the answer came back, "I don't want to go to school, Dad." The father was persistent and again knocked and said, "You must go to school." The answer again came back, "I don't' want to go to school!" "Why not?" asked the father. "There are three reasons," came the reply. "First, I find school boring; second the kids tease me terribly. Third I simply hate school." Then the father responded, "You have given me three reasons for not going to school, I will give you three that say you must attend. First, it is your duty, second you are 45 years old, and third you are the principal."

Father de Mello's story and the thesis of his book is that people today spend too much time hiding from the truth; they want to run away and play with their toys. People today are happy to put their head in the sand, like the proverbial ostrich, and refuse to see the reality before them. People are unaware of the duties and responsibilities of their life; in many ways people are unwilling to pay the price for what they want. They simply want things and refuse to accept the consequences of their desires and needs.

The Christian life well-lived will ask much of us. As G.K. Chesterton once wrote, "The Christian ideal has not been tried and found wanting. It has been found difficult and left untried." We cannot run away and hope that things will magically be made whole and new. That is the dream world of John who at 45 years of age refused to accept the reality of his life. Scripture presents us with a great challenging question: what price am I willing to pay to be a disciple of Jesus? Am I ready to wake up, do my duty, and not count the cost?

St. Luke (14:25-33) presents us an image of Jesus that most of us would rather not hear. The Lord gives the crowds and we who live two thousand years later three specific and hard-to-accept conditions for all who seek to live the Christian life and be his true followers. First, Jesus says, "Whoever comes to me and does not hate father and mother, wife and children, brothers and sisters, yes, and even life itself, cannot be my disciple." Most of us find Jesus' words to be not only challenging, but in conflict with his general message of love and peace. We must understand the Semitic use of hyperbole and the meaning of hate. Rather than demonstrating anger or hostility toward a family member, Jesus is saying that if a conflict exists the demands of discipleship must take precedence over the most sacred of human relationships. What does that mean practically? If family members, friends, or associates pull us away from our relationship with Christ, then we must forego our human contacts or even sever ties with others. The Lord must be primary in our life.

Jesus' next challenge is equally severe: "Whoever does not carry the cross and follow me cannot be my disciple." No one seeks problems and difficulties, but they will come. Jesus challenges us to bear the cross and not take shortcuts in life. We may fall into conflict with others, fail in school or work, have to suffer the pain of separation, loneliness, serious illness or death, but if we go around these obstacles, we will never reach the finish line of life. We must do our best to negotiate the hurdle. Only then can we continue the race that leads to eternal life.

Lastly, Jesus challenges the world's fascination with materialism: "None of you can become my disciple if you do not give up all your possessions." This comment strikes at the very heart of contemporary society. To be disciples places us in direct conflict with our world. A television commercial a few years back stated, "Who says you can't have it all?" Jesus says that the accumulation of things can lead to our destruction. Today we all want the latest and greatest of everything. We want the newest and most stylish clothes; we need to obtain the most up to date cell phone. We "must" experience the most recent fad and participate in all the right events with all the right people. But Jesus is asking us, what is more important--these things or your relationship with me? If we are honest, we would have to say that many times we concentrate on the material world and because of our choice fail Jesus' test. The created world has priority; the Creator and his Son receive only what is left of our attention.

Jesus does not simply state the conditions for discipleship; he goes one step further and asks if we have calculated what it will cost to be his followers. The Lord uses two short parables to ask if we have weighed the consequences of our actions: "For which of you, intending to build a tower, does not first sit down and estimate the cost, to see whether he has enough to complete it? ... Or what king, going out to wage war against another king, will not sit down first and consider whether he is able with ten thousand to oppose the one who comes against him with twenty thousand?" (Luke 14:28, 31) Although the consequences for failure in these stories differ greatly, the message they proclaim is the same--have we calculated what the price of being a disciple? Have we measured the outlay on our time, talent, and resources? Are we willing to do what is necessary to be a follower or are we content to be like John in Anthony de Mello's story and hide from the reality of God's call?

We need the wisdom of God to find the strength necessary to follow the Lord without counting the cost. Wisdom literature in the Hebrew Scriptures is filled with passages which speak of our need to place our trust in God's wisdom. The author of the Book of Proverbs (3:5-8) states, "Trust in the Lord with all your heart, and do not rely on your own insight. In all ways acknowledge him, and he will make straight your paths. Do not be wise in your own eyes; fear the Lord and turn away from evil. It will be a healing for your flesh and refreshment for your body."

St. Paul understood the need to calculate the cost of his relationship with Jesus. He had measured the price for himself and found that he considered all rubbish when compared with his relationship with Christ. Paul witnessed to the cost of discipleship, and he told others to do the same. In his letter to Philemon Paul writes his friend, who is a well-to-do Christian in Colossae, asking him to do the right thing and accept his escaped slave Onesimus back as a brother in the Lord. Philemon was forced to measure the cost of following Jesus. In this case the cost might be ridicule from his fellow patricians for taking back a slave. But Jesus' commandment of love was more important. Only God's wisdom will allow him to do the right thing and not count the cost of following Jesus' lead in demonstrating mercy and forgiveness.

What price are we willing to pay to be disciples of the Lord? We have many examples in Scripture, history, and daily life of those who have suffered much in their quest to follow the Lord. The price may be high, but the reward is even greater. St. Paul has said it well, "Eye has not seen, ear has not heard, nor has it so much as dawned on man what God has prepared for those who love him." (I Corinthians 2:9) Let us not count the cost; let us follow in the path of Jesus and find eternal life.

Contemporary Prophets Speak—Are We Listening?

On March 24, 1980, St. Oscar Romero, Archbishop of San Salvador, was celebrating Mass at a cancer hospital operated by a group of religious sisters. Immediately after the consecration, gunmen entered the rear of the chapel, a hail of bullets rang out, and in another moment the archbishop lay dying in a pool of his own blood. St. Oscar was a man who spoke for his people. He spoke for human rights; he spoke out against those in the government who made decisions that favored the rich and elite at the expense of the poor. He spoke for land reform; he spoke out against injustice. St. Oscar spoke with authority; he spoke the truth; he spoke with love. St. Oscar Romero was a prophet.

It seemed from his earliest days that Romero was destined to be a priest. He was born in 1917 in an eastern mountain village of El Salvador and at age thirteen entered the minor seminary. A brilliant student, he was assigned to Rome for his theological training and was ordained there in 1947. He returned to his native land and was an instant success in ministry, first in parochial work and later in higher education. In fact, he was so successful that he was raised to the position of auxiliary bishop after completing work in education and parishes.

The 1960s was a difficult time for many in the Church and so too for Oscar Romero. His rather traditional and conservative theological perspective was tested when many changes came to the Church in the wake of the Second Vatican Council But he negotiated the changes well so that by the early 1970s he was a strong advocate for many groups who found themselves on the fringes of the Church and society. In 1977 he was appointed Archbishop of San Salvador, the primatial see of the country. Romero was a man who truly heard the cry of the poor and acted upon his conviction that the Church must serve all people. He promoted land reform for peasants, spoke out against government death squads, and in general advocated Catholic principles of social justice. He spoke out when the masses were oppressed through decisions pointedly made to assist the rich. Romero was fearless and spoke out despite threats against his life, shortened through the hate of others. His courageous actions and words demonstrate how God's word continues to be voiced in contemporary society.

If we have the eyes to see and the ears to hear, we can recognize the presence of prophets in our midst today. When we hear the word prophet what images and names come to mind? Possibly some think of great evangelists, such as the character of Elmer Gantry in literature, who stands on the street corner with Bible in hand and preaches hellfire and damnation for those who refuse to reform their lives. Others may think of the door-to-door sale of religion. We may not agree with the theological perspective of many of these groups, but we certainly must respect their courage and zeal in their efforts to proselytize. The names of prophets that come to mind are familiar to all: Isaiah, Jeremiah, Ezekiel, or possibly one of the so-called minor prophets--Amos, Zephaniah, or Jonah. What is a prophet? A prophet is one with the rare and special privilege to speak God's word with great authority. But the privilege of the prophetic voice incurs significant responsibility as well.

Scripture describes the office and mission of the prophet in Hebrew society. Moses, the great liberator of the Israelites and their first prophet heard the cries of the people for a representative to speak God's word: "The Lord your God will raise up for you prophets like me from among your own people; you shall heed such prophets." (Deuteronomy 18:15) Prophets are tasked to speak God's word and to do so fearlessly. They speak with authority, proclaiming God's word as it is revealed to them, but they do so with the knowledge of the responsibility that comes with their office: "Anyone who does not heed the words that the prophet shall speak in my name, I myself will hold accountable. But any prophet who speaks in the name of other gods, or who presumes to speak in my name a word that I have not commanded the prophet to speak--that prophet shall die." (Deuteronomy 18:19-20).

Jesus was the preeminent prophet for as the Son of God he spoke from personal knowledge of the Father. The Gospel evangelists describe Jesus' teaching and how the people were spellbound by what they heard. Jesus' teaching was new and different; it was authoritative. (Mark 1:21-22) Jesus' message was challenging, yet he proclaimed it, as St. Paul suggests, regardless if it was convenient and inconvenient. (II Timothy 4:2) He was courageous because he spoke God's word not when it seemed to be acceptable or appropriate in the ears of the hearers or when he would receive a favorable hearing. Rather, often Jesus' message raised conflict; it shook people up. Jesus' message was challenging to the people's sensibilities; their zone of comfortability was rocked severely. Some heeded Jesus' message and became his followers. Others disregarded or were indifferent to the message and others still were violently opposed to what they heard and orchestrated his death.

Moses, Isaiah, Ezekiel, and Jeremiah were some of the great prophets of the Old Testament. They spoke God's word as it was presented to them; they spoke with authority and did what God asked of them. Jesus was the preeminent prophet because he knew the Father. Lest, however, we think that prophecy ended with Jesus, we can look at people like Sts. Oscar Romero and Teresa of Calcutta, and the Anglican archbishop from South Africa, Desmond Tutu, to see that contemporary prophets are in our midst. In the Church there are courageous people who today challenge us and serve as prophets. Some speak out on behalf of the unborn; some speak for the rights of the elderly. Some are advocates for the rights of prisoners and others speak for the poor, the homeless, the destitute, and others who have no little or no voice in our society. Are we listening to these voices, or is the message we hear too harsh, or do we feel it is not applicable to us? Do we listen and face it when people speak the truth, or do we cover our ears and run from the message because it is too challenging?

There are many others in our contemporary society who serve as prophets and probably don't even realize it. Parents have been given special authority by God to proclaim the Lord's word, in speech and action to their children and thus serve as prophets. Mothers and Fathers must take responsibility in proclaiming God's word, whether it is a word of discipline, praise, or love to their children. Teachers, coaches, and mentors also have the rare privilege and the significant responsibility to act as prophets through the instruction, encouragement, guidance, and admonition they give to those placed in their charge. All under the tutelage of parents, teachers, coaches, and mentors must listen to the voice of God that comes to them from these contemporary prophets.

Contemporary prophets abound in our society. Some may be archbishops, some may be pastors, but most are everyday people we know, love, and encounter. Let us, therefore, consider our call to speak God's word; let us be prophets. May we be Christ to one another. St. Teresa of Avila has succinctly and beautifully presented the challenge to us: "Christ has no body on earth, but yours, no hands no feet but yours. Yours are the eyes with which Christ looks with compassion for the world. Christ has no hands but yours." May we believe, act, and proclaim the same!

GETTING THE WHOLE STORY

Anaturalist and a small group of youth set out on a hike through the wilderness. As the group walked, they experienced many sights, noises, and smells. About every 15 minutes the naturalist stopped the group and asked, "Tell me what you saw and heard?" Invariably the young people would describe only a fraction of what they experienced and for the most part what they mentioned were consistent throughout the hike, demonstrating that they, while clearly attracted to some things, barely noticed others. Their purview was limited.

Possessing an attitude of openness that allows one to have a broader perspective and clearer picture of various events, ideas, and perspectives, the lesson the naturalist sought to communicate to his young charges, was certainly in the mindset of Jesus during the time of his public ministry. Christ realized that a diversity of opinions and ideas could aid people to get the whole picture and, by that view, assist them to make better and wiser decisions. While Jesus clearly reached out in a preferential way to the children of Israel, his fellow Jews, he did not do so to the exclusion of others. On the contrary, as St. Luke (10:14) reports, he traveled to the regions of Tyre and Sidon. St. Mark speaks of Jesus going to Gerasene territory and there encountering Legion (Mark 5:1-20). He interacted with people on all levels of Hebrew society, from the elite to those who were unseen and possessed no voice. He realized he would never be able to get the whole story and to understand any ongoing situation without talking with people on all sides and all fronts. He chose Matthew, a tax collector, and thus a collaborator with the dreaded Romans, who was despised by his fellow Jews. He even chose Judas knowing that one day he would turn traitor and inaugurate the process that would lead Jesus to the cross.

The openness of Jesus to new ideas, possibilities, and people, was sharply contrasted by the narrow mindedness of the religious elite of his day. He chastised small-minded individuals when he said, "For this people's heart has grown dull, and their ears are hard of hearing, and they have shut their eyes; so that they might not look with their eyes, and listen with their ears, and understand with their heart. (Matthew 13:15) Jesus' critique of the religious elite of his day was centered on their apparent inability to see beyond their own purview. In a self-centered and rather arrogant manner, the religious elite put forth the dictates and laws of society as they understood them. The Scribes and Pharisees could only view the world in their own narrow way. Their "tunnel vision" closed their minds to all other possibilities. Thus, they viewed the world in a rather skewed fashion.

The more open method of Jesus is clearly the one marked out by Christianity as the path to follow. Yet, the tendency for many is to see what we want to see, hear what we want to hear, and believe what we want to believe. Nothing outside what we have come to expect or understand as normal or proper has any merit in our lives. Clearly, there are many standards. There is first and foremost the law of God; there is Church teaching to keep us on the proper path. There are certain laws which society has over the course of civilization deemed proper and acceptable. Still, there is room to dialogue and through the process learn from each other. We cannot be like the youth on the wilderness hike who could only see and hear what they considered important.

Getting the whole story, understanding all the aspects of any question or decision usually requires an individual to go beyond their own needs and desires. Initially one must be able to broaden their attitudes and associations. All people have a perspective, an attitude, an opinion that is generated over time and, from the person's perspective, certainly works. Yet, right-thinking people, who are simply different than us, may possess another perspective on the same idea. Having the ability to "walk in the shoes of another" allows one to see and hear a different side of the story. It is quite comfortable and rather easy to simply hold tightly to our own perspective, but we can learn much from others and receive a much better understanding of the issue or question by having a broader attitude. Next, we must be willing to accept that there are different ways to accomplish the same purpose. As the expression goes, "There are several ways to skin a cat." Too often people express the belief that it is "my way or the highway." A particular method may be beneficial and help a person or group, but it is not the only way to achieve a common end. Thus, a sense of appreciating varied ways of achieving ends is important. It is also imperative that we learn how to associate with people beyond our personal friends and those with whom we wish to associate. We make friends and associate freely with those with whom we have common attitudes, ways of acting, and perspective. We will never see other possibilities around us if we do not take the time to engage people who are different than us. We have all heard the expression that diversity is the spice of life. It applies not only to food, but to human associations. People who grow up with different experiences, cultural backgrounds, and general philosophies of life can aid each other. But if we only freely associate with a limited group, then we are like the children on the nature hike; we will see and hear only what we want to perceive.

Getting the whole story takes extra time and effort but it's something we must do. Too often we shortchange ourselves and others by not investigating more fully, but rather going on often limited and at times inaccurate information. We need to open our minds and our hearts to appreciate differences of opinion and various methods of operation more fully. Then and only then will we completely grasp the story as it comes to us, in its full measure, and not simply what we want to see, hear or believe. We will then be able, as the famous song from the musical "Godspell" says, "See thee more clearly, love thee more dearly and follow thee more nearly, day-by-day-by-day."

God's Wisdom or the World?

Once upon a time there was an old man who lived on the outskirts of town. He had lived there so long that no one knew who he was or where he had come from. Some thought that he had been a very powerful king, but that was many years ago. Others suggested that he was once famous, rich, and generous, but he had lost everything. Still others said that he was once very wise and influential. There were even some who said he was holy. The children in the town, however, thought he was an old and stupid man, and they made his life miserable. They threw stones at his windows, left dead animals on his front porch, destroyed his garden, and yelled nasty words at him at every opportunity.

Then one day, one of the older boys came up with an idea to prove once and for all that those who thought he was a former king, or rich, famous, and generous, or wise and influential, and most especially those who considered him holy, were all wrong. No, he truly was just a stupid old man. One boy knew how to catch a bird in a snare. He told his friends that he would catch the bird and together they would go to the old man's home and knock on the door. When the man answered the boy would ask, "Old man, do you know what I have hidden behind my back?" Now he might guess that it is a bird, but with the second question I will get him. I will ask him if the bird is alive or dead. If he says dead, I will allow the bird to go free, but if he says the bird is alive, I will crush it to death with my hands. Either way he will prove he is only a stupid old man.

The children thought it was a great plan. Thus, the older boy caught the bird and together they went off to the old man's house and rudely knocked on the door. The man opened the door and seeing the large gathering of children realized something was up. The boy spoke quickly, "Old man, do you know what I have hidden behind my back?" The old man looked at the children one by one and out of the corner of his eye he saw a white feather fall to the ground. He answered, "Yes, I do. It's a white bird."

The children's eyes grew large. How could he know it was a white bird? Maybe the people in town were right all along. The older boy was not to be deterred from his goal and quickly asked the second question. "Well, that was a good guess, but is the bird alive or dead?" Again, the old man looked with sad eyes at each of the children. Finally, his eyes met those of the boy. He answered, "That depends on you; the answer is in your hands."[1]

Certainly, the old man was filled with wisdom and knowledge. Not only could he "out fox" the children, especially the boy, at their own game, but he was wise enough to be able to teach them an important lesson at the same time. We have the choice to do good or evil. We have the chance to choose the wisdom of God or that of the world. Which will you choose?

The Hebrew Scriptures provide many examples of how the Lord laid before humanity distinct options that require us to choose between God and the world. The Genesis account of creation (2:4b-3:24) related how God gave Adam and Eve all that they could possibly need or want. Yet, they were not satisfied. Satan tempted them by claiming they could be like God, but in reality, they were being asked to choose the world over God. They took the bait; they chose unwisely, seeking ambition over what they had been given. The result was the disorder and wickedness in the world, what many contemporary theologians call the "original sin" as it is the common lot of all. None can escape from this reality. Later in the Pentateuch, God, in a conversation with Moses, places another fundamental choice before the great deliverer. We read in Deuteronomy (30:19b-20): "I have set before you life and death, blessings, and curses. Choose life so that you and your descendants may live, loving the Lord your God, obeying him, and holding fast to him; for that means life to you and length of days, so that you may live in the land that the Lord swore to give to your ancestors, to Abraham, Isaac, and to Jacob." God is telling Moses that the choice for God is a choice for life; to choose the world is a formula for death. This fundamental choice is placed before the rulers of Israel and Judah numerous times by the many prophets sent by God. In short, the message of the prophets in a basic choice. Isaiah, Jeremiah, Amos, Hosea, and all the others placed before the ruling elite the choice to follow God or the way of the world, manifest by false gods, such as Baal, or even more common, the false avenues of power, wealth, and prestige.

God did not simply place choices before the Hebrews but showed the people how to make wise and proper decisions. When Jesse paraded before Samuel his sons to see which one God had chosen by God to replace Saul, he did not consider the youngest, David, because he of his youth and ruddy complexion. In other words, he did not "look the part." God, however, corrected this attitude saying to Samuel (I Samuel 16:7), "Do not look on his appearance or on the height of his stature, because I have rejected him; for the Lord does not see as mortals see; they look on the outward appearance, but the Lord looks on the heart." God is telling Samuel and Jesse that they must not look at what the world considers important when selecting a king, but what God deems valuable. As always, the choice is clear--the world or God.

In his ministry, Jesus also provided many examples of the need to choose God over the world. We recall the story of the Pharisee and the tax collector. The former thought himself important because of his perceived righteousness, while the latter only beat his breast and admitted his sinfulness. Jesus is clear (Luke 18:14), "I tell you this man [the tax collector] went down to his home justified rather than the other; for all who exalt themselves will be humbled, but all who humble themselves will be exalted." Humility comes from God; arrogance comes from the world. The parable of the man with a super abundance of wealth (Luke 12:13-21) is another example of making the choice between God and the world. All the man seems to be concerned about is where to store his great wealth; he seems totally oblivious to the source of his prosperity. Thus, his life will be taken. Jesus concludes, "So it is with those who store up treasure for themselves but are not rich toward God." In the story of the rich man, traditionally known as Dives, and the beggar Lazarus (Luke 16:19-31) we recall how the former seemed unconcerned about the beggar until it was too late. He made his choice and so too will his family have to choose God or the world. All the Synoptic evangelists (Matthew 19:16-30, Mark 10:17-31 and Luke 18:18-30) report the story of Jesus' encounter with the rich young man who was challenged to divest himself of his wealth. Again, in essence it is a choice between God and the world. Jesus provides a great challenge to those who are attached to the world: "Truly I tell you, it will be hard for a rich person to enter the kingdom of heaven. Again, I tell you, it is easier for a camel to pass through the eye of a needle than for someone who is rich to enter the kingdom of God." Jesus continued, "For mortals it is impossible, but for God all things are possible." (Matthew 19:23b-24, 26b) Clearly Jesus is telling his disciples that they must choose God and not the world. Lastly, Jesus himself was given the challenge of choosing the world or God. After his baptism he chose to go to the desert to prepare himself for his public ministry (Matthew 4:1-11, Mark 1:12-15, Luke 4:1-13). There Satan tempted him with the three great challenges that have always faced humanity: power, wealth, and prestige. In each case Jesus rejected the world, saying that the things of God were more important. We must choose the same.

Free will, that quality along with the ability to think, which separates us from the rest of God's creation, always must be used judiciously and wisely. We must choose well and wisely, but unfortunately this is not always the case. Thus, we might ask, why does the world suffer? Why do pain, problems and suffering exist in such abundance? We all believe that God is all good, all love, full of compassion and all powerful. This is how we define God. Thus, the question bears repeating, why does our world suffer? Why do wars exist, and people die in innocence? Why do people in positions of public trust commit acts that cause others not only to lose faith in the individual, but in the system as well? Why do people fight one another and the only question between them is the color of their skin, their political preference or religious belief?

The basic answer to these challenging questions is personal choice, our free will to choose the wisdom of the world or that of God at any time in any way. Soren Kierkegaard, the famous nineteenth century existentialist philosopher and theologian, based his thinking on the concept that faith is a matter of choice, our personal decision in finding God. This personal decision, our free will, is why the world suffers. It is free will that allows the drunk to drive and kill others. It is free will that allows people in public service to break the law and thus lower the integrity of the system. It is free will that places certain members and groups in society on the fringe and does not allow them to participate. Free will moves us closer to or further from God. As Kierkegaard wrote, it is our decision; faith is our choice. As God said it to Abraham, "I place before you death and life; thus, choose life." (Deuteronomy 30:19)

Too often we willingly choose the world and, thus, death, but if we wish we can choose the wisdom of God and life. Yes, we must use our gift of free will wisely, to always choose God's wisdom over that of the world. Often, we hesitate; we are unsure how far we can go or how much we are willing to risk. Thus, we balk and miss opportunities. A little story illustrates how our tendency to hesitate can lead to loss. Three wise men were encouraged to experience what others called the cave of wisdom and life. They made careful preparations for what would be a challenging and arduous journey. When they reached the cave, they noted a guard at the entrance. They were not permitted to enter the cave until they had spoken with the guard. He had only one question for them, but he insisted that they answer only after discussing it with each other. He assured them they would have a good guide to lead them through the various regions of the cave. His question was simple, "How far into the cave of wisdom and life do you wish to go?" The three travelers discussed the question and then returned to the guard. They said, "We do not want to enter very far. We only want to venture far enough to say we have been there." The response of the guard manifested none of the disappointment that he felt as he summoned a guide to lead them into the cave. Then he watched as they set out to make the return trip back to their own land.

Much of the life we are given by God is our choice. The decisions and the choices we make will in many ways determine our future path. Let us, therefore, consider the options that stand before us and have the courage to go forward, confident of God's presence with us. May we always choose wisely the wisdom of God. If we can our reward in heaven will be great.

KEEP YOUR EYE ON THE GOAL!

In the days of the great sailing ships, it was common for the captain to hire a few young men who would serve as cabin boys during the voyage. One of the tasks of these cabin boys was to periodically climb the mainmast to the top crows' nest and serve as a lookout when the ship approached land or if there was some need to observe the distant horizon. Often when these young lads began their ascent of the mainmast, they made the mistake of looking down. When they did so, the height, combined with the periodic rocking of the ship, made the lads dizzy, too often leading them to fall and either be severely injured or die. Thus, they were always instructed by some of the older crew members that when they made their ascent, they were to always keep their eye on the crows' nest, the goal which they sought.

Keeping one's eye on the goal was not only good advice for cabin boys; it has been and always will be solid instruction in living the Christian life. Salvation History is essentially the story of how God instructed the Jews and their ancestors in faith, the Christians, to keep their eyes on the goal, namely maintenance of their relationship with God. The Scriptures contain numerous examples of those who successfully kept their eyes on the goal and, in the end, achieved their desired end.

Abraham and Moses were asked by God to take on significant tasks and they completed them successfully by keeping their eyes fixed on the goal. Abram, we are told, was a wandering Aramean, a nomad from the land of Ur (Genesis 11:27-12:9). God's plan of salvation began in earnest way when he came to Abram and asked him to journey to an unknown land. He was told that he would be the father of a great nation. However, he and his wife, Sarah, were older, not, at least in normal circumstances, at the age to conceive and bear children. Despite the uncertainty of responding to an unknown God, Abram, whose name was expanded to Abraham, kept his eye on the goal, doing whatever what was asked. He was even willing to sacrifice his son, Isaac, his one chance of progeny (Genesis 22:1-14). By keeping his eye on the goal, he became the first great patriarch and the father of a great nation, as God had promised.

Hundreds of years later Moses was also given a Herculean task. Called by God in the desert, in the form of a burning bush that was not consumed (Exodus 3:1-22), Moses was asked to lead the Israelites back to their homeland. The task was anything but easy. He had to deal with the stubbornness of Pharaoh and possibly even more distressing the frequent complaints from his own people as they wandered rather aimlessly, due to their disobedience, spending forty years in transit to the Promised Land. Yet, despite the many forces arrayed against him, Moses kept his eyes firmly fixed on the goal and, like Abraham, achieved his end.

Unfortunately, the Hebrew Bible also narrates the failures of many leaders in Israel to keep their eyes on the goal, leading to disaster for the Jewish community. After God destroyed all their enemies and the people were settled in the Promised Land, infidelity to God and his commandments began almost immediately. The people turned away from God, leading to their destruction at the hands of their enemies. God sent judges, such as Gideon, Deborah, and Samson to rescue the people and for a short time they returned to God. In the end, however, they continued to fall away from their goal. After the establishment of the monarchy and the reigns of David and Solomon, the rulers of the Northern Kingdom of Israel and the Southern Kingdom of Judah lost their vision and worshiped false gods, as well as mistreating the most vulnerable within Hebrew society. God's displeasure with these rulers led to the loss of the Northern Kingdom to the Assyrians and the exile of Judah to Babylon for fifty years. Failure to keep their eye on the goal thus brought much pain and even destruction and death to the Hebrews.

The inability of those placed in positions of authority in ancient Israel to maintain their attention on their goal must be contrasted with the absolute obedience and proper direction of Jesus Christ. Jesus kept himself focused on the goal and never considered the price he would pay. Jesus' call to the apostles must indeed have been strong for we are told that they "immediately" left their livelihood and family to be his followers. Yet, these first followers came to realize that their discipleship required them, like their master, to keep their eyes fixed on the goal. It would not be an easy road. On the contrary, Jesus warned his followers: "I am sending you out like lambs into the midst of wolves." (Luke 10:3) However, Jesus pointed them toward the proper path to achieve their goal: "Enter through the narrow gate; for the gate is wide and the road is easy that leads to destruction, and there are many who take it. For the gate is narrow and the road is hard that leads to life, and there are few who find it" (Matthew 7:13-14). Jesus called his disciples to be dedicated; he challenged them to keep their eyes on the goal. On one occasion Jesus told a band of would-be followers that their discipleship must be complete. He asked one person to follow, but the individual asked permission to bury his dead father. Jesus responded, "Let the dead bury their own dead; but as for you go and proclaim the kingdom of God." Another said he would follow, but asked permission to bid farewell to his family. Jesus told that man, "No one who puts hand to the plow and looks back is fit for the kingdom of God." (Luke 9: 59-62) People today might feel that Jesus' reaction was rather harsh, but he was only describing the need for complete dedication to purpose; he was asking his followers to keep their eyes on the goal. The Lord put it very directly when he said, "If any want to become my followers, let them deny themselves and take up their cross and follow me. For those who want to save their life will lose it, and those who lose their life for my sake will find it." (Matthew 16: 24b-25)

Jesus' demands for his followers were exemplified in his own life. Whatever the goal was, whether short-term or longer, Jesus never flinched from moving forward and doing what was necessary. He was not deterred from curing people on the Sabbath, even though the law said such action was forbidden. He did not refrain from speaking his mind, whether that was in the synagogue in Nazareth, conversations with the Scribes and Pharisees, or chastising Peter, his personal choice to lead the nascent Christian community. He did not avoid conflict; he never "sugar-coated" his message, that stated clearly that the road will be difficult, and priorities must be straight. Jesus was very clear telling his disciples: "Whoever loves father or mother more than me is not worthy of me; and whoever loves son or daughter more than me is not worthy of me; and whoever does not take up the cross and follow me is not worthy of me." (Luke 10:37-38) Jesus never shied away from doing what was difficult, whether it was overturning the tables of the money changers in the Temple, or courageously walking the Via Dolorosa to his own ignominious death.

The challenge Jesus gave to his first followers is still present in the twenty-first century. In fact, in some ways the trial may be greater. Our goal, whether we think about it or not daily, is to return home to God. That long-term goal is achieved by shorter-term objectives, each of which requires our attention and focus. The allurements of contemporary society, whether they are the generic ideas of secularism and relativism, or the more specific things of materialism, power, and prestige seek, almost daily, to derail us from moving in a clear and positive direction toward our goals. Thus, we must not look down, as the experienced sailors taught the young cabin boy when climbing to the crows' nest, but rather look up and keep our eyes set on the goal. We may feel left out of contemporary society, but our goal is not in this world, but rather an eternal existence with God, the one from whom we came. Therefore, let us keep our eyes clearly fixed on the goal; the rewards may not be as plentiful today, but will be found in the eternal life to come.

LIVING IN THE PRESENCE OF JESUS

Unbeknownst to many Roman Catholics today, one of the "superstars" of the fledgling television industry of the 1950s was Bishop Fulton Sheen. Serving in those days as the auxiliary Bishop of New York, Sheen rivaled "Mister Television" Milton Berle with his highly rated show, "Life Is Worth Living." Always broadcast live, Bishop Sheen dazzled his audiences with his ability to capture their interest with timely and challenging shows that forced people to reflect upon various aspects of their lives. In one show, titled "The Theology of the Rat Race," Sheen described how contemporary people can never seem to live in the moment; they are either bogged down in the past or living in future expectation. He suggested that when we fail to live in the present moment, we miss so many opportunities to encounter God in the various ways that the Lord manifests himself to us.

Living in the present moment and capturing the possibilities that each day brings is a lesson that is clearly taught by Scripture. When John the Baptist began his ministry, he told those who were willing to listen that there was a need to reform their lives and to begin anew. For him there was no better time to be converted, to transform one's life than the present moment. People came to John asking what they needed to do now to prepare for the arrival of the Christ. He responded by saying, "Whoever has two coats must share

with anyone who has none; and whoever has food must do likewise."
(Luke 3:11) Tax collectors and soldiers were also given advice on
their preparations. In essence, however, John told the people that they
needed to do something now; there was no need to wait. Jesus was
clearly one who took every opportunity to make the present moment
special. He did not dwell in the past, such as the sin of the woman
caught in the act of adultery (John 8:2-11) and he rarely spoke about
the future, save his own impending death and the future arrival of the
Holy Spirit. Rather, Jesus concentrated on the people who came to
him and the needs they brought at that moment. He wasted no time
to cure lepers (Mark 1:40-42; Luke 17:11-19), the woman with the
hemorrhage, the daughter of Jairus, (Mark 5:21-43) and the blind
man, Bartimaeus (Mark 10:46-52). He acted immediately to change
water into wine, saving the day for the newly married couple (John
2:1-11); he met the need placed before him to feed 5000 with five
loaves and two fish (Matthew 14:13-21). Jesus took advantage of
every opportunity to teach and by his actions to show the love of God
to all. As the expression goes, the grass did not grow under Jesus'
feet for he never wasted a moment in his daily efforts to inaugurate
the Kingdom of God in our world.

Living in the present moment is difficult for many and the reasons
are multiple and often complicated. Some people live in the past;
they are unable to move beyond experiences that brought triumph
or defeat. Some who have achieved great distinction continue to
bask in the aura of that former glory, falsely believing that some
additional recognition or credit is due them today for what was done
in the past. While we should and certainly do acknowledge the great
accomplishments of individuals, those who achieved such accolades
too often perceive that there is no more to be done; they have made
their contribution. If such an attitude leads to cynicism toward the
present or future, or a sense of entitlement, then one might rightly ask
"What have you done for me lately?" Too often as well past hurts or
painful experiences keep us from living in the present moment. We

simply cannot let go of what has happened, to ourselves or others. We live in a state of misery, too often wallowing in self-pity or asking the perennial question, "Why did God allow this to happen?"

While some hold too tightly to the past, others live only for the future. This can happen in common and more significant ways. As we commute to work on Monday, we are thinking of what we will do during the next weekend. As we live our day-to-day routine, we look forward to our next vacation or opportunity to get away. These very common ways of living in the future are, unfortunately, accompanied with instances of people who look only to the future, seeing no hope or possibility in the present moment. In both cases, too often people miss individuals, opportunities, and events that the present moment brings. Encountering people, we did not expect and taking the time to interact with them indeed can be a great blessing. Being sufficiently open to unanticipated events or opportunities can provide learning experiences of which we had never dreamed. To be unduly tied to the past or the future results in a life of "what could have been."

Living in the present moment and accomplishing what can be done today can be highly beneficial. Opportunities arrive at our front door and knock seeking entrance. They come in various forms, including our brothers and sisters who travel the same road of life. Procrastination is a constant threat to living in the moment; we say, "Why not wait for tomorrow?" However, the better attitude is to achieve today what is possible. We must take advantage of the moment and all the possibilities it brings. If we have our health, time, and opportunity why should we not act?

Bishop Fulton Sheen dazzled American television audiences in the mid-1950s with his thirty-minute live broadcasts that aided people to live in the present moment. The past is a great teacher; we can learn from our mistakes as well as our triumphs to make the future better for ourselves and our world, but we must not forget the opportunities the present moment brings. Jesus never missed an opportunity to act; he referenced the past and predicted his own future, but he lived in the present moment. Let us have sufficient wisdom to gain what we can today, realizing that the experiences of the present can give us perspective on the past and greater and better tools to live in the future.

LIVING THE CHRISTIAN LIFE TODAY: A FORMULA FOR SUCCESS

W hat was the most destructive day in the history of Christianity? After pondering this weighty question, one might arguably answer the day Jesus Christ was crucified, today celebrated as Good Friday. From the point of ecumenism, others might suggest 1054 when the break between the Orthodox traditions and Roman Catholicism became cemented. Others still might point to October 31, 1517, the day Martin Luther tacked his famous "Ninety-Five Theses" to the front door of the Cathedral in Wittenberg, Germany. For those centering on more contemporary Catholicism, one might suggest January 2002 which opened the infamous "Pandora's Box" to the sex abuse crisis in the Church.

When this challenging query was first posed to me, my questioner gave his own response: The worst day in Christianity came in February 313 with the publication of the "Edict of Milan," Emperor Constantine's proclamation, which for all practical purposes overnight transformed Christianity in the Roman Empire from being proscribed to the religion of the state. My initial reaction to this response was "How could recognition of the Church be seen as a negative?" In the discussion that followed, my friend suggested that Constantine's proclamation, that moved Christianity from the shadows to the light, a positive move indeed, brought unforeseen problems. Without intending to do so, Constantine's edict made Christian discipleship too easy. During the centuries when the practice of Christianity was proscribed, being a follower of Jesus required determination, perseverance and a willingness to suffer. Overnight, through the Edict, many of the hardships of being a Christian were instantly removed; the challenge of the Christian life was greatly eased.

The freedom brought by the "Edict of Milan" in the Patristic Church finds new challenges in today's secular, freethinking, and overly open society. To be a faithful Christian, to be a follower of Jesus Christ today is indeed a great challenge for it forces us to violate the norms that most of society considers operative and appropriate. Living the Christian life today requires us to have a relationship with Jesus, to know him and to be in communication with him. Once we gain sufficient knowledge and are in proper communion with Christ then we can begin to follow him through a life of dedication, demonstrable perseverance, fulfillment of responsibilities and manifestations of faith.

Our Relationship with Jesus

Relationships of any nature begin by building our knowledge of those with whom we seek communion. Enhancing our knowledge of family, friends, colleagues at work, even neighbors down the street allows us to better understand them, allowing us to draw closer to people, making us more serviceable to each other. We would never seek advice, service, or treatment from any professional if we did not believe that the individual was conversant in the latest technologies, medicines, or interpretations of the law. If for whatever reason one person wants to get to know one another better, knowing more about that individual will greatly facilitate one's chances.

Similarly, if we want to have a better relationship with Jesus, we need to improve our knowledge of him. Yet, while average people usually say they seek an enhanced relationship with the Lord, few are willing to take the necessary time and effort to know Christ better. We rely far too heavily on our knowledge of the Church from the last time we had any formal Christian education, whether that was through private schools or parish religious education programs. We can and must do more and better if we wish to walk more closely and faithfully with Jesus. Opportunities to enhance our knowledge are all around us, but they require our time and effort. National and local (diocesan) newspapers as well as very readable magazines provide us with information on many levels and various topics. The Internet, through such serviceable sites as Zenit.com and others provide a daily (if one wishes) summary of the important events and peoples in contemporary Catholicism.

There is no substitute for better knowledge of Christ in order to enhance our relationship with him, but this must be combined with better communication, which lies at the heart of any relationship. Married couples, friends, teammates, even colleagues at work must be in good communication for relationships to flourish. Today we experience an overload of communication. This is especially manifested in the technological revolution that has produced cell phones, the Internet, and all the various social media associated with it. Literally today people carry their whole lives in their hand; their phone is the source of communication with the outside world. Many people, especially the younger generation, cannot wait for their next "injection" of communication.

Contemporary people are experts in communicating with one another, but, unfortunately, this does not always translate to great communication with God. Like everything that is worthwhile, communication takes time and so we must find time, carve it out, if necessary, to speak with God each day. The Lord deserves our time; we cannot shortchange our communication with him for to do so places us in danger. In our communication with God, we must speak from our hearts, not simply from our heads and mouth. God knows the ideas in our heart as well as those manifested more overtly. In our daily communication with the Lord, we must not only speak, but listen for God's response. As a wise old religious sister once told me "We have two ears and one mouth and thus we should listen twice as much as we speak." We constantly speak, but we seldom listen for God's response. We may be very fortunate and receive God's answer through a theophany such as Moses' observation of the burning bush that was not consumed. More likely however, the answer will probably be received in the heart, through life experience or events. Either way we must be listening for the Lord's response.

Following Jesus: Dedication, Perseverance, Responsibility, and Faith

Knowledge of Jesus and enhancing our ability to communicate with him is central to living the Christian life, but what is necessary to be good and faithful followers of the Lord? The process must begin by our commitment to dedication. Success in any endeavor requires our dedication and so too with living the Christian life. Great sports teams or individual athletic performances require dedication. Great artists, musicians, painters, dancers, and actors must be completely dedicated to their disciplines. Success and great achievement in any endeavor can only be reached by a sense of dedication, manifested most generally in time and effort.

What does dedication in the Christian life entail and how is it manifested? First, dedication requires us to follow God's law. The law, whether articulated in the Bible or through the Natural Law, is known; we know what is correct and proper. In order to follow the law, however, it may be necessary to stand strong against outside pressure, especially in contemporary life, which constantly gives us a message of what society claims is right and proper, yet is often contradictory to God's law. Dedication will probably mean going against the flow, not being accepted by the majority, and even being

101

unpopular or ostracized. But Jesus warned his disciples about this in his famous Beatitudes (Matthew 5:11-12), stating: "Blessed are you when people revile you and persecute you and utter all kinds of evil against you falsely on my account. Rejoice and be glad for your reward is great in heaven, for in the same way they persecuted the prophets who were before you."

Dedication means total commitment; one cannot count the cost of being a contemporary disciple of Jesus. We are called to die to self so that others may have more. As just one example, St. Maximillian Kolbe literally manifested this reality by substituting his life for another prisoner in Auschwitz, the infamous Nazi death camp. Our call to commitment will probably not be so great, but in any case, we are called to pick up our cross and follow in the footsteps of the Lord. Jesus was very clear: "If any want to become my followers, let them deny themselves and take up their cross and follow me. For those who want to save their life will lose it, and those who lose their life for my sake will find it." (Matthew 16:24-25) Jesus summarized the dedication we must manifest in his timeless words: "Enter through the narrow gate; for the gate is wide and the road is easy that leads to destruction, and there are many who take it. For the gate is narrow and the road is hard that leads to life, and there are few who find it." (Matthew 7:13-14)

Dedication that requires us to be countercultural, not count the cost of our discipleship, and enter through the narrow gate is indeed difficult, especially in a society where acceptance is paramount. The road less traveled may not be popular and will require more of us, but the greatest accomplishments for most people in life never came via the easy route. On the contrary, those triumphs of which we are most proud in life required us to do more, to work, sacrifice, and raise the bar to higher levels. It did not come easy, but it was worth every ounce of our effort. If you want to do well in school, you must study; if you want to succeed in work, you must take the time and manifest the effort that signifies your dedication. If we slack off, in any endeavor, we will not achieve the end we seek. The same is true to be a follower of Jesus; dedication is necessary.

We must be dedicated, but this great quality must be sustained with our perseverance. The Christian life requires us to never give up but to stridently move forward. When knocked to one's knees, either proverbially or literally, the Christian has no option but to stand up, dust oneself off, and continue to walk the road. The road of discipleship will seldom be straight, unencumbered, and without a few chuck holes and detours. Relationships of all sorts, including our relationship with the Lord, go through rocky times, but perseverance is necessary. Remember the rather tenuous relationship between Jesus and his chosen chief apostle, Peter. The Gospels portray Peter as the one who does not fully understand why Jesus must die; he is the one who when the Lord needs him most denies Christ three times. Yet, as described in John chapter 21, Jesus gives Peter a second chance. The Lord never gave up on his relationship with Peter and he will never give up on any of us. Francis Thompson in his epic poem, "The Hound of Heaven," aptly analogizes Jesus to one who leaves no stone unturned in a diligent search for us. Jesus is the good Shepherd, the one who leaves ninety-nine perfectly good sheep in the desert and searches for the one who has strayed away. Since Jesus continually perseveres in reaching out to us, we are called to do likewise in our outreach to him.

There will be times when we do not understand what is happening; we might even question God. We cannot understand why something has happened--the illness, injury, or death of a colleague, friend, or relative. We cannot understand why the inhumanity of some is so destructive to the decency of others. We ask why our plans did not work out as we forecast. We must always remember, however, that God's ways are not our ways, and his time is not our time. Perseverance is necessary to be a follower of Jesus, to live the Christian life today.

After dedication and perseverance, the third element to a successful Christian life today is to meet our responsibilities, to ourselves, to others, and ultimately, of course, to God. Responsibility is something we learn from our earliest days. We are taught that when given certain privileges, responsibility comes with it as a package. When we are young and receive the privilege to go out with our friends, we must take seriously the responsibility for our actions, realizing that failure to be responsible could jeopardize the privilege we have received. If we wish to be a member of a club, athletic team, or fraternal organization we must follow the creed, the rules of that group. If you want the freedom and other privileges that come from being a citizen in a democratic nation, we must be responsible for our behavior and make it consistent with the laws of the land.

Christianity indeed gives us numerous privileges, but with those privileges come significant responsibility. We have the privilege of the Word of God, the sacraments, the Church, and all its many groups that provide support. We revel in such privileges, even taking them too often for granted, but the significant responsibility that comes with such privileges must not be ignored. These responsibilities mean taking seriously what the Church teaches and carrying it out in our daily lives. To be a responsible Christian means to be an active participant. When we attend Mass are we ready to celebrate and not simply sit there disinterested, waiting for the time to pass, thinking about what we plan to do that afternoon or the next day. A responsible Christian life means frequenting the sacraments, especially confession, which is far too often neglected in our contemporary Church. All people are sinners and, therefore, need to be reconciled to the Church and to God, the two elements provided by the Sacrament of Reconciliation.

The Christian life requires us to be dedicated, persevere in all our endeavors, and be responsible, but without the unifying glue of faith to unite these important qualities, our quest will never be complete. What precisely is faith; how can it be defined? While many good answers could be chosen my favorite response comes from the Letter to the Hebrews 11:1: "Now faith is the assurance of things hoped for, the conviction of things not seen." Through the journey of life there are many things for which we hope. When we are young, we hope for good grades in school, to be successful on the athletic field, to gain admission to the college of our choice, and to marry the person of our dreams and raise a family. Later in life we hope for success in the professional world, to raise our children properly, the opportunity to enjoy the world in which we live, and when appropriate to retire and enjoy the fruits of our labor. We always hope for good health and for world peace. There are many things that we cannot see, yet we believe. We have a conviction about these invisible, but very believable things. We cannot see God, but we believe; we cannot understand the concept of the Trinity, yet we believe. We cannot predict the future, but we believe it will bring both goodness and challenges. St. Paul tells us that without faith we are lost. He knew what he was talking about, for he was lost until Christ appeared to him on the road to Damascus and gave him the gift of faith.

Conclusion

Living the Christian life has never been easy, but the challenges that it presents make us better prepared and able to not only live today, but to prepare ourselves for a return home to God at the end of our days. To satisfactorily be a follower of Jesus begins by better knowing the subject of our attention and finding ways to better communicate with him. Four distinct, yet related, qualities form the recipe for success in living the Christian life today. First, Christians must be totally dedicated. Such dedication will probably necessitate going against the mainstream flow, to enter through the narrow gate, realizing that it is the one path to life. We must be people of perseverance, never giving up, but always striving to go further and find better ways to be a disciple. Christians are called to be responsible, realizing that the great privilege of being a follower of Jesus demands significant responsibility. Our dedication, perseverance, and responsible attitude are wrapped together by being a person of great faith, believing what cannot be seen or touched, yet with full conviction professing our trust through all we do and say. The journey will not be easy, but the Lord never promised his followers an easy path. Rather, he promised the cross, but in a very real way the cross becomes our only hope. Thus, always live in hope, as we daily walk as disciples of Jesus.

THE CALL TO EVANGELIZATION

Jesus' last words to his apostles as recorded by St. Matthew (28:19-20a) were: "Go therefore and make disciples of all nations, baptizing them in the name of the Father and of the Son and of the Holy Spirit, and teaching them to obey everything that I have commanded you." The Lord's exhortation to go forth in his name, baptizing and teaching, has served as the basic rationale for Christian evangelization throughout the Common Era. Historically two basic evangelistic theories have been utilized. Acculturation, a more aggressive method that held little or no value in the culture and religious practice of those to be evangelized. This method, which imposed the culture and religion of the evangelizer, was the general concept utilized in Latin America by the Spanish. Inculturation, a more conciliatory method that sought to work within cultural and the religious environment of the people to be evangelized, was used by the French in the Great Lakes region of North America. Although vastly different in approach, these two ideologies held one common goal: to carry out the edict of Jesus by bringing the light of the gospel message to the entire world.

The evangelization efforts of countless peoples over the centuries have brought Jesus' message to all continents; there are few people in the world who have not been introduced to the Christian message. Yet, the call to evangelization in the twenty-first century is no less valid or important. Indeed, while people may know and even claim that they practice the gospel message, nonetheless there exists a need to re-evangelize the world, both individually and communally. Thus, Jesus' message to his apostles continues to challenge us to follow their lead as evangelizers of the world. The mission is the same, but the techniques must be different. A description of two modern evangelization models, active ministry, and servant can prompt us to resurrect in our own hearts and minds the need to fulfill Jesus' final command.

A Traditional Understanding of Evangelization

At its root, evangelization is the process by which one assists another to draw closer to God. This is accomplished most profoundly by preaching Christ's message of love which is articulated repeatedly and profoundly in the Gospels. Jesus inaugurated his public ministry by going to the synagogue in Nazareth, his hometown, and stating that the prophecy of Isaiah was fulfilled in his presence. Initially all spoke well of him and were amazed at his teaching, but when he challenged them, their Janus-faced attitude prevailed, and they sought to hurl him over a cliff. (Luke 4:16-30) Here the message of Jesus was proclaimed, but it seems that did not make a difference in the lives of those who heard his words. Similarly, the gospel may be preached, but evangelization does not happen unless some change or transformation is affected in the listener. Thus, evangelization necessitates some form of conversion, not generally a one-shot transformation as happened to St. Paul, but a more ongoing daily effort to find the proper road to God.

Traditionally evangelization, the conversion of one's person to the mission and message of Christ, has been practiced through some popular images. During the "First Great Awakening" in early eighteenth-century America, itinerant preachers such as Jonathan Edwards, George Whitefield, and John Wesley, traveled near and far to proclaim the message of Christ. Street preachers, like those who stood in the public square or on a busy corner and proclaimed a particular message, have certainly been popular throughout history. Sinclair Lewis' protagonist Elmer Gantry portrays this evangelical style in a poor light, but Billy Graham's ministry and the rosary crusade of Father Patrick Peyton, CSC, present more positive views. The mission bands of such religious communities as the Paulist Fathers, Redemptorists, Dominicans, and Jesuits, to name only a few, were very popular during the middle decades of the twentieth century. We also are aware of the "door-to-door" evangelization of some Protestant denominations, such as the Mormons and the Jehovah's Witnesses. We may not follow with their theology or feel we have the energy or capacity for this latter type of evangelization, but one must certainly respect the zeal and courage these groups demonstrate in their ministry.

New Models of Evangelization

History has clearly demonstrated the efficacy of the evangelistic efforts, but there are certainly other ideas and means that can be utilized to bring the message of Christ to others and transform their lives. One such model, "Active Ministry," seeks to bring others to God by fulfilling Jesus' command to preach the Gospel to all nations. In this way we go forward with confidence, realizing that we are not alone; Jesus is with us always in our efforts. A second method, "Servant Model," suggests that we can bring people closer to God by serving others in humble ways. As Jesus suggested, it is the meek, humble, and lowly who will find peace in God's kingdom.

Active Ministry Model

A brief story can be used to aptly illustrate the Active Ministry model. Three young people were discussing various versions of the

Bible. One young man said, "I like the New American translation. It is easier to read, clearer, and uses language to which I can relate." Another young man stated, "I like the Jerusalem Bible. It is also easy to read and is quite poetic; it is very helpful in my prayer. A third person, a young woman, responded a bit differently: "I like my mother's version best. She translated the Bible into action so I can utilize it in everyday life" The story illustrates the efficacy of practical example, the basic concept that our actions speak louder than words.

Manifesting good example and thereby being an active minister, is a technique of evangelization in which all can participate for it is a basic responsibility of baptism. When Jesus called the apostles to become his followers, he did so personally and by name. As the Scriptures recount, he said, "Follow me." These men, we are told, immediately left family and occupation and became his closest and most trusted disciples. In a similar way, the day we were baptized our names were pronounced before the Christian community for the first time. It was our call from the Lord to live a life of active industry. When Jesus first proclaimed his mission, he reiterated the words of the prophets. Likewise, we go forth, having been called by the Lord and seeking to re-proclaim the basic and repetitive message of love found on the lips of Jesus in the New Testament. Jesus' call to the apostles was specific in name, but generic in expectation and responsibility. Similarly, our call was specific, but we have a general responsibility associated with this call to seek holiness and to share that with our brothers and sisters. In other words, we are called in an active way to draw people closer to Christ, to be evangelists.

One might ask how active ministry can be seen as a process of evangelization? As explained above, evangelization requires conversion, which is a process, not an immediate self-transformation. Thus, each action of our lives that positively manifests the message and mission of Jesus to others adds to the process of conversion and thereby to evangelization. Consider how many times you have been inspired by the actions of others. Sometimes what we observe is colossal or heroic; many times, however, simple and mundane tasks can be equally powerful. Nothing is too small or insignificant for all actions that emulate the pattern of Jesus' life can be instructive and helpful. Who of us has not been forced to pause when we see the faith of one who kneels in prayer before the Blessed Sacrament or faithfully grasps a rosary in hand, on the bus or train, or simply walking down a busy city street? The actions of others force us to pause, to reflect, and to think. We are challenged to ponder our own lives, to get involved, to seek other avenues that can aid our progress to God and, whether we think about it or not, draw others closer to the Lord as well. Such actions inspire us to move closer to God, to be converted and renewed.

Our ministry, seen in a generic sense and not simply in a formal religious setting, has the same impact and influence on others that the good example we observe has on us. Our ministry truly is a vehicle which others use to find God and, therefore, is a powerful tool of evangelization. Our example aids others; it aids us as well. We find a sense of fulfillment which can only happen in doing the work of God.

Servant Model

As with our discussion of Active Ministry, a story can be used to illustrate the basic concepts of the Servant Model of evangelization. An Army chaplain came upon a wounded young soldier lying in great pain in a foxhole. With Bible in hand, the chaplain offered the wounded man a word of consolation: "Son, can I read some words of encouragement to you from the Good Book?" The soldier did not respond verbally but began to shift about as if he were very uncomfortable. Dutifully, the chaplain found a bedroll lying about on the battlefield. He rolled it up and placed it under the man's head as a pillow. Again, he was just about to ask if the soldier wanted to hear from the Bible when the young man whispered, "I am so thirsty." Again, the chaplain hurried off, found a canteen, and then helped the man sip some water. A third time the chaplain prepared to make his overture, but now the wounded man began to shiver; he was obviously cold. Without thinking, the chaplain stripped off his own field jacket and laid it over the wounded man as a blanket. Then, almost on command, the young soldier looked the chaplain in the eye and said, "Chaplain, if there is anything in the Good Book that will help an individual do more for another then you have already done for me, then please read it. I want to hear it." This story powerfully illustrates the efficacy of being a servant, to willingly and without pretense give oneself to another. Jesus proclaimed this same message to his apostles. In responding to an argument among them as to who was the greatest, he said, "Whoever wishes to be great among you must be your servant and whoever wishes to be first among you must be your slave; just as the Son of Man came not to be served but to serve, and to give his life [as] a ransom for many." (Matthew 20:26-28)

Society today, especially in the hustle and bustle of the business world, does not fully appreciate the value of servitude. Rather, one might say we are brainwashed or indoctrinated, into the belief that making an impression upon others is imperative. Young people need to carry impressive records to obtain admission to the college of their choice and later find a job to exercise the skills and talents they have honed and obtained. Working people of all stripes and of all ages must be impressive, not only to secure employment, but to maintain it and to move up the corporate ladder. Clearly, impressions are a necessity in our world today; this cannot be denied. But who are we trying to impress and why? This is the key question.

The process of making an impression upon others can lead to many problems and drives us away from the virtue of service. "Getting ahead" leads often to the tendency to step on those around us. However, if we simply act on our own perceived agenda, with no thought to the needs of others, then the impression we leave may be just the opposite of that which we desire to give. Impressions based on power, wealth, and prestige, the three great temptations posed to Jesus in the desert as he prepared for his public ministry, are many times negative. We may be somewhat sheltered because of the structures of our life from falling prey to the temptation to wealth, but prestige and power stand at the door seeking admittance to our house. We must be constantly vigilant to assure that our drive to impress those above us in the chain of command does not in the process bring injury to our fellow travelers and peers seeking to make ends meet in the world.

A life of service does not make headlines of the papers very often, but it does make a great impression on others and, therefore, serves as a great vehicle for evangelization. Certainly, there are powerful examples, like St. Teresa of Calcutta, who have so impressed the world with a life of service that their names are known with affection universally. However, generally the service we perform is like that of the Army chaplain, simple, every day, and often random acts of kindness that hopefully characterize our life. The conversion we hope to affect in ourselves and by extension others through our service can be likened to the to the "life" of a water pitcher. When first purchased the pitcher was shiny white, with an imprint of pink and blue flowers on the side. After many years of service, it became chipped after hundreds of washings it was only a faint impression of its former glory. Similarly, we are like worn water pitchers, created by God for a specific and special purpose, but one that can generally be classified in the role of service. Through our service we become beautiful not because we are kept on the shelf where we will not be marred, but because we have been used for God's purposes.

The witness value of being a good servant is incalculable. The example we set will be recognized for its goodness and valued highly by others. What we do speaks clearly of our priorities. To labor on behalf of others sends a missive that people are important--a clear message of evangelization. Living for others, which in essence is the life of service, makes people stop and look at the highly hedonistic society in which we live. As Jesus says the greatest is the person with sufficient courage to serve others.

Few of us will be famous servants, but all of us have the common responsibility to help others and draw them closer to Christ. We have the common vocation to be evangelists. One way to view our common Christian responsibility is once again illustrated by a purposeful story. One day a woman decided to prepare stew for dinner. The potatoes she needed were located in the cellar. She descended the steps from the kitchen into the darkened cellar. Light shone into the space from a small window. She went to the corner of the room and opening the bag of potatoes found that several had grown small green branches from their eyes. She wondered how this was possible since there was no light in this space. Just then the light from the small window reflected off a highly polished copper kettle that was hanging from a metal holder. Now realizing how the light had struck these potatoes she reflected, "I'm not a preacher; I'm not a teacher. But I can and must be a copper kettle Christian, reflecting by word and action, the message of Jesus to others." Regardless of our apostolate, status in life, age, or any other factor, we all have the opportunity, even the duty, to be copper kettle Christians. This is our Christian call; this is the call to evangelization.

SEEKING EXCELLENCE IN LIFE

The year 2004 will always be remembered as a banner year, one of excellence for the Boston Red Sox. After 86 years of frustration the "curse of the bambino" was broken, and the Sox became World Series champions. The excellence on the field that year may have been inspired by the story of one of the team's greatest heroes of yesteryear, Ted Williams. As those who follow baseball know batting 400 in the major leagues is quite a feat. In fact, that last player to do so was Ted Williams, but his accomplishment was not done the easy way; Williams had guts and was a man of excellence. Ted entered the last day of the 1941 season with 179 hits in 448 official at bats. When you do the math, his average was .39955. In major league baseball if a player's average is more than halfway between one value and a second, the higher figure is used. Thus, officially Ted entered the final day, a scheduled doubleheader with an official average of .400. Thus, Williams' manager came to the slugger and suggested that he sit the day out, since the games had no bearing on the Red Sox season. The last .400 hitter was 11 years prior, and the manager felt Ted should not take a chance of having a bad day at the plate. But Williams told his manager, "If I am going to be the batting champion and possibly bat .400, I am going to win it like a champion." Ted played both games of the doubleheader and he got six hits in eight trips to the plate to raise his average to .406.

Ted Williams had guts, the courage of confidence. He was a man who demanded excellence in himself.

The miracle season of the 2004 Boston Red Sox and the true story of one of baseball's legends provide a challenge to reflect upon excellence in life and the motivation we have in doing what we do. St. Paul was a man who demanded excellence, in himself and others. Not content with the mundane mediocrity he saw in the Christian community at Colassae, he wrote to that nascent group (3:1): "So if you have been raised with Christ, seek the things that are above, where Christ is seated at the right hand of God." Paul demanded excellence from himself as well as others. He was never a burden to anyone and exhorted those in the communities he founded to act in a similar way. He wrote in II Thessalonians 3:11-13: "For we hear that some of you are living in idleness, near busybodies, not doing any work. Now such persons we command and exhort in the Lord Jesus Christ to do their work quietly and to earn their own living. Brothers and sisters, do not be weary in doing what is right." Paul's message is clear; we must demand quality and excellence from ourselves; laziness is to be avoided at all costs.

The prophet Malachi (4:1-2), writing to the Hebrews in Judah after their return from exile, also speaks of excellence. The prophet labels those who are arrogant as evildoers. These will be cut down and burned like stubble in the field. In contrast, however, those who revere the name of God will rise on the healing wings of the sun. In other words, those who have taken the easy road will be cast off; those who choose the more difficult path will find life with God. In the Sermon on the Mount (Matthew 7:13-14), Jesus puts it this way: "Enter through the narrow gate; for the gate is wide and the road is easy that leads to destruction, and there are many who take it. For the gate is narrow and the road is hard that leads to life, and there are a few who find it."

We are all called to live lives of excellence. We are always challenged to do our best, regardless of time and circumstance. We are called to excellence in our work ethic. How do we approach what we do, at work, in school, on the athletic field, in relationships with one another? Are we content merely to do what is necessary, to get by? Do we seek only the lowest common denominator, a level that will not get us in trouble with anyone else? Are we expecting others to pick up the slack for our inattention or laziness? Or are we, as Paul and Malachi suggest, people who set the bar higher and seek new heights and broader horizons? Do we encourage others by our ethic to follow our lead to be more productive and seek greater things? We must seek excellence in opportunity and challenges as well. When opportunities come our way do we pass them by or do we engage them, at least somewhat and find the grace therein? Are we content to simply be who we are and do what we have always done, or can we seek the excellence of challenge that calls us to move away from a staid existence and to a find new avenues for our talent? We must seek excellence in faith and its expression. When celebrating the Eucharist are we fully engaged? At Mass, do we sing with full throat and respond to the priest with a sense of enthusiasm and purpose? When the readings are proclaimed and homily preached do we give our full attention? Do the readings and homily have our full attention? Are we continuing our religious education through our reading of religious books or articles? Do we know what is going on in our local diocese and the Church universal? Are we content to be adults in body but youth in our knowledge of the Faith? Think what would happen if we never matured in our knowledge for our role in the secular world? While simple faith is a beautiful attribute, it is important to understand not only what the Church teaches, but why it teaches it. Excellence in faith is not only knowledge, but also prayer as well. Are we content with a couple of rote prayers in the morning or evening? Can we not move to Paul's higher realm with new prayer forms, a retreat or faith sharing?

We have been gifted in so many ways and, therefore, we should seek to maximize what we have. We should seek excellence in the material, cultural, and spiritual realms of our lives. Jesus proclaims in Luke's Gospel (12:48b), "From everyone to whom much has been given, much will be required; and from the one to whom much has been entrusted, even more will be demanded." In a similar way the Hollywood blockbuster "Spiderman II, presents a powerful message. " Ben Parker, the uncle of Peter Parker, alias Spiderman, tells his nephew who wants out of his role as a superhero, "Great power demands great responsibility." We have all been given great power in many and multiple ways. We must be people of excellence and not waste what we have been given.

The challenge to be a person of excellence is significant. We may not think we are up to the task. After all, why work so hard? Clearly an exhortation to work hard is present, but we must also remember that Jesus is with us in every moment, but most especially the most trying and difficult times. Speaking of the end times (Luke 21:18), the Lord tells his apostles that they will suffer, "But not a hair of your head will perish." If we strive for excellence, doing our part, God will always do his part.

Ted Williams demanded much from himself; but is this not the norm for champions? Inspired by Williams' heroic 1941 .406 batting average and understanding the clear message of Scripture, let us strive for excellence in every aspect of our lives. Let us be like Christ who challenged others to raise themselves to his level. The challenge is great, but the gift of eternal life is worth every effort. Our response is awaited!

Seeking the Greater Good

"Four score and seven years ago, our fathers brought forth on this continent a new nation conceived in liberty and dedicated to the proposition that all men are created equal. Now we are engaged in a great civil war, testing whether that nation or any nation so conceived and so dedicated can long endure." These words of President Abraham Lincoln proclaimed at the dedication of the Gettysburg National Cemetery will always be remembered by students of American history. The year was 1863; the nation was embattled in the great Civil War. After 87 years of unity, the great house, the union, was divided. It was the task of Lincoln to reunite the Union and make it one, but he would not do it at the cost of his convictions.

America's Civil War was contested over several issues, but at their heart the issues centered upon states' rights, most especially the practice of slavery. As a constitutionalist, Lincoln supported the nation's foundational document which states that all rights not expressly granted to the Federal Government are given to the states, but he believed slavery was not an issue for the government, but rather was an intrinsic evil that needed to be exorcized from the nation. For Lincoln the fact that the nation was divided over the issue of slavery was of less consequence than the principle of its abolition. Lincoln certainly wished to preserve the Union and move the nation forward, but if preservation did not include the freedom of African slaves, then division was necessary.

Abraham Lincoln was a man of principal, and he did not allow the threat of division to cloud his vision. At his first inauguration on March 4, 1861, he could see that the signs of the times might produce war between Americans, but nothing was so sacred to him as the principals upon which he stood and in which he believed. He proclaimed, "I, therefore, consider that in the view of the Constitution and the laws, the Union is unbroken; and to the extent of my ability, I shall take care, as the Constitution itself expressly enjoins upon me, that the laws of the Union be faithfully executed in all the states."

Judging between what is good and what is of greater good is often a decision we must make. Choosing what is right and upholding our convictions, even in the face of adversity is a courageous act, and one of the great challenges of the Christian life.

Scripture teaches us important lessons on the need to be firm in our beliefs and always choose what is right. For the Hebrew people the law was the base foundation from which all their beliefs and ethics were drawn. Adherence to the law and "doing the right thing" were synonymous. Possibly the best example that is described in the historical, prophetic, and wisdom books of the Hebrew Scriptures (Old Testament) is maintenance of the Sabbath, the third commandment of the decalogue: "Remember the Sabbath day and keep it holy. Six days you shall labor and do all your work. But the seventh day is a Sabbath to the Lord your God; you shall not do any work -- you, your son, or your daughter, your male or female slave, your livestock, or the alien resident in your towns. For in six days the Lord made heaven and earth, the sea, and all that is in them, but rested the seventh day; therefore, the Lord blessed the Sabbath day and consecrated it." (Exodus 20:8-11; also, Deuteronomy 5:12-15) For the Hebrews the law was sacred, and maintenance of the Sabbath was absolute. This is what God had commanded and it was imperative to uphold the Lord's edict and its purpose of giving praise to God. Yet, despite what seems to be absolute, we must read further to know if God asks more of us.

As a good practicing Jew who understood and valued his heritage and the Law, Jesus would have been the last to willingly violate his ancestral tradition. Yet, in the Gospels we hear how he acted upon a higher good. Jesus often challenged the law, especially the absolute edict of Sabbath observance. St. Mark relates how Jesus walked through the grain fields on the Sabbath and ate of its produce. Then he entered the synagogue and encountered a man with a withered hand. He challenged the Pharisees, "Is it lawful to do good or to do harm on the Sabbath, to save life or to kill?" (Mark 3:4) Jesus realized that the minds of the religious leaders were closed to his purpose and work. Their closed attitude did not allow them to learn the lesson Jesus so badly wanted them to understand and make part of their lives: "The Sabbath was made for humankind, and not humankind for the Sabbath." (Mark 2:27) Essentially, Jesus told his contemporaries, and we who live today as well, that there is a higher good, something even more important than strict compliance with the law. The Sabbath, the law, is given to free us and serve our needs, not chain us from doing what is good.

Jesus was courageous and stood against adversity, especially against the narrow-minded view that many of the religious leaders of his day possessed. We recall how he rejected the verdict of condemnation that the Scribes and Pharisees had placed upon a woman caught in the act of adultery. When queried about his opinion in the matter, Jesus responded, "Let anyone among you who is without sin be the first to throw a stone at her." Jesus' challenge was too much for these religious leaders. John reports, "They went away, one by one, beginning with the elders." (John 8:7b-9) Jesus was not afraid to challenge the system when he knew a higher good needed to be achieved. He never compromised his convictions and what he knew was the right thing to do.

St. Paul was certainly a man of firm purpose and strong conviction. He traveled the eastern Mediterranean world on three extensive missionary journeys in his attempt to proclaim the message of Jesus that came to him initially at his conversion on the road to Damascus (Acts 9:1-9) and his sojourn in Arabia (Galatians 1:11-2:1). Imprisonments, beatings, shipwreck, even being stoned could not dampen his fervor nor weaken his conviction. Standing against adversity, proclaiming the sometimes-difficult word, and challenging prevailing norms were almost daily events for this great apostle. Thus, when he tells the Christians at Corinth, a community he knew well having lived with them for a considerable amount of time during his travels, to stand firm in their conviction, he spoke from his experience. Encouraging his friends he wrote, "We are afflicted in every way, but not crushed; perplexed, but not driven to despair; persecuted, but not forsaken; struck down but not destroyed; always carrying in the body the death of Jesus, so that the life of Jesus may also be made visible in our bodies." (II Corinthians 4:8-10)

The many responsibilities and complications of daily life often place us in positions where we must make choices that are unpopular with others. When Abraham Lincoln made the decision, based on his conviction that slavery was evil, to engage the South and not allow this practice to continue, he became in certain sectors very unpopular and, I am certain, suffered much. Life events bring many encounters when we are forced to make unpopular choices that cause us to suffer. When parents are forced to exhibit "tough love" and challenge their children about the company they keep or the habits and behavior they exhibit there will be some suffering along the way. It is difficult when an employer is forced to tell an employee that his or her work is not up to standards and that if improvement is not forthcoming soon that a termination notice will follow. When teenagers must challenge their peers about the use of alcohol, drugs, and inappropriate sexual relations the words many times will not be well received. People who have the courage to challenge others will be considered "out of it" and placed on the fringes by those who are "in" with all the important people. Countering the prevailing norms of our complicated world will not be easy; it will cause us lots of anguish and pai. We might suffer greatly. But let us not forget that Jesus upheld a higher order and maintained his convictions at great expense, namely his rejection by his own people and ultimately his ignominious death by crucifixion. If we wish to be true followers of Jesus, we can expect no better.

The Christian life led in emulation of Jesus will never be easy, but rather will be filled with numerous challenges that will require us to make significant decisions. We may be forced to violate the norm of our organization, business, or even family tradition to do what we know is right, that which constitutes a higher order. Through much prayer and celebration of the sacraments we will receive the grace needed to strengthen our will to uphold our convictions and to stand strong against sometimes strong opposition. Let us take courage from the actions of Abraham Lincoln, the words of St. Paul, and most especially the life of Jesus to manifest lives worthy of our call and consistent with the Lord's message of love and peace. Our reward will be eternal life.

Negotiating the Storms of Life: Challenges and Benefits

For nine months in 1940, London and its environs were in the eyes of a great storm. The infamous "Blitz" when the German Luftwaffe pounded the English capital, seeking to terrorize the people and bring Great Britain to its knees, was a time of great distress. Initially for 57 straight days German warplanes dropped bombs and incendiary devices, leveling many areas of the city, and seeking to break the will of the British people. Then for the next six months, German air raids continued periodically. However, one man stood in the eye of the storm and would not be broken. Winston Churchill, who had served the British government in various capacities for many years, became prime minister only a few months prior to the onslaught. During a period of terrible suffering Churchill brought calm and courage to his people. The morning after a raid Churchill was often seen walking through the rubble, almost daring the Germans to attack. He brought hope to a people who were living a nightmare that killed almost 45,000 British citizens. Churchill could not be swayed by his advisors to stay away from the fray or to hide from the onslaught. On the contrary, he lived through the daily raids with his people, famously stating, "If the British Empire and its Commonwealth last for a thousand years, men will still say: '**This was their finest hour**.'"

Winston Churchill stood in the eye of a massive storm, but he never flinched. Not only did he have personal strength and conviction, but most assuredly he must have believed that the British cause was just and, therefore, to resist and stand against the tide at all costs was imperative. Churchill stands as a significant historical example of an important theme that we hear in Scripture, namely that we must, through our faith in God, be able to stand against the various storms through which we must pass, both personally and as a society.

The Storms of Life in Scripture

The Book of Job is clearly a text which describes the personal storm of a man of faith. Job was a wealthy man. He possessed lands, material possession, a large and beautiful family and great faith. But the Lord allowed Satan to take all of Job's great wealth away, to place him in the eye of the storm and see how he would react. We read how Job was visited by three of his friends who discussed his plight with him. Through these conversations, the Lord speaks to Job as he endures this great storm in his life. While Job was tempted to curse God, and wavers, in the end he holds strong and weathers the great storm of his life. Because of his great faith the Lord restores to Job all his former riches and greater, so much so that as the book concludes, "In all the land no other women were as beautiful as the daughters of Job." (Job 42:15a)

The Gospel of Mark (4:35-41) presents a classic story of weathering the storm. We hear that Jesus and his disciples are crossing the Sea of Galilee in a small boat. This was a routine evolution; the four evangelists report similar crossings on numerous occasions. The Sea of Galilee is not a large body of water; it is possible to look across its east-west expanse quite easily. Nevertheless, violent storms can arise on this body of water. Mark describes one of the storms as Jesus and the apostles are crossing from east to west. The evangelist tells us that Jesus was asleep "on a cushion." Apparently, the Lord is not concerned; he has no fear. When a storm arose, however, the apostles wake him and ask, "Teacher, do you not care that we are perishing?" (Mark 4:38b) In essence they are pleading, "Please do something about the situation." Jesus immediately calms the wind and sea, but he did not let the opportunity to lovingly yet forcefully chastise his chosen inner circle, the apostles, challenging their lack of faith. He said to them "Why are you terrified? Do you not have faith?" (Mark 4:40) Jesus' action convinced the apostles that he was indeed God. As Mark records their words, "Who then is this who even wind and sea obey him?" (Mark 4:41b)

All of us have endured many storms in our life. Some, probably most of them, are personal storms. We may have failed at some endeavor, whether that was in school, or in business, or even a personal relationship. Storms arise through financial hardship, illness, or injury, either personally or to a loved one. Storms arise when we fail to achieve a goal or do not rise to the expectations of others. Many other storms arise in our life that are more communal in nature. Historically, the United States has withered many storms, especially armed conflicts such as the Civil War as well as the infamous twentieth century wars, World Wars I and II, Korea, Vietnam ,and continuing into the twenty-first century with conflicts in Iraq and Afghanistan. We have gone through the Great Depression and more recently the 2008 economic decline. Most assuredly the whole world has gone through arguably the greatest worldwide storm in history with the Covid-19 pandemic.

Many times, the storms of our lives appear to be overwhelming. Certainly, that must have been what Winston Churchill and the British people thought in 1940 when bombs daily lighted up the night sky for two months, and then continued for another half year. But the British champion, Winston Churchill stood in the breach and would not allow his nation to succumb to such a storm. Similarly, we must not allow storms that attack our lives, whether personally or communally, to defeat us. We have the one person in our corner who can always be counted upon to be our champion. His name is Jesus Christ.

St. Paul emphasizes this reality when writing to the Christian community at Corinth, a group of people he knew well from his long visits to the city. He tells them that it is through Christ's love for them that he weathered the storm of his life, enduring death, but rising so that we could live not for ourselves, but to promote Jesus' message and mission. While human resolutions can be helpful, ultimately it is through our total confidence in Jesus Christ and his ability to weather the storms that threaten our lives that ultimate solutions will be found (II Corinthians 5:14-17). Jesus calmed the storm on the Sea of Galilee when the apostles cried out to him; Jesus will calm the storms of our lives if we have the courage to do the same.

What have been some of the challenges of the storms we have faced, especially the recent international pandemic? Certainly, our routine, job, and especially interaction with people have been radically altered. For those fortunate to keep their jobs, many were forced to work from home. Children were forced into remote learning and the world learned quickly about "zoom." Psychologically the pandemic has altered the way we think. For many, trust in institutions, individuals, and even our faith has been challenged. Our mental attitude and approach to our day-to-day life has been changed. Challenges to our faith have been abundant. Active participation in the sacraments was taken away for the majority; the television Mass became the norm. As we slowly move back to a pre-Covid-19 environment we have the challenge to build back our lives. How have our relationships with others shifted or changed? What have we learned about ourselves or others?

While difficult, challenges do bring benefits, even if at times they are hard to find. Think about the greater appreciation you have for the ordinary and routine in your life. When things are commonplace, they become mundane and our appreciation for them is less, but when these same routine things are missing, their value becomes that much more apparent. At Mass, even after returning in many regions to physical attendance, the lack of music, empty holy water fonts, no hymnals, the inability to shake hands or demonstrate some active sign of peace to another, heightened our awareness of the simple yet important things. The pandemic has prompted us to re-evaluate our lives and to consider what is truly significant and what is extraneous. We have had the opportunities to grow in different ways, to try things that we have never attempted, to seek new vistas and avenues in life. We can learn an important lesson from the words of St. James (1:2-4): "Consider it all joy, my brothers, when you encounter various trials, for you know that the testing of your faith produces perseverance. And let perseverance be perfect, so that you may be perfect and complete, lacking in nothing."

Conclusion

Storms of various natures, both personal and societal, force us to place our lives on pause, to interrupt where we are and what we are planning to do. How have we dealt with these situations? Do we view these realities, these interruptions and pauses, whatever their nature, as problematic? Or can we view them as opportunities for growth and movement in different directions? Weathering great storms can give us much food for thought for our relationship with God and others. Have we appreciated all the many ways God interrupts our lives, placing them on pause, allowing us to see new vistas and possibilities, or do we simply grow angry that the status quo which we know so well has been interrupted? What have we learned from the very storms of our life? What have these experiences in life taught us?

The pandemic has been a unique experience for all of us. It may take some effort, but we need to spend the necessary time in prayer and reflection to ask ourselves what have we learned and what do we still need to learn from this common human experience? The pandemic has affected different people in varied ways; there is no common denominator other than our lives have been placed on hold. We have been living through an interrupted life. We can learn a lesson, however from history, the specific example of Winston Churchill, and certainly from Scripture that placing our life on pause, experiencing an interruption, large or small, presents many opportunities. If we have not taken the opportunity to contemplate our response, it's not too late. God has brought us an opportunity, not necessarily one we chose or even desired. Nevertheless, the possibility of good things in the future is present. We only need to be open to find them.

THY WILL BE DONE

In his famous book *The Great Divorce*, the prominent British writer, C.S. Lewis, describes two types of people in the world, based on their response to God's call. One group says to God, "Thy will be done." The other group proclaims to God, "I am going to do it my way." These two groups illustrate the two basic responses to the Lord's call, the two fundamental ways of answering the challenge to be his disciples. Many fall in step, seeking as best they can, to follow the path provided by the Lord. Others, on the other hand, taking personal control of the situation, follow their own devices, which are often contrary to the desire of God. Wisdom and experience help us to understand our need to follow God's call, proclaiming "Thy will be done."

Scripture provides numerous examples, both in the Hebrew Bible and the New Testament, of people of great faith who have followed the call of the Lord, although possibly not initially. The message of the prophets, both the 15 with so-called "named" prophets and those others, like Elijah and Elisha, who spoke God's word but not in a formal book of the Bible, was a call to fall in place and follow the invitation of the Lord. Rather than speaking of future events, the prophets proclaimed their words, for the most part, to the ruling elite in Israel and Judah who were responsible to lead the people and follow the Mosaic Law. Many times, dissatisfied with the actions of the kings and other elites, in both nations, God sent prophets who chastised those in positions of power for their failure to follow the path which God had laid out for them and to be responsible for the people in their care. Rather than following the dictates of the Law, the ruling elite often conducted affairs and governed in ways that were leading the people astray. In essence they were saying to God, "I am going to do it my way." The prophets themselves found their task to be difficult and often initially sought to run away, feeling themselves unqualified or in other ways unsuited for the task God had planned for them. Jonah was told to go to the people of Nineveh and warn them of their impending doom, but initially he balked, stowing away on a ship in the hopes that God might not find him. But, as they say, Jonah "got the message" when the great storm at sea and his capture by the "large fish" convinced him of his need to follow the call of the Lord. It took some twisting of his arm, but finally Jonah said, "Thy will be done." Isaiah, proclaiming God's word to the Southern Kingdom of Judah, felt unworthy of his call, claiming that he was lost "a man of unclean lips, and … [living] among the people of unclean lips." Yet, God purged his feelings of inadequacy and in the end, Isaiah could triumphantly proclaim, "Here am I; send me!" (Isaiah 6: 5, 8) Similarly, Jeremiah, claiming youth and inexperience, tried to run from the call of the Lord, but God responded "Do not be afraid of them, for I am with you to deliver you. … See, today I appoint you over nations and over kingdoms, to pluck up and to pull down, to destroy and to overthrow, to build and to plant." (Jeremiah 1:8, 9b, 10)

The New Testament also provides ample evidence of the need to follow in the footsteps of the Lord, but again some needed to be convinced. Nicodemus, after his conversation with Jesus (John 3:1-21), eventually became one of the Lord's disciples, but conversion was necessary. Undoubtedly the most famous and significant person who eventually said, "Thy will be done," was St. Paul. He describes himself as one who "was violently persecuting the church of God and was trying to destroy it." (Galatians 1:13b) Yet, as the one chosen by the Lord to bring the message of salvation to the Gentiles, Paul came to consider his former way of life as loss. He proclaimed, "More than that, I regard everything as loss because of the surpassing value of knowing Christ Jesus my Lord." (Philippians 3:8)

The example of familiar personages in both the Old and New Testaments, serve only as additional evidence to the most basic model of obedience found in Jesus. In his famous "Bread of Life Discourse," Jesus states, "I have come down from heaven, not to do my own will, but the will of him who sent me." (John 6:38) Jesus never took the attitude "I am going to do it my way," but to the very end was completely obedient to the will of his Father. Even his impending suffering and death could not sway him from his loyalty. His words in the Garden of Gethsemane were indeed powerful: "My Father, if it is possible, let this cup pass from me; yet not what I want but what you want." (Matthew 26:39b)

The challenge of C.S. Lewis in his famous novel, the trial negotiated successfully by so many in the Scriptures, is the same test we wrestle with daily. Christians want to do the will of God, but the obstacles and various barriers to follow in the footsteps of the Lord are indeed numerous and often high. Following in the footsteps of the Lord, truly being able to proclaim, "Thy will be done," requires total trust in Jesus. The world offers so many people, material things, and ideas, all of which are enticing and invite us to follow. It seems "foolish" to take a chance on an unseen and intangible God. Yet, experience, as the greatest teacher, helps us to look at our lives and realize the emptiness and hollowness of seeking to do things our way, rather than following the lead of the Lord. Placing our total confidence and trust in God will never be easy, but then it was not easy for Jonah, Isaiah, Jeremiah, or Paul. It was not easy for Jesus either, but they all came to realize, as they say, "through the back door," that their our own thinking and ways led nowhere they sought to be. Following the way of the Lord, however, allows us to find our way home. Let us have the strength and courage to do the same in our lives. The reward will be eternal life!

PART III: THE CHALLENGES OF MINISTRY

INTRODUCTION

As we journey with our Lord, Jesus, our basic Christian vocation to live a life of holiness, incurs significant responsibility. While this obligation can be manifest in many ways, generally we are called to minister to others, and by doing so serve not only our brothers and sisters but Jesus Christ. In past generations the concept of ministry was, in the minds of many, reserved for priests, religious, and a few dedicated lay men and women who may have served the Church in a more professional way. However, the Second Vatican Council very clearly challenged all members of the Church, described as the people of God, to do their part to build the Kingdom in our world. The "Decree on the Apostolate of the Laity" from Vatican II, is clear with its challenging words: " There are innumerable opportunities open to the laity for the exercise of their apostolate of evangelization and sanctification." It is no longer acceptable to simply "go to church on Sunday," and understand this to be all that is required. Rather, we are all called to minister as contemporary disciples of Jesus Christ.

Ministry takes many forms; there is no one method, action, or formula that the faithful should follow in being active ministers. Certainly, some endeavors are specifically pointed toward meeting the needs of others. Those who have the desire, time, and opportunity to assist the poor and those who are less fortunate in our society may find their ministry with the St. Vincent de Paul Society and similar groups, both on national and parochial levels. Others who are gifted in education can serve youth through religious education programs. Still others might serve in liturgical ministries as lectors, Eucharistic ministers, acolytes, or members of a choir. Let us not forget the numerous secular organizations, including fraternal orders, local soup kitchens and food banks, and various senior citizen outreach programs that can utilize our time, talent, material wealth, and opportunities to serve others. Recall as well that we certainly serve in many routine, ordinary, even mundane ways. A kind word or gesture, a random act of kindness, or even a simple "thank you" will be beneficial to others as well as ourselves. As the expression goes, "kindness returns."

Part III of this volume, "The Challenges of Ministry," addresses the many trials found as ministers in our complex twenty-first century society. In essence our efforts at ministry seek to complete the work of Jesus, the one who came to serve and not be served. We are first called to respond to the invitation of the Lord. We must learn to be people of action and reject the tendency toward ambivalence or laziness. We must possess sufficient trust in the Lord to enter fully into the life of ministry. Rather than simply testing the waters, we need to dive in fully. We must also realize that anything we do in the Lord's name is always appreciated. The simple acts we perform, while seemingly insignificant to us, may be very noteworthy to others. Ministry calls us to lead others to Jesus. We must do our part, assured that Jesus will do the rest. Let us, therefore, get to work!

$100 FOR GOD: THE CHALLENGE TO GO THE EXTRA MILE FOR THE LORD

One Sunday as I stood in the sacristy speaking to the lector and music minister before the Mass that we would celebrate in 10 minutes, a man, in my mind from his appearance a homeless individual, stepped through the sacristy door. In a very calm, dignified, and even prayerful way he said to me, "Father, can you give this to Father Bill or Father Jim for the building fund?" He placed in the palm of my hand what appeared at first to be a $20 bill. I told the man, "Certainly, sir, I will make sure your kind donation goes to the right people." As quickly as the man appeared, he calmly walked from the sacristy, down the steps, and out into the parking. After he left, I gave the money to the music minister, knowing he would encounter the pastor later that morning. To my great surprise, however, what the man had placed into my hand was not a $20 bill but five $20 bills. I asked those in the sacristy, "Am I correct, is that man homeless?" They responded with a collective, "Yes," which prompted me to say, "How can he afford to give the parish $100 when he is living on the streets?" Again, those with whom I was conversing answered, "He has done this in the past. The priests here have helped him, and he wants to show his gratitude." It happened so suddenly and unexpectedly that it prompted me to pause. Knowing that the basic theme of my forthcoming homily was centered about doing more, going beyond our comfort zone, and giving not only from our excess but from our own wants and needs, the whole incident provided much food for thought.

How far are we willing to go, how deep can we dig to meet the trials of ministry that come our way? This challenging question is certainly raised by the above narrative, but it is also described in Sacred Scripture. Jesus puts the challenge very forthrightly when he said to the rich young man who had followed all the commandments, "You lack one thing; go sell what you own, and give the money to the poor, and you will have treasure in heaven; then come, follow me." (Mark 10:21) We are told the young man went away sad for he had many possessions. Tradition tells us that St. Anthony of the Desert heard these words, followed them literally, and became a hermit, an anchorite, the forerunner of monasticism and by extension religious life in general.

The challenge to dig deeper and go further in our discipleship is expressed by Jesus in other ways. Jesus says that if our eye or hand is problematic and causes us to sin, we should rid ourselves of the offending organ (Matthew 5:29-30) Certainly, Jesus is speaking metaphorically of priorities, proclaiming that nothing should come before our relationship with him. The Lord also speaks very clearly that the Christian life and thus our life of discipleship will not be easy. On the contrary, we are promised just the opposite: "If any want to become my followers, let them deny themselves and take up their cross daily and follow me. For those who want to save their life will lose it, and those who lose their life for my sake will save it." (Luke 9:24-25) In other words Jesus taught us to dig deeper go farther and do more. We are challenged to go beyond our comfort zone in our service of others. We should not forget how Jesus challenged his disciples to go the extra mile: "If anyone wants to go to law over your shirt, hand them you coat as well; should anyone press you into service for one mile, go with him two miles." (Matthew 5:40-41)

The Extra Mile in Practice

Quite obviously the applications of Jesus' challenge, manifested in my unexpected experience before Mass, are many, but general ideas can be addressed. How have we gone the extra mile in our efforts to be present to people? We have all experienced people who we might label "high maintenance." The tendency, from our experience, is to avoid such people and situations claiming to ourselves that we have better and more useful things to do. While in some cases, this may be true, our basic vocation as Christians is to be present. Through our baptism call, in some ways we proclaimed our time is others' time. Going the extra mile often necessitates using the precious time we have and giving it to others. Often, we are exhausted from our daily tasks and responsibilities. We certainly do not need to be martyrs and we do not need to save the world; Jesus did that once and for all on the cross. We need to rest and re-energize to be effective in our baptismal call. Going the extra mile means being more generous with our time. I once heard an appropriate aphorism: "We have 24 hours in the day, how we use it is up to us."

Another clear way to go deeper is how we prepare for our ministry, whatever form it might take. I recall as a young priest being rather shocked when the pastor of the parish in which I was serving announced to me after dinner on Saturday evening that he was going over to the office to prepare his homily for the next day. While people work with different schedules and prepare in varied ways, it seemed to me that Saturday night preparation was the last minute. This event raises the question of how we prepare for our daily work. Are we focused on the job at hand, the situation before us, or are we thinking about other matters, that while possibly important personally, are not related to our work responsibilities? How do we prepare for our work as ministers of Christ and his Church? We must all individually ask ourselves what is the depth and degree of our preparation?

Digging deeper in ministry also may require us to do more, go to unexpected places and engage people and situations we might not want to encounter. It may be the case that we do not possess the requisite skills for certain challenges. Not everyone can counsel others, be a teacher, or visit the ill and infirmed. People in every vocation find themselves periodically in situations they never wanted and probably felt totally inadequate, but whether it is a family situation such as dependency or the need to serve as a caregiver or a business situation that requires time, travel, and gaining new talents, those who were required to change, accommodate, or add another dimension to their life did it because it was necessary.

Preparation for the Extra Mile

Assisting others in the name of Christ and the Church, like many aspects of life, can be at times routine, but the challenge to go the extra mile can arise without notice or warning. Thus, we need to be prepared. We need to take the time that is necessary to prepare for the unexpected. Recall the parable of the wise and foolish virgins. Those who were prepared while the bridegroom was delayed entered the wedding feast, but the foolish, those who were not prepared were left out. (Matthew 25:1-13) While most see this as the need to prepare for the unexpected call to life eternal, it can also be applied to our day-to-day Christian challenges as well. We prepare for such eventualities by our daily prayer, mental and physical preparedness, and working constantly to advance our relationship with God. Busyness cannot be an excuse to not find time for our "daily talk" with the Lord; spiritual direction should not lapse in our life. We need the counsel of those who can check on our spiritual foundations. Similarly, we need to keep mentally and physically "in shape." Reading and some physical exercise should be part of our daily routine. The popular Catholic writer and lecturer, Matthew Kelly, puts it simply yet profoundly," Be the best version of yourself." If we prepare well, then we can answer the call to go the extra mile.

A chance and totally unexpected encounter with a homeless man who dug deep, giving all he had to assist the local parish, should prompt all who are privileged to bear the name Christian, God's people, the Church, to consider how we go the extra mile for others. It will probably not be easy, but then it was not easy for Jesus. If we seek to be his disciples and do his work in our world, we must expect nothing less than his experience. But we have his promise as well. Jesus said, "For those who want to save their life will lose it, and those who lose their life for my sake and for the sake of the gospel will save it. "(Mark 8:35) St. Paul puts it so powerfully and beautifully: "What no eye has seen, nor ear heard, nor the human heart conceived, what God has prepared for those who love him." (I Corinthians 2:9) May we never tire of going the extra mile for others. Jesus willingly went to the cross so that we could find life. How far we are willing to go for others is totally up to us. May we be generous in our response.

ACT ON YOUR FAITH

The Great Depression was undoubtedly one of the darkest hours in American history. Beginning with the great stock market crash in October 1929, the United States, almost overnight, found itself in an economic death spiral of unparalleled magnitude. Fortunes accumulated during the halcyon days of "the roaring 20s" were lost, people were thrown out of work and despair gained the upper hand in the minds of the individual American where confidence had earlier reigned supreme. Unemployment in the United States rose from 3.1% in 1929 to 24% in 1932. Labor income during the same period dropped 42%.

The need for action had never been greater and all eyes turned to Washington, D.C. and President Herbert Hoover for answers. Hoover was a champion of American individualism. For him compassion was understood as it had traditionally been understood for decades in United States—people helped each other. Families, communities, and fraternal orders met the needs; financial bailout was not the responsibility of the Federal Government. But as much as Hoover believed in this ideology, the nation's economic status and with it the plight of the individual worker only grew worse.

In March 1933 a new charismatic president, Franklin Delano Roosevelt, came to the White House offering the American people fresh hope through what he called the "New Deal." Roosevelt believed the government could not hide behind tradition and say, "It's always been done this way," as had his predecessor. Unique difficulties required new and special solutions. Thus, with rapid pace Roosevelt during his famous first "100 days" introduced and convinced Congress to pass a whole series of initiatives (15 in total), geared toward restoring economic prosperity and human pride, all which attempted to return people to work and relieve the daily suffering that the prolonged Depression had created. The New Deal created an alphabet soup of agencies and government offices that initiated the needed recovery. The National Industrial Recovery Act (NIRA) was the basic program. The Agricultural Adjustment Act (AAA) aided farmers; the Federal Emergency Relief Administration (FERA) met the immediate needs of the poor and unemployed. The Public Works Administration (PWA) and Works Progress Administration (WPA) were designed to get people back to work on a government subsidy.

President Roosevelt was not content to hide behind "what had always been done" but boldly went forward and acted. He did what needed to be done, as innovative as it was. He saw the need and acted. While people may argue historically about FDR, he was unquestionably a man of action who did what was necessary; he was not concerned with precedence.

The implementation of Franklin Roosevelt's New Deal is a good example of a central message in the New Testament, namely that we cannot hide behind laws and preset ways of doing things but must act on God's word as it comes to us and do what is necessary to meet the needs of God's people.

The law was central to Judaism, providing the basis for all decisions, and the rule by which people lived. Yahweh gave the law to Moses on Mount Sinai. Nothing was more important. Moses told the Israelites, "Give heed to the statutes and ordinances that I am teaching you to observe. You must neither add anything to what I command you nor take anything from it but keep the Commandments of the Lord your God with which I am charging you." (Deuteronomy 4:1b-2).

The centrality of the law continued into the time of Jesus, a good practicing Jew. However, the Lord brought a fresh perspective. Jesus told the Pharisees and experts that they had used the law as a shield to keep them from doing what is more important. (Mark 7:1-8) The Jewish religious leaders were guilty of hiding behind the law as an excuse for disregarding the needs of the poor and others who needed their assistance. It was very comfortable for the Pharisees to observe the outward dictates of the law, but they failed to go the next step and think of others.

Jesus' challenge to the Pharisees was great, but St. James gave an equally significant one in his powerful epistle. As the Pharisees hid behind the law, James (1:22) challenges his readers: "Be doers of the word and not merely hearers who deceive themselves." The deception of the Jewish religious leaders was that they were content to adhere to the letter of the law without acting upon it. Similarly, Herbert Hoover, while I am sure well-intentioned, was content to do what others before him had done; he was unwilling to be proactive.

We live in an action-oriented society, but unfortunately most of the things we do are for ourselves and not for the common good. We are not willing to go the extra mile and think of innovative ways in which we can serve and assist. We say, I have always done it that way, why should I change now? I have neither the time nor the energy necessary to do something different. There are times as well that we hide behind other people, rules, tradition, or other convenient means to avoid action. At work, for example, if there is some problem that needs resolution, we at times say, "I can't do anything about it; it's the company's or my boss' responsibility to fix it." In our local community we back away from challenges we face, saying, "I am only one voice; I have nothing positive to contribute." We vote with our feet and do little or nothing to assist. In our families we aim to keep peace and bring calm to problematic situations. We hide behind the façade of ignorance or inability in our failure to act. There are numerous challenges within our contemporary Church. What are we doing to remedy them? One might rightly say, "It's tough to fight City Hall," whether that be the government or the Church. But if we simply remain passive resolutions will not be found. If such an attitude had prevailed in the early 1930s the Great Depression and its consequent human misery would have been much more severe.

Let us, therefore, not stand idly by, but rather do what is necessary to fix the problems we face as individuals, family, community, or Church. Let us as James says act on the word and not merely listen. The road will not always be easy, but we can expect nothing less than the way our Master trod. Let us follow Jesus' lead, to death but eventually to resurrection and eternal life.

ACTION: THE CURE TO AMBIVALENCE

The first 20 years of the Cold War witnessed some interesting posturing and revelations on the part of the Soviet Union and the West. One of the most obvious and flagrant actions on both sides was the widespread manufacture of nuclear weapons, enough quite certainly to destroy the earth several times over. Both East and West manufactured arsenals of nuclear weapons that led to the political theory of Mutually Assured Destruction (MAD), the idea that through nuclear deterrence neither superpower would initiate a nuclear confrontation because retaliation would bring utter destruction to both sides. During this period of history, in a surprising revelation, the Soviet leader who emerged after the death of Joseph Stalin, Nikita Khrushchev, when speaking to the Politburo, criticized Stalin's policy of death camps, including his mass elimination of unwanted peoples. As he spoke, one brave member of the audience, in a heckling tone, berated the Soviet leader asking, "Where were you when these events took place? Why did you do nothing?" Khrushchev stopped his speech and then through the dead silence asked, "Who is challenging me? Speak up!" The silence in the Politburo chamber was deafening; no one was willing to admit that he was the one who had interrupted the Premier. Thus, Khrushchev continued, addressing the heckler, "I was like you. I was too afraid for myself, so I failed to act."

Inaction, our failure to do what is necessary in any situation, can often be a serious problem, especially today. People are reluctant to get involved, perceiving that their actions will not be properly received, or some might not understand our actions or motives. Sometimes, as well, people refuse to spend the time that action and involvement require. Thus, not only are responsibilities not met, but injustice and many other problematic situations can arise simply because one will not take the time to act.

Jesus was bold and active on behalf of others; he did not worry about what people thought or whether his actions would be acceptable by those in positions of power and authority. On the contrary, he acted when it was necessary, heedless of the consequences. The Jewish law with respect to Sabbath observance was clear and straightforward, yet Jesus violated its precepts on several occasions. All three synoptic evangelists narrate the story of Jesus walking through standing grain and eating it on the Sabbath (Matthew 12:1-8, Mark 2:23-28, Luke 6:2-5). Not only did Jesus and his followers break the Sabbath, but the Lord had the audacity to claim: "The Sabbath was made for humankind, and not humankind for the Sabbath; so, the Son of Man is Lord even of the Sabbath." (Mark 2:27-28). Jesus' strident actions to assist those in need, heedless of Sabbath regulations, was also evident in his cures of the man with a withered hand (Matthew 12:9-14, Mark 3:1-6), paralytics (Luke 13:10-17 and John 5:1-18), and a man with dropsy (Luke 13:10-17). Jesus boldly acted in defense of the woman caught in the act of adultery (John 8:1-11). Exposing the hypocrisy of those who accused her, Jesus once again demonstrated his willingness to act; he refused to be silent. When the Temple, the Jews' most sacred space, and from Jesus' perspective his Father's house, was being used as a marketplace, he demonstrated righteous anger, by overturning the tables of money changers and exclaiming, "My house shall be called a house of prayer; but you are making it a den of robbers" (Matthew 21:13). Clearly, Jesus was not silent when he experienced or saw injustice, people in need, or perceived that the standard and conformist response was inadequate or inappropriate.

The boldness exemplified by Jesus in word and action has been demonstrated by numerous people throughout the apostolic era. The resurrection event transformed Peter from one who denied the Lord three times to one who was willing to proclaim his faith boldly and unabashedly in Jesus. When faced with an order to stop preaching, he courageously responded, "We must obey God rather than any human authority" (Acts 5:29). Stephen, the first martyr, was equally strident, refusing to be cowed by threats and admonitions from others. Rather, he was willing to sacrifice his life for what he believed (Acts 6:8-8:1). St. Paul, after his dramatic conversion along the road to Damascus, (Acts 9:1-9) reversed directions completely, moving from being a great persecutor of Christians to the chief advocate of Jesus' message. He traveled the Eastern Mediterranean world on three missionary journeys, preaching the word, establishing Christian communities, and possibly most importantly writing several letters that today serve as the base for Christian theology. Paul did not let adversity, especially as he experienced it in Ephesus; Philippi, and Corinth, to sway him from his mission. Rather, he continuously and doggedly acted on his belief, serving as the first and greatest evangelist and theologian of Christianity.

Throughout the Christian era, men and women of great faith have demonstrated by their actions an active faith, realizing that ambivalence is not acceptable for the one who truly professes Jesus Christ as Lord. During the English Reformation, St. Thomas More refused to compromise his beliefs even when his opposition to King Henry VIII's policies landed him in the Tower of London. As the playwright Robert Bolt has appropriately described him, St. Thomas was "A Man for All Seasons," never counting the cost for proper action. More recently, Martin Luther King Jr. refused to compromise his strident belief in nonviolent protest to effect change. Even when members of his own camp believed that a more aggressive method was necessary, Dr. King refused to budge.

The challenge of Jesus Christ, to be a person of action and refuse to be ambivalent in situations that call us to act, is as relevant today if not more than ever before. Both on a personal and a communal level, Christians are called to action, to stand against the tidal wave of secularism and relativism that seeks to drown our voice. As individuals we cannot stand idly by when we find ourselves in situations, at work, school, or casual encounters, where people or groups are being maligned. We cannot remain silent when values that our faith professes are put aside as passé or irrelevant because society has "moved beyond" supposedly outdated ideas and beliefs. To be a person of action, to refuse to stand aside, but rather to speak and act in support of the Church will be costly. We may lose a friend, feel ostracized or marginalized; we will probably feel like a minority. But, like Jesus and other great people of faith have demonstrated, we cannot count the cost for our belief, but rather must stridently profess the truth, knowing, as Jesus says, that the truth will set us free (John 8:32). If we do not suffer at least to some degree for our faith, then most probably we are not living the Christian ethic to its fullest degree. We must remember Jesus' words, "If any want to become my followers, let them deny themselves and take up their cross and follow me. For those who want to save their life will lose it, and those who lose their life for my sake will find it." (Matthew 16:24-25). As a community, the Christian faithful also have a significant responsibility. What are we willing to do to address the many significant issues which plague our society—homelessness, poverty, ignorance, racism? We cannot solve the world's problems overnight, but the adage applies: Think globally, but act locally. Our local communities need our action, not our ambivalence, in moving toward resolution of our societal ills.

Christianity calls us to action in a world where attitudes such as political correctness, fear of offending others, or an unwillingness to become involved in a situation often prevail. In his book *Seek*

First the Kingdom, Cardinal Donald Wuerl referenced Pope Benedict XVI, suggesting that contemporary culture's tripartite "isms" -- secularism, materialism, and individualism-- require our response. On numerous occasions (over 100 times) Jesus refers to the Kingdom of God as something we must build. Thus, we cannot stand idly by when the Church is inaccurately or unfairly represented in the press or conversation, when Church teaching is maligned or ridiculed as irrelevant for today's society. We must act and provide a counter voice when teachings and traditions, based on natural law, those foundational to Christianity from the apostolic era, are summarily discarded to accommodate "modern" ideas or individual ideas, tastes or preferences. Our baptismal call and the privileges that come with it also mandate that we take seriously our Christian responsibility to be people of action. To be ambivalent about the world in which we live is a complete abdication of our commitment to contemporary discipleship. We have only one option; we must act.

Nikita Khrushchev's challenge to those in the Politburo was like that given, in word and action, by Jesus and many men and women of faith throughout the Christian era. The increasingly complex modern society in which we live is somewhat frightening to many, but it affords us an opportunity, as difficult as it might be at times, to truly live the Christian life to which we have all been called through baptism. Let us see in the words and actions of Jesus and our ancestors in the faith the inspiration we need to be people of action, never counting the cost for speaking the truth, but with a confident realization that our words and actions will set us free and bring faithful Christians to life eternal.

ANSWERING GOD'S CALL

Villiam Jennings Bryan, one of the most famous political figures in American history, yet little known today, was truly a man who answered the call. Bryan was born in Salem, Illinois in 1860, at the dawn of the Civil War. He received his education at Illinois College and Union College of Law in Chicago and began practicing law in 1883. He moved to Nebraska and became very popular with local people in Lincoln as an advocate for those with little or no voice in society. Content to continue his law practice, Bryan was convinced by local citizens to run for congress, serving two terms from 1892-1896. He was a great proponent of the Populist cause of coinage of silver and gold as a solution to the economic depression which struck the United States in 1893. His famous "Cross of Gold" speech, supporting bimetallism, delivered at the 1896 Democratic National Convention, was so persuasive that at the young age of 36 he was nominated to run for President. He lost that election to the Republican William McKinley, but he continued to answer the call. Four years later the Democrats again asked him to run and again he lost.

Despite his failure to win the presidency, the fame of William Jennings Bryan grew through his great speeches and oratorical style which became legendary. He traveled throughout the nation to promote the policies for which he stood. In 1901 Bryan founded the

150

Commoner, a weekly newspaper published in Lincoln that advocated progressive political causes. In 1908 the Democrats asked their champion to run for president a third time. The result was a third loss, this time to William Howard Taft. Defeat could not dissuade Bryan from assisting others in need and thus he accepted President Woodrow Wilson's invitation to serve as Secretary of State. He served with distinction from 1913 to 1915, but after the United States became hostile toward Germany he resigned under protest, believing the administration's action to be immoral. He was the champion of many popular causes, leading the fight for the popular election of United States senators and standing at the forefront of the women's suffrage movement which culminated in the nineteenth amendment to the Constitution. Bryan was also active in the temperance movement and fought for prohibition.

The final episode of his life quite possibly is the one for which he will be most remembered. In 1925 Bryan again answered the call, this time from the Protestant fundamentalist faith he followed to leave retirement one last time and be the champion of religion in the famous 1925 Scopes "Monkey" trial in Dayton, Tennessee. John Scopes, a high school biology teacher, was accused of teaching the scientific theory of evolution in his classroom, a practice that was against the state law passed that very year. Bryan was counsel for the prosecution, defending the fundamentalist Protestant cause. Clarence Darrow, the famous jurist from Chicago, was Scopes' defense counsel. The famous play and equally popular movie "Inherit the Wind" tells the story of this famous trial. Scopes was convicted; Darrow had been defeated. William Jennings Bryan had earned his last hurrah as he died one week after the trial ended. He was a man who, to the very end, answered the call.

From the dawn of human civilization, God has been asking his people to answer the call. Responding to God's call, Salvation History has many stories of people who were asked to accomplish difficult tasks. Noah built the ark to save his family and preserve humanity and God's creation of the animal kingdom. Abraham left his homeland, went to a foreign place at the bid of the Lord, and now we honor him as the father of a great nation, the Hebrew people. Moses led the Israelites out of bondage in Egypt and the many judges answered the God's call to rally Israel at a time of national need. The prophets too answered the call of the Lord, even when they believed themselves not qualified for the job. Jeremiah was only a youth and ill-prepared, but God told him, "Before I formed you in the womb I knew you, and before you were born, I consecrated you; I appointed you a prophet to the nations." Even though the prophet worried about his youth, God responded, "Do not say, 'I am only a boy'; for you shall go to all to whom I send you. Do not be afraid of them. For I am with you to deliver you." (Jeremiah 1:5-7) We recall how Amos (7:14-15) did not want the task God gave him: "I am no prophet, nor a prophet's son; but I am a herdsman, and a dresser of sycamore trees, and the Lord took me from following the flock, and the Lord said to me, 'Go, prophesy to my people.'" In all these cases God asked something difficult, time consuming, and possibly fear-filled of men who considered themselves ordinary, unqualified, and simply not right for the job. Yet, in faith they all answered God's call and, in the process, wrote chapters in the great account of Salvation History.

Jesus of Nazareth chose twelve unlearned, rather ordinary men, at least in all the ways people today would judge qualifications, for a very difficult task. He called these men, fishermen for the most part, one-by-one to join his mission and they all agreed without hesitation. These men had no idea what the call would entail, but they joined nonetheless, so impressive and powerful was the call of the Lord. At first the call was passive; all that the apostles were required to do was walk with the Lord and listen to his words. But then Jesus added more to the stakes; the call became active when he sent them out, two-by-two on mission to do the Lord's work. They went without staff, money, change of clothes, or food. In other words, they went forth in faith that all that would be necessary for the task would be provided. They were to preach the Good News, effect cures, and lead people to Jesus. They obviously did their work very well; the Church today exists because of their efforts.

We have all been called individually by name and collectively by community to answer God's call. The call first came at baptism. Our name was announced to all the Christian community that day; we became members of this special body of faith which we call the Church. We were called that day, although we most probably did not realize it, to service, to ministry, to an active pursuit of God. We live that call as a community. The community needs our input. If we sit around and do nothing, allowing everyone else to do what is necessary, then we have missed the call. In the process we have missed the opportunity of a lifetime to show the face of Christ to others.

What exactly is the call that all Christians are challenged to answer? It is the call of the prophets and the apostles; it is a call to proclaim God's message of peace by all that we say and do. It is the call to be holy people who live in a manner others would wish to emulate. It is the call to do what God asks of us, always and be joyful in our actions. This, quite obviously, is not a simple task. That is why it is necessary that all of us be involved, in some way, in going forth to actively answer God's call.

We can answer the call of God in many ways. Each person must determine what the answer will be. Whatever the answer, it must be an active participation! Like the patriarchs and prophets, we may not consider ourselves to be qualified; we may not want the job. But we must answer God's call, as freely and immediately as did the apostles, for our benefit now and for the needs of our world. We must answer the call to make the Kingdom come, now and to eternal life.

Answering the call of the Lord has always been a great challenge and so it is today. There will be many obstacles that society will throw into our path. We may be ridiculed by friends and colleagues for the words we say and the actions we do; we may feel unqualified for the task, submit to laziness or cowardice, or simply not want to participate. Answering God's call will not always be fun, but many of the greatest accomplishments and, thereby satisfactions, in life have been done through challenge. G. K. Chesterton, the famous British essayist and convert to Catholicism, once wrote in *What's Wrong with the World*, "The Christian ideal has not been tried and found wanting, it has been found difficult and left untried." Thus, while it is important to always try and find the bright side of every event and discover the good in every action, the reality is that many things we are asked to do by God will not be fun. It is generally not fun to visit a sick relative, neighbor, or business associate in the hospital, but to do so means answering God's call. It is difficult and not fun for parents to discipline their children, to provide them with "tough love" when enabling another is much simpler, but that is answering God's call. It isn't easy to take the ethical way in work practices when we are pressured to take short cuts that might hurt another or be unfair, but that is answering God's call.

God is calling, are we answering? Go, Jesus says, preach the Good News, heal the sick, help others. The road of discipleship will be filled with many potholes, twisting turns, and obstacles, but we can and must go forward with faith. Why? We have God's promise of success: "Know that I am with you always, until the end of the world." (Matthew 28:20b)

COMPLETING THE MASTER'S WORK

C lassical music provides some significant examples of great musical compositions that were never finished by their composers. Wolfgang Amadeus Mozart, a perennial favorite with many, never completed his magnificent Requiem Mass. Franz Schubert, who like Mozart lived only a short life but produced over 600 works of music, wrote only two movements of his eighth symphony. Orchestras today still play this great composition, appropriately known as the "Unfinished Symphony." Living in the latter nineteenth and early twentieth centuries, the Italian opera composer Giacomo Puccini also left a master creation unfinished, but, fortunately for the world his students, known as his disciples, finished their master's work.

Giacomo Puccini was in his day the star of the opera world, attaining great fame, not only in his native land of Italy, but throughout the world. It was quite common to hear people along the streets of any great city whistling or humming one of the many popular melodies from such great works as Tosca, La Boheme, Madama Butterfly, Manon Lescaut, and Gianni Schicchi.

Toward the end of his life Puccini took on a significant challenge, the composition of another great opera. Using a libretto by fellow Italian Renato Simmoni, who adapted a work of the eighteenth-century Venetian playwright Carlo Gozzi, Puccini tackled the composition of Turandot, the story of a gallant young man, Calaf, in his efforts to win the hand in marriage of the stern, mysterious, and seemingly cold Chinese Princess Turandot. Puccini was in his sixties when he began the opera's composition. For four years he labored long and hard, but he was a very sick man and knew his time was running out.

Puccini returned home to God before his master work was completed, but because he was a famous man, he had many friends, including a cadre of loyal students, his disciples. These young men and women did not allow their master's great work, his *magnum opus,* to lie unfinished. Thus, they gathered, studied the text of the opera, and then began the difficult task of finishing their master's work. In 1926, two years after his death, Puccini's greatest work, "Turandot," was performed for the first time, appropriately enough at Milan's La Scala Opera House with Arturo Toscanni, the most famous conductor of the day, at the podium. When the opera reached the point where Puccini's work ended Toscanni paused, set down his baton, turned to the audience and said, "Thus far the master wrote, but he died." after a moment of silence, the famous conductor again picked up his baton, and with tears in his eyes said, "But his disciples finished his work." Thunderous applause was heard as the opera continued; the work of the master had been completed.

In some important ways Giacomo Puccini's life paralleled that of Jesus, who was sent by God to be with us for a certain amount of time to initiate a mission. Like Puccini, who was sent by God to delight our ears with beautiful music, so Jesus was sent to show us how to lead good and holy lives, to demonstrate the presence of God in the world. We know, however, that Jesus was not able to complete his mission, a reality that the Lord himself knew. Jesus prepared those who were called his disciples to complete his work. He taught them, through parables in his public preaching and in a more straight forward manner when they were away from the crowds. The Lord gave them a coherent and powerful message and then he sent them out two-by-two to begin the task of building the Kingdom of God on earth. He told them, "The harvest is plentiful, but the laborers are few; therefore, ask the Lord of the harvest to send laborers into his harvest." (Luke 10:2) These disciples were sent with what Jesus knew they needed. They did not require money or extra clothing, the things people generally believe are necessary on journeys. No, Jesus sent them forward with the promise of the prophets of old and the refinement of their message which Jesus proclaimed. When he proclaimed God's word to the Hebrews upon their return from exile, Isaiah (66:12-13) summarized the Good News which Jesus later made explicit: "For thus says the Lord: I will extend prosperity to her like a river, and the wealth of the nations like an overflowing stream; and you shall nurse and be carried on her arm and dandled on her knees. As a mother comforts her child, so I will comfort you; you shall be comforted in Jerusalem." Jesus knew what was necessary to carry on his work and it was not the things of the world, but rather the things that only God can provide.

Jesus knew that the work he asked his followers to do would not be easy. When he sent them forward, he cautioned them, "See, I am sending you out like lambs into the midst of wolves." To deal with the problems that would come he armed the disciples with the greatest of all messages. Jesus wanted the people to know that God would always take care of them, but equally importantly was the missive that discipleship would not be easy. As Jesus said more than once, "If any want to become my followers, let them deny themselves and take up their cross and follow me. For those who want to save their life will lose it, and those who lose their life for my sake will find it." (Matthew 16:24-25) Yes, being a follower of Christ and doing our share to complete the Master's work will cost us. Writing a half generation later, St. Paul knew precisely what Jesus meant when he said, "May I never boast of anything except the cross of Our Lord Jesus Christ, by which the world has been crucified to me, and I to the world." (Galatians 6:14) To be a follower, to go out on mission, to do our share to complete the Master's work will lead us to the cross.

Jesus sent his followers out on mission. He called the seventy-two forward to do their part to build the Kingdom. Prior to his Ascension, He commissioned the apostles: "Go therefore and make disciples of all nations, baptizing them in the name of the Father and of the Son and of the Holy Spirit, and teaching them to obey everything that I have commanded you." (Matthew 28:19-20a) Today we, a contemporary band of twenty-first century disciples, are asked to go forward and do our share and shoulder the burden, in completing our Master's work. We go into an often-hostile world and sometimes we hesitate; we choose not to get involved. At times we say, "O, ministry, that is for those who have the time or the talent; I will simply choose to follow and let others lead." Such an attitude is counterproductive and does nothing to advance the cause of Christ in our world. If we are not going to do the work, who will? St. Teresa of Avila, the famous sixteenth century Carmelite mystic and religious reformer once wrote, "Christ has no body on earth, but yours, no hands, no feet but yours. Yours are the eyes through which Christ sees with compassion for the world. Christ has no hands or feet but yours."

Yes, Jesus is calling us to go forward. We have been trained and we have the requisite skills and knowledge; now we must develop the proper attitude. Giacomo Puccini's students, his disciples rejoiced in the opportunity to share their Master's life. Let us have the same attitude and never be complacent about serving the Lord. A little story, I believe, illustrates the challenge we face today:

Fred Everybody, Thomas Somebody, Peter Anybody, and Joe Nobody were neighbors, but not the type that most want to know. They were odd people and difficult to understand. The way they lived their lives was a shame. These men all went to the same church, but most would not have wanted them as parishioners. Everybody went fishing on Sundays or stayed home and conversed with his friends.

Anybody wanted to worship, but he was afraid that Somebody would not speak with him. Thus, guess who went to church--that's right, Nobody. Actually, Nobody was the only decent one of the lot. Nobody did the parish census; Nobody joined the Parish Council. One day there was a call in the parish bulletin for people to apply for a position as a teacher in the Religious Education Program. Everybody thought Anybody would apply; Anybody thought Somebody would apply. So, guess who applied? You are right, Nobody! Let us not have the attitude of a nobody, but rather, knowing we are the hands and feet of Christ, let us answer the challenge, pick up the cross and do our share to complete the Master's work.

THE CROSS OF LIFE

In the fifteenth century a rural village near Nuremberg, Germany was home to a family with 18 children. The family was poor, but despite the difficulty of making ends meet, two brothers in the family still held a dream, namely, to pursue their talent as artists. With the financial situation bleak, the two boys came up with their own solution to their dilemma. They agreed to toss a coin with the loser going to the local mines to work so he could support the other while he attended art school. When the first was finished with his training, he would support the education of the other, either by sale of his art works or by going to the mines himself. Thus, one brother went off to the dangerous mines while the other went to the art academy. After four years the young artist returned triumphantly to a homecoming dinner. All the family gathered to celebrate. The artist rose from the table during the meal to drink a toast to his beloved brother for his years of sacrifice. He said, "Now Albert, it is your turn to go to the Academy and pursue your dream; I will support you."

Albert sat at the table and tears began to flow down his cheeks. He began to repeat, "No, no, no." Finally, Albert rose, wiped the tears from his face and holding his hands out in front of him said softly, "No, brother, it is too late for me to go. Look at what four years in the mines has done to my hands. The bones in every finger have been crushed at least once and I suffer from arthritis so badly

160

that I cannot even hold a wine glass properly to return your toast, much less make lines on a canvas with pen or brush. No, brother, for me it is too late."

Then, one day, many years later, to pay homage to his brother who had sacrificed so significantly for him, the great artist Albrecht Durer painstakingly drew his brother's hands with palms together and crooked fingers pointed skyward. He called his powerful sketch simply *Hands*, but the entire world almost immediately opened its heart to this masterpiece and renamed his great work and tribute of love *The Praying Hands*.

The story of the creation of Albrecht Durer's master drawing depicts how far one man was willing to go for another. Albert Durer's sacrifice for his brother gave the world a treasured masterpiece. God's voice, heard through the words of Scripture, calls us to consider how far are we willing to go for another, how much can we sacrifice to assist others and promote the work of Christ in our world?

The task of being a prophet was inherently difficult. God called certain people to proclaim a hard and often stern message to the Hebrew religious leaders, stating that they had many times failed in their responsibilities to the people. The reaction of the prophets to God's call varied, but in the end, they were forced to sacrifice greatly in order to fulfill God's command. Some prophets, like Jonah, Hosea, Jeremiah, and Isaiah did not believe themselves qualified for the job and protested to the Lord. We recall Jonah attempting to flee from God only be swallowed by the great fish and later spewed forth on the land to continue his mission (Jonah 1:1-2:10), and Jeremiah's (1:6) plea of inadequacy, "Ah, Lord God! Truly I do not know how to speak, for I am only a boy." Isaiah (6:5) considered himself unworthy of the call: "Woe is me! I am lost, for I am a man of unclean lips, and I live among a people of unclean lips." Some were angry at God because their task caused them great pain. Jeremiah (20:7) told God, "O Lord, you have enticed me, and I was enticed; you have overpowered me, and you have prevailed. I have become a laughingstock all day long; everyone mocks me." Habakkuk (1:2-3) voiced a similar lament: "O Lord, how long shall I cry for help, and you will not listen? Or cry to you, 'Violence!' and you will not save?' Why do you make me see wrongdoing and look at trouble?" In all these cases, despite the difficulty and pain, the prophets did as the Lord bid them. They sacrificed their wants and desires for others.

The Pauline corpus and Acts of Apostles are filled with examples of what the Apostle to the Gentiles endured to proclaim God's message and bring many to conversion. Paul was imprisoned on three occasions, writing some of his most powerful letters while under such duress. He was stoned in Lystra (Acts 14:19), shipwrecked three times (II Corinthians 11:25), imprisoned in Philippi (Acts 16:16-24) and Jerusalem (Acts 22:22-30) and placed under house arrest in Rome (Acts 28:16). He traveled the Eastern Mediterranean world on three long and arduous missionary journeys. Thus, Paul knew of what he wrote when he asked the Romans to offer their bodies as a living sacrifice (Romans 12:1). From the day of his conversion on the road to Damascus (Acts 9:1-9) to his eventual journey to Rome and death, Paul gave freely of who he was and what he might be so others would come to know Jesus. He continually asked people to reach beyond themselves, as he challenges the Colossians (3:1) to seek "higher realms," looking to the standards of God and not those of humanity.

Listening to Paul we might wonder what is the will of Christ in our lives? The specifics will vary from person to person, but undoubtedly the general call is one of personal sacrifice for the needs of our brothers and sisters. Immediately after placing Peter at the head of his nascent Church, Jesus tells the disciples his will: "If any want to become my followers, let them deny themselves and take up their cross and follow me. For those who want to save their life will lose it, and those who lose their life for my sake will find it. For what will it profit them if they gain the whole world but forfeit their life? Or what will they give in return for their life?" (Matthew 16:24-

26). Yes, the message is clear, Jesus desires that we sacrifice for one another.

God's message, as articulated in the Scriptures is clear, but its execution is often difficult. We live today in a world that is centered on self. The common good is seemingly always secondary to our personal needs and desires. While many of us make significant efforts in caring for family members and friends who are ill, infirmed, or otherwise in need of our assistance, or we reach out to the specific needs of the poor in our parish or civic community, we many times fail in a more generic sense. We are unwilling to endure the sacrifice that is necessary to promote the common good. Americans are highly resistant to compromising their lifestyle so our brothers and sisters in other lands, or even the poor in our own cities and towns, can have even the basic needs of life. We refuse to entertain ideas and policies that might cost us some something, but in the end could benefit our local community in greater measure. We say we want to assist when we see the evening news and observe the massive problems of the world, yet we hesitate when the cost is personal and asks more than simply giving from our excess. If we want to effect change in our world, we must think globally but act locally, as surely as Albert Durer willing sacrificed so his brother Albrecht could become a famous artist.

Jesus' message is clear, there is a need to pick up the cross and follow in his footsteps. Christ willingly went to the cross for our sake. He gave up his personal autonomy, stripped himself of his dignity, and gave all so that we might have life. St. Paul says it so powerfully in his famous Christological hymn in the Letter to the Philippians (2:6-8): "Though he was in the form of God, [Jesus] did not regard equality with God as something to be exploited, but emptied himself, taking the form of a slave, being born in human likeness. And being found in human form, he humbled himself and became obedient to the point of death--even death on a cross." May we have the courage to profess and act the same!

DIVE IN: YOU CAN TRUST JESUS

O n warm summer days it is quite common to search for the nearest pool, lake or possibly the ocean to find a cool and refreshing place. Yet, for most of us, when we enter the water to "cool off" we generally do so in a very hesitant way. We walk into the shallow end of the pool or slowly enter from the shore of a lake or ocean. The water is cold and the shock of simply "diving in" seems all too much. Thus, we gradually, with hesitance, enter. However, we generally find that if we simply dive in, despite the initial shock, we rapidly adjust and are ready to enjoy the coolness and pleasant feel the water gives almost immediately.

Our hesitancy to dive into the cool water on a warm summer day is, unfortunately, too often repeated in our relationship with God. We hesitate, are cautious, fearful of what our full and unhesitating response to the Lord may entail. This reality has been illustrated numerous times in Scripture. Many of the prophets of the Hebrew Bible were hesitant to accept the call of the Lord. Isaiah claimed, "Woe is me, I am lost, for I am a man of unclean lips, and I live among a people of unclean lips." He needed to feel purged of his inadequacy to receive God's call as a prophet. In the end, however, he could proclaim, "Here I am … send me." (Isaiah 6:5, 8c) Jeremiah, when called by God, protested, "I know not how to speak; I am too young." (Jeremiah 1:6). Eventually, however, Jeremiah prophesied to the Southern Kingdom of Judah. Amos, who prophesied to the Northern Kingdom of Israel, proclaimed, "I was no prophet, nor have I belonged to a company of prophets. I was a shepherd and a dresser of sycamores." (Amos 7:14)

Similarly, the New Testament provides several examples of people who hesitated when called by Jesus. In Luke 9:57-62 Jesus speaks of three people who hesitated when called. The invitation to follow the Lord is extended, but the response is tepid at best. One says he will follow but Jesus responds, "Foxes have dens and birds of the sky have nests, but the Son of Man has nowhere to rest his head." A second man wants to follow but asks to bury his father. Jesus only responds, "Let the dead bury their dead." A third person wants to follow but wishes to take leave of his family. Jesus answers, "No one who sets a hand to the plow and looks to what was left behind is fit for the Kingdom of God." Again, in Luke 14:16-21, Jesus tells a parable which addresses the consequences of hesitancy in following the call of the Lord. A great dinner has been prepared and the guests are told to come, but each has an excuse. One having just purchased a field asks to be excused so he can examine it. A second invitee has purchased five yoke of oxen and asks leave to evaluate them. The third has just been married and thus responds, "I cannot come." In anger and frustration, the host of the dinner tells his servants to go to the streets and invite "the poor and the crippled, the blind and the lame." The master concludes, "None of those who were invited will taste my dinner." The ramifications of hesitancy lead to being shut out of the Kingdom. Nicodemus in his famous conversation with Jesus (John 3:1-21) was rather hesitant as well. He only came to Jesus at night, fearful of what the Sanhedrin, of which he was a member, or other leaders of the Jews might think. In the end, Nicodemus gets the message and is converted, but his hesitancy was palpable.

The hesitancy of the Hebrew prophets and others described in the New Testament can, fortunately, be countered by examples of an immediate response with its corresponding rewards. The call of Jesus was indeed powerful for the apostles. We are told in the various stories of their call that they immediately responded, dropped everything to become his followers (see Matthew 4:18-22, Mark 1:16-20, John 1:35-51, Luke 5:1-11, 27-28). All three synoptic evangelists (Matthew 9:20-22, Mark 5:25-34, Luke 8:43-48) report the courage of a woman afflicted with a hemorrhage for 12 years. She was fearful but did not hesitate to come to Jesus, confident that simply touching his clothes would bring her a cure. Her faith was rewarded. In Matthew (8:5-13) and Luke (7:2-10), we hear of a Roman centurion, a pagan, who nonetheless did not hesitate to approach Jesus. The Lord complements him on his faith and grants his request. Upon hearing that Jesus was passing, Bartimaeus, the blind man, unhesitatingly asked to receive his sight. Jesus grants his request telling him, "Go your way; your faith has saved you." (Mark 10:46-52)

We have all heard the expression, "He who hesitates cannot win." This can be applied to many facets of life. If we wait too long on some business proposition, the opportunity may be lost or be secured by a competitor. If we wish to be more proactive in a social setting but sit back and allow others to go first, the goal we have set for ourselves might not be achieved. If we wait around for opportunity to knock, we will find ourselves left out in the cold.

The call of the Lord is ever present and too often we hesitate before we respond, if we answer at all. We're a bit unsure of what the call may entail, what it may mean for our present or future. Following the call of Jesus will cost us, but if we have the faith demonstrated by the apostles, the woman with the hemorrhage, the centurion or Bartimaeus, we can be confident that the results will be beneficial to us. Nothing in life is free and thus answering the call of the Lord will force us to change a plan or two, go somewhere or do something we might not have expected to do, but then St. Paul reminds us (I Corinthians 1:25) "For the foolishness of God is wiser than human wisdom, and the wisdom of God is stronger than human strength."

We need to have confidence that our full and unhesitating response to the Lord will, in the end, prove beneficial. While it is wise to be wary of the world's many allurements, we can be confident with God for he will never lead us astray. Paul writing to his friend Timothy (II Timothy 2:11-13) expressed this reality in this way: "This saying is sure. If we have died with him, we will also live with him; if we endure, we shall also reign with him; if we deny him, he will also deny us; if we are faithless, he remains faithful--for you cannot deny himself." Let us be confident and not wade into our relationship with the Lord. Rather let us dive in and today reap the benefits of building the Kingdom of God in our world.

LEADING PEOPLE TO JESUS

In a small town there lived an old man who was quite ill and resting in the local hospital. Those responsible for his care noticed that he was quite agitated; there seemed to be something he wanted to say, but he was unwilling to tell them. Therefore, officials at the hospital summoned the man's son who came to speak with his father. In speaking with his son, the old man told him about an incident that happened many years ago, when he was a teenager. It seems that late one evening he and some of his friends went to the crossroads of their town. In those days, before sophisticated signs, there were arrows made of wood that gave the direction and distance to nearby towns: Marshall was 5 miles to the west; Clifton was 3 miles to the east; Springville was 7 miles straight ahead. The boys, as a prank, changed the signs, hoping to confuse people. Now, as an old man, literally dying and prepared to meet God, he was very worried about how many people he had sent in the wrong direction.

This little tale provides a good illustration of the daily Christian challenge to do our best to always point people in the correct direction, toward Christ, and eternal life. On the surface this might sound like a rather simple task; who would intentionally point people in the wrong direction? Yet, unknowingly at times, through our actions and words, we send people away from God. When we do not set a good example, when our words and actions are inconsistent, the message sent is inconsistent with our Christian call.

Fortunately, we have many wonderful examples from Scripture of people who have pointed others in the proper direction and done a good job to lead others toward God. The ancient patriarchs of the Jewish people are certainly good examples. Abraham and Moses were given extremely difficult tasks by God. The former was asked to leave his place of birth and the life he knew to follow a God who was unknown to him. He was challenged to accept the covenant which God set before him with the promise that he would be the father of a great nation. His inaugural work to place the Jewish people on the proper path was the first major step in Salvation History. Moses' mission was also a great challenge. His many encounters with Pharaoh were followed by the task of leading the people through the desert to the land promised them by God. It took 40 years to reach the Holy Land, but that was only because of the infidelity of the people, not because Moses did not direct them in the proper way. Clearly, Jesus, through his teaching, and basic law of love directs people toward his Father; he provides a roadmap that if followed brings us back to God. He shows us how to live and gives us a new commandment of love as the base upon which the example that we set for others must be firmly rooted. It is from this foundation that the direction to God can be found.

We have good examples as well of the gifts and tools we need to direct people toward God, but, unfortunately, too often we fail to use these gifts properly to carry out our basic Christian vocation as evangelists. For most, I suspect, evangelization is a concept perceived to be an outreach to non-Christians or those who do not know of God. This reality still exists, but for our first world society there is a crying need for re-evangelization. While the reasons are many that churches have many empty pews and many of the basic sacraments are underutilized or ignored, one can never discount failure to demonstrate good example as one major reason. Sometimes our failures are at work; we simply hold the party line which is often not Christ-centered. It takes courage to do the right thing and point people in the proper direction, but therein lies the challenge. At times our failure is in our community or neighborhood. We are not good citizens or neighbors; our effort and example are needed, and we are "missing in action." Sometimes, indeed, our failures are associated with the Church. We are highly critical of the hierarchy or certain teachings. Our rebellious attitude is detrimental to the Church's mission.

Setting a good example, and by such action, directing people to the proper course to Christ and eternal life is a critical part of our common vocation to holiness. A good example of providing good direction by setting good example is found in the story from the heydays of Christian evangelization of the African continent. Four Christian missionaries were sent to the nation of Upper Volta (Bukina Faso today) in west Africa. Their presence was something of a novelty in a nation that at the time was 90% Muslim. These missionaries were sent to help with many projects which made life more livable for the local people. One day the four were diligently engaged in digging a well. As they dug into the dirt a Muslim holy man walked by and observed their efforts. "Who are you?" asked the holy man. "We are Christians," came the response from the missionaries. "So, you are followers of Jesus, the great prophet?" continued the holy man. "No," answered the missionaries, "we are followers of Jesus, the Son of God and our Savior," came the response. As the missionaries continued to dig into the earth, the water table was reached. Water began to fill the hole and eventually overflowed onto the land. The Muslim holy man was amazed at what he witnessed. He again asked, "Are you digging this well for Jesus?" "No," said the Christians, "we are digging this well for others, in imitation of Jesus." The holy man continued his way. The next Friday in the mosque the man was telling the story of his encounter with the Christians to some of his close friends. They too were amazed at what they heard. Then the holy man said, "These Christians dug for others and found a great body of water, maybe they have found the truth as well!" May we as well by the example we set, lead others to the truth.

MINISTRY: THE WORK OF ANGELS

E ach year as the warm days of summer turn to the coolness
and bright colors of autumn, the Church celebrates the work
and ministry of angels. We begin this two-fold celebration on
September 29 with the feast of the Archangels—Raphael, Michael,
and Gabriel. We conclude three days later, October 2, honoring the
myriad of Guardian Angels whom the tradition describes as assigned
by God to each man and woman. The Scriptures speak of how angels
are sent to assist in God's plan of salvation. They bring messages,
accompany the faithful along the path of daily life, and fight the
battles of God. We who seek to minister in Christ's name are called
to do likewise.

A Celebration of Angels

In celebrating the Archangels on September 29, the Church
reminds us of three special messengers who were sent to accomplish
very specific tasks. The Book of Tobit, one of the classics of the seven
apocryphal texts of the Hebrew Bible, tells the story of Raphael, who
was sent by God to accompany Tobias in his quest to find medicine
to cure the blindness of the latter's father, Tobit. Raphael's task is to
lead, guide, and protect his young companion in his quest. Along the
way Tobias experiences many adventures, finds love and marriage,
and in the end secures the medicine his father needs. Thus, he achieves

many goals, receives numerous blessings, and completes his mission. This is made possible because of the archangel's guidance. Raphael has served his purpose well; he has carried out the mission God gave him to accompany, guide, and protect Tobias from harm.

While Raphael's mission from God was to guide and direct, Michael was sent to fight God's battles. The short Letter of St. Jude describes Michael in an argument with Satan over the body of Moses. While Michael does not make any pronouncement against the devil he does say "May the Lord rebuke you," (Jude 1:9b) indicating the false nature of Satan's argument. In the apocalyptic Book of Daniel (12:1) Michael's role is much more proactive. He is described as "the great prince, guardian of your people." In his vision, Daniel describes the classic confrontation between good and evil at the end of time. Michael is the great champion of the people; he stands ready to greet those who rise from the dead and experience God's great victory over evil. The New Testament continues to reveal Michael's role as a champion for God. Revelation 12:7-9 reads,

> Then war broke out in heaven; Michael and his angels battled against the dragon. The dragon and its angels fought back, but they did not prevail and there was no longer any place for them in heaven. The huge dragon, the ancient serpent, who is called the Devil and Satan, who deceived the whole world, was thrown down to earth, and its angels were thrown down with it.

Michael serves the special and unique role to fight God's battles against evil.

Clearly the most prominent and best-known of the archangels is Gabriel, the one who delivers special messages to those favored by God. We first hear of Gabriel through St. Luke's depiction of the Annunciation: "In the six-month, the Angel Gabriel was sent from

God to a town of Galilee called Nazareth, to a virgin betrothed to a man named Joseph, of the house of David and the virgin's name was Mary. And coming to her, he said, 'Hail favored one! The Lord is with you.'" Gabriel continued, "Do not be afraid, Mary, for you have found favor with God. Behold, you will conceive in your womb and bear a son and you shall name him Jesus. He will be great and will be called Son of the Most High and the Lord God will give him the throne of David his father, and he will rule over the house of Jacob forever and of his kingdom there will be no end." (Luke 1:26-28, 30-33) We next encounter Gabriel in Matthew's gospel. While the evangelist does not specifically name the angel, tradition suggests that the message delivered to Joseph that he, Mary, and Jesus must flee from the wrath of Herod: "Arise, take the child and his mother, flee to Egypt, and stay there until I tell you. Herod is going to search for the child to destroy him" came from Gabriel. Later, after the crisis has passed, once again Gabriel comes to Joseph instructing him to return to Israel. (Matthew 2:13b, 19-20) The messages that Gabriel delivered were obviously highly significant and, thus, the Lord entrusted them to a special carrier.

Three days after celebrating the archangels the Church provides us the opportunity to honor the unnamed angels who guard and protect each one of us. While not a prayer that youth today memorize, still the "Prayer to the Guardian Angel," says something powerful for our faith and belief in God's abiding protection for us: "Angel of God my Guardian dear to whom God's love entrusts thee here. Ever this day be at my side to light, to guard, to rule and to guide. Amen." The Scriptures describe these special "Guardian Angels" to have several special functions. The "Q source" common to Matthew (4:1-11) and Luke (4:1-13) describes the angels' watching over Jesus during his great temptation in the desert. When tempted to throw himself off the parapet of the Temple, Jesus responds, "He will command his angels concerning you, and with their hands they will support you, lest you dash your foot against a stone." (Matthew 4:6b) John's Gospel and the Book of Revelation describe these angels as ministering in God's presence. In John's apocalyptic vision found in Revelation 8:2-11:19, while the angels ascend and descend on the Son of Man (John 1:51), they stand before God and minister to his needs Angels are also present as Jesus describes the Parousia in Matthew's Gospel (24:29-31). In the parable of the weeds (Matt 13: 24-30), we learn that at the end of the age, "The Son of Man will send his angels, and they will collect out of his kingdom all who cause others to sin and all evildoers. They will be thrown into the fiery furnace where there will be wailing and grinding of teeth." (Matt 13: 41-42). Similarly, when describing his return, Jesus says that "He [Jesus] will send out his angels with a trumpet blast, and they will gather his elect from the four winds, from one end of the heavens to the other." (Matt 24:31)

Ministry: The Work of the Angels

The tasks assigned to both the three archangels and the many unnamed guardians who stand ready to assist in carrying out God's will, are the same duties of those privileged to minister to God's people. Like Raphael, we are called to accompany others along the road of life. What a privilege we have as Christians to accompany our brothers and sisters through the daily occurrences of life. We are called to respond especially when difficulties, tragedy, or other life circumstances and events place heavy burdens or even cut down those we know. It is during such times that we fulfill the work of Angels and in many ways as well, become the Christ to others. We recall the famous words at the end of the anonymously written poem, "Footprints": "My son, my precious child, I love you and I would never leave you. During your times of trial and suffering when you see only one set of footprints, it was then that I carried you." Yes, we walk with our brothers and sisters during times of great challenge, but we also accompany them and celebrate each triumph and moment of joy. We serve as did Raphael and the many unnamed "guardians"

175

who watch over us and stand ready to assist us whenever the need arises.

Besides walking with our brothers and sisters, we must also be the ones, like Gabriel, who bring the message of Christ to others. This important responsibility can be manifested in several beautiful and powerful ways. We are called to bring Christ's message of love and compassion, as well as his more challenging missive of keeping our priorities straight, to the people with whom we walk the Christian path of life. The written word can also be an effective way to present the message of Christ to others. As Gabriel brought both good news and warning at different times to the Holy Family, so we have the task to present God's message in a contemporary vein to Christians today. But, lest we think that words are the only vehicle, we must always remember the adage, "Actions speak louder than words." We must recall how St. James exhorted the nascent Christian community to "ante up" and communicate the message of Jesus by living an active faith: "What good is it, my brothers, if someone says he has faith but does not have works? Can that faith save him? If a brother or sister has nothing to wear and has no food for the day and one of you says to them, 'Go in peace, keep warm and eat well,' but do not give them the necessities of the body, what good is it? So also, faith of itself, if it does not have works is dead." (James 2:14-17)

As we accompany others in word and deed, we are also called upon to fight Christ's battles in our contemporary world. Indeed, this may be the most challenging of all responsibilities. Walking with others in need does not require significant "backbone" for this is a natural action of ministry. However, to stand against the onslaught of secular society, to boldly and consistently proclaim that there are absolute truths articulated by God, and to be willing to suffer because of your stance, will be extremely challenging for anyone. In essence, like Michael who fought physical battles in support of God, we are asked in our contemporary world to be countercultural and refuse to compromise beliefs and standards that have been hallmarks of Christian and more specifically Roman Catholic faith for centuries.

This latter responsibility of fighting Christ's battles has been a central part of ministry from the very beginning and one that Jesus predicted. In the Acts of the Apostles, Peter stands ready to suffer as he boldly proclaims his faith amidst a sea of external opposition and hatred in the Jewish community. (Acts 4:5-12) Similarly, Paul, preaching to the Gentiles, was stoned, suffered shipwreck, and was rejected by many. Yet, he could boldly proclaim to his friend Timothy, "Proclaim the word; be persistent, whether it is convenient or inconvenient; convince, reprimand, encourage through all patience and teaching." (II Tim 4:2) Jesus realized that his followers would suffer, but reminded them that despite the pain, their efforts would be rewarded (Matt 5:1-12). He left them with the knowledge that, despite the opposition one may face and the apparent lack of success one might achieve, in the end, "Take courage, I have conquered the world." (John 16:33c)

Conclusion

The Church's celebration of angels, those who assist in God's work is, in many ways, an annual opportunity for those who minister to reflect on our fidelity to the people we serve, in imitation of the work of angels. The Scriptures speak of how the angels accompany men and women, sharing in the triumphs and defeats of life, fighting God's battles today and proclaiming God's word to others. Jesus is counting on us, as he does the angels. Let us not disappoint him!

PLAYING "SECOND FIDDLE" IS OKAY WITH GOD

People attend motion pictures for various reasons. Some go because the theme, whether it is a courtroom drama, comedy, science fiction, or another genre is attractive. Others attend because of the leading actor or actress in the movie. When they were in their prime, I saw all the pictures starring Jack Nicholson or Gene Hackman, simply because these actors were in it; I would still go to see any movie which featured Meryl Streep or Denzel Washington. A great performance by a leading actor or actress can certainly make a difference.

When we watch a movie, whether in a theater or on television or even today "streaming" on a computer, when the story has ended, and the performances of the leading characters have concluded we proverbially "make for the exit." Either we physically leave our seat in the theater, we turn the channel of the television or click the mouse on our computer to move to some other function. However, when we turn our attention away, the movie has not ended, for the names of literally hundreds of people, most behind the scenes, and about whom the audience cares little and knows nothing, roll across the screen. While the moviegoer may know nothing of these numerous "behind-the-scenes" individuals, one should not make the wrong conclusion that their efforts are unimportant. On the contrary, without

178

their contribution, whether that be as a sound engineer, makeup artist, costume designer, or a myriad of other necessary functions, the story line of the movie and the more obvious starring roles of the named actors would not be possible. Those working behind the scenes, those who one might say "play second fiddle" in the grand scheme of moviemaking are, nevertheless, very important in the overall production; they must not be forgotten.

Judeo-Christian history provides several different examples of people who have made significant contributions, although less visible and appreciated, that made possible the work and efforts of the more "star" performers. When we hear the story of the Exodus of the Israelites from Egypt, the great superhero is Moses. True enough, he took the lead and was the one who suffered the most, initially at the hands of Pharaoh, and then later the constant complaints of his own people as he led the Israelite community during its 40 years sojourn to the Promised Land. Yet, there were a few very important "co-stars," whose contributions were integrally important to Moses' ultimate success. The great deliverer's mother took the chance of floating her son in a papyrus basket down the river Nile. Had she not taken the chance to save her son the Exodus would not have happened. Aaron, Moses' brother, was the former's spokesman since he was gifted with speech and Moses was not. Without Aaron, Yahweh's repeated messages to Pharaoh would never have been communicated and the power of God, as experienced in the great plagues, would never have been manifested.

Undoubtedly the most famous "second fiddle" in Christian history is John the Baptist. As is often the case in popular music concerts, John was the warm-up act for the main attraction, namely Jesus. Yet, John's role, while that of a precursor, not a superstar, was very important. Jesus recognized this himself. While John said, "He must increase; I must decrease," (John 3:30) Jesus reminded his followers that no man born of woman was greater than John the Baptist (Matthew 11:11). John's role as a voice crying in the desert,

"Prepare the way of the Lord. Make straight his paths," (Mark 1:3) set the stage for the starring role that Jesus played in Salvation History. The Church in a very real way acknowledges the critical role of John by celebrating him on two different occasions, June 24, his birth, and August 29 his death.

Another significant "behind-the-scenes player" was St. Joseph. It is noteworthy that none of the four evangelists report even one word from Joseph's lips, yet his supporting role as Jesus' foster father allowed Christ to mature in an environment that prepared him for his public ministry. St. Joseph's role, like that of John the Baptist, was secondary, but nonetheless vitally important in the overall master plan of God, Salvation History.

Contemporary society exalts and at times almost worships the stars, winners, those who stand in the lead roles in society. Whether it is the Hollywood scene, college or professional sports, politics on local, state, or national levels or the tycoons of business, people today concentrate on those who stand at the top. We are almost brainwashed to believe that only by association with those deemed "important" can we ever move up the ladder of recognition ourselves. We place so much attention on those who are the stars that we too often forget or at least negate the significant contributions made by those outside the spotlight.

Concentrating on the stars, to the detriment of the cast of thousands who support them, might prompt us to feel at times very empty about ourselves. Few of us will be found on the front pages of local let alone national newspapers or magazines; even fewer of us will be the subject of some historical essay or book. Thus, we might consider our contribution to be of lesser or insignificant value, especially when compared with those in our society whom history will remember or note. We don't want simply to be an asterisk in history, yet in the grand scheme of things this is where most of us will lie.

However, we must take consolation and realize a sense of joy and pride in playing second fiddle. In the mid-twentieth century the then popular conductor of the Philadelphia Orchestra, Eugene Ormandy, when asked what the most difficult position in the orchestra was, answered: "Oh, second fiddle is the most difficult. I can get plenty of people to play first violin, but not second." Ormandy realized that while the second violins might not carry the melody, nevertheless without them the beauty and the greatness of the composition played can never be experienced.

Let us, therefore, not be in any way disappointed that life might find us playing the role of "second fiddle." Some of the greatest and most significant personages in Judeo-Christian history did the same. Without people like Aaron, John the Baptist, and Joseph Salvation History would never have found its apex in Jesus Christ. So, the next time you watch a movie, don't leave when the credits start rolling, but rather appreciate the contribution these "hidden" people have made. For most of us it is our role as well, but one if done well, will help us to build the kingdom of God in our world.

Ministry: Answering the Call of Jesus

Baptism, the first and fundamental sacrament, provides many privileges and challenges. Through baptism we become members of the family of Jesus Christ. As Christians we are privileged to be his followers, to receive the sacraments of the Church, to be brothers and sisters with our fellow travelers, all of whom are seeking to find Christ and eternal life when the Lord calls us home. The privileges of the Christian life, offered through baptism, are many and blessed are we who have been given these opportunities.

While the privileges of the Christian life are many, so too significant responsibility is part and parcel of the life of the baptized. In the popular superhero movie, "Spiderman," Ben Parker challenges his nephew Peter, alias "Spiderman": "Great privilege incurs great responsibility." The privileges of life bring responsibility. The privilege of being born in the first world comfort of the United States brings significant responsibilities as citizens of this nation—responsibility to follow the laws of the land, to vote for our elected officials in a representative democracy, and to be active in our community seeking to better the day-to-day life of our fellow citizens. The privilege of material prosperity necessitates the responsibility to share that abundance with those less fortunate. The privilege of intellectual acumen requires that we aid those who find certain concepts or ideas difficult to grasp. Those with the privilege of physical prowess and athleticism must be willing to instruct and coach others with lesser skills. Those with the privilege of time have the responsibility of utilizing their gift by visiting and assisting others who are without companionship or feel too burdened to meet some of their daily responsibilities.

Ministry, whether it be the work of a priest or religious, a professional layperson, or a dedicated volunteer, is indeed a privilege. We are privileged to work alongside and in union with Jesus Christ. When Jesus left the world, he only initiated the kingdom; it is our task to do what we can with the time, resources, and expertise we possess to complete the work of Jesus the master. Jesus' great commission: "Go, therefore, and make disciples of all nations, baptizing them in the name of the Father and the Son, and of the Holy Spirit, teaching them to observe all that I have commanded you," (Matthew 28:19-20) asks us to do what we can to bring the kingdom closer to its fulfillment. We are to answer the call of the Lord.

God's Call in Scripture

God's plan to minister to his people has been manifested throughout Salvation History. Even before God's plan had taken its first major step toward the redemption of the world, the Lord called Noah for the Herculean task of preserving the world. The Book of Genesis tells us, "The Lord saw how great was man's wickedness on earth and ... he regretted that he had made man on the earth and his heart was grieved. ... I will wipe out from the earth the men whom I have created ... and also the beasts and the creeping things and the birds of the air, for I am sorry that I made them." (Genesis 6:5-7) However, Noah found favor with God and thus was told to build an ark of gopherwood. Together with his family, Noah was instructed to gather one male and one female of all species to preserve the world.

God told Noah, "I will establish my covenant [with] you." (Genesis 6:18) Noah's fidelity to the Lord and his command preserved God's creation, allowing Salvation History to proceed.

The Lord's challenge to answer the call to follow him was formally initiated through the invitation of God to Abram. The Lord challenged him, "Go forth from the land of your kinsfolk and your father's house to a land I will show you. I will make of you a great nation and I will bless you." (Genesis 12:1) Dutifully and seemingly without hesitation, Abram responded to this challenge from a God he did not know or understand. Yet, he obviously did so with great faith. As Genesis recounts, "Abram put his faith in the Lord, who credited it to him as an act of righteousness." (Genesis 15:6) Abram's (later Abraham) response initiated a covenant between God and his Chosen People, the Jews, a contract that found its apex in the life and mission of Jesus Christ.

Like Abraham, his ancestor in faith, Moses received the call of God to be the great deliverer of his people from slavery in Egypt. Moses' encounter with God in the desert, the theophany of the burning bush that was not consumed, initiated the call. The Book of Exodus presents no specific evidence that Moses, like Abraham before him, had any knowledge of God. Raised by the Egyptians, Moses' initial encounter with the Lord (Exodus 3: 1-10) presented a great challenge. God said to Moses, "I have witnessed the affliction to my people in Egypt and have heard their cry of complaint against their slave drivers, so I know well what they are suffering." Thus, the Lord commissioned Moses, "I will send you to Pharaoh to lead my people, the Israelites, out of Egypt." (Exodus 3:7, 10) Understandably, Moses was a bit hesitant, but the Lord told him, "I will be with you." (Exodus 3:12a) Moses' faith and trust that God was indeed with him, together with the manifestation of the ten plagues, placed the Israelites on the long road to freedom in the Promised Land they had abandoned several centuries prior.

As Salvation History continued to move forward, God called many prophets to proclaim his message. The invitations to the prophets were at times met with skepticism and some reservation, but in the end these men of faith answered the Lord's call to speak on his behalf. Isaiah felt unworthy of the Lord's call: "Woe is me; I am doomed! For I am a man of unclean lips, living among a people of unclean lips, yet my eyes have seen the King the Lord of hosts!" (Isaiah 6:5) Purged of his apparent inadequacies, the prophet is ultimately able to proclaim, "Here I am, send me." (Isaiah 6:8b) Jeremiah tells us that before he was born the Lord had a plan for him: "Before I formed you in the womb I knew you, before you were born, I dedicated you, a prophet to the nations I appointed you." As with Isaiah, Jeremiah felt inadequate, complaining, "Ah, Lord God! I know not how to speak; I am too young." Nevertheless, God commissioned Jeremiah, "See I place my words in your mouth! This day I set you over nations and over kingdoms, to root up and to tear down, to destroy and to demolish, to build and plant." (Jeremiah 1:5-7, 9b-10) Amos, a shepherd from Tekoa, was sent to the Northern Kingdom of Israel to preach a message of social justice. Because he felt threatened, King Amaziah sought to banish Amos to the Southern Kingdom of Judah, but the prophet, admitting his inadequacies nevertheless answered the call: "I was no prophet, nor have I belonged to a company of prophets; I was a shepherd and a dresser of sycamores. The Lord took me from following the flock, and said to me, 'Go, prophesy to my people Israel.'" (Amos 7:14-15)

New Testament manifestations of the call of the Lord to minister in Christ's name are equally plentiful and powerful. From the moment of his conception, John the Baptist was directed toward his ministry as the precursor of Jesus Christ. When the angel of the Lord appeared to John's father, Zechariah, he told him, "He [John] will be filled with the Holy Spirit even from his mother's womb, and he will turn many of the children of Israel to the Lord their God. He will go before him in the spirit and power of Elijah to turn the hearts of fathers toward [their] children and the disobedient to the understanding of the righteous, to prepare a people fit for the Lord." (Luke 1:15b-17) John echoed the words of Isaiah, "Prepare the way of the Lord, make straight his paths." He challenged people to reform their lives, and to "produce good fruits as evidence of repentance." (Luke 3:8) John's ministry and staunch opposition to the immoral life of King Herod led to his execution, but he fulfilled God's plan, fading from view, and bringing Jesus into the light. John stated his role clearly, "He [Jesus] must increase; I must decrease." (John 3:30)

The call of the first apostles is powerfully narrated by all four of the evangelists. Both St. Mark and St. Matthew narrate the call of Peter and his brother Andrew and the sons of Zebedee, John and James. Jesus came to these fishermen, calling "Come after me, and I will make you fishers of men." (Matthew 4:19; Mark 1:17) The immediacy of their response, leaving everything—family, friends, occupation--to follow Christ suggests that the Lord's call was indeed powerful, one that could not be ignored. The perception of unworthiness exhibited by the Jewish patriarchs and prophets was also evident with the apostles. St. Luke describes the call of Simon Peter and the great catch of fish (Luke 5:1-11) As with his ancestors in the faith, Peter felt unworthy of the call. While according to Luke Jesus had earlier cured Simon's mother-in-law of a fever, and thus presumably the future chief apostle was aware of the Lord's power, nonetheless Peter was dumbfounded at the catch of fish. Falling at the knees of Jesus he said, "Depart from me, Lord, for I am a sinful man." Still, he, along with James and John, Simon's partners, "brought their boats to the shore, ... left everything and followed him." (Luke 5:8b, 11)

Arguably the most dramatic call, a true *volte face*, moving from one direction in life to another is the call of Saul of Tarsus, who became the famous St. Paul, apostle to the Gentiles. The Acts of the Apostles tells us that Saul was an avowed enemy of Jesus' followers. He consented to the execution of Stephen, the first martyr (Acts 8:1).

We learn one chapter later that Saul "still breathing murderous threats against the disciples of the Lord" was on his way to Damascus to bring back in chains to Jerusalem "any men or women who belong to the Way." (Acts 9:1-2) As he drew close to his destination, Saul was felled by a flash of light and heard Jesus' challenging words, "Saul, Saul, why are you persecuting me?" (Acts 9:4) Blinded for three days, Saul was eventually reconciled and baptized, leading to his ministry as the first and foremost apostle to the Gentiles. The detailed description of Saul's (now Paul) three long and arduous missionary journeys through the Eastern Mediterranean world and his journey to Rome, (Acts 12:25-28:31) preaching the message of Christ and establishing Christian communities wherever he went, is a story unparalleled in Christian history.

How Have We Been Called by the Lord?

Through the privilege of baptism, all Christians have incurred a significant responsibility to respond to the call of the Lord. Depending on our vocation in life, as a celibate religious, single person or married with family, the responsibility is the same while the manifestations will obviously be different. Too often it is perceived that responding to God's call through ministry is essentially the privileged work of those who have dedicated their lives through the evangelical counsels of poverty, chastity, and obedience. While quite obviously priests and religious, not only through their vows, but their style of life have sought to minister in Christ's name in a more formal way, all people who bear the name Christian are challenged to listen for and respond to the call of the Lord.

The clerical and religious life, by its nature, presents more time and opportunity to serve God's people directly. The challenge, therefore, for these people is not finding the time or opportunity, but rather seeking new, possibly innovative ways to bring the Lord's message to our society which, unfortunately, becomes more secular and less God-centered with the passing of time.

God's faithful people, the Christian community at large must do their part to bring the salvific message of Christ to others. Professional ministers such as priests and religious certainly provide an important and, in many cases, life giving example, but most people of faith only experience a "professional" sense of ministry on Sunday. Encounters with priests and religious in schools, hospitals, and social service agencies occur daily, but most prominently and regularly through the faithful's weekly attendance at the celebration of the Eucharist. Thus, it is imperative that faith-filled laity, with great fidelity to Jesus Christ, and the Church, boldly step forward to answer the Lord's call, in their daily walk toward life eternal. We can "preach" the word of God with our mouths, but actions speak very loudly. We all, know the popular dictum, "Actions speak louder than words." St. Francis of Assisi has famously been quoted, "Preach the Gospel and when necessary, use words." The power of example can never be overstated. People we encounter are either drawn closer to or pushed further way from the message of Christ by what they observe in us. Our responsibility is indeed great and, thus, we need to daily remind ourselves of the need to put forward our best effort, in word and deed.

Conclusion

The privilege of being a Christian brings with it great responsibility. As with every endeavor in life, we always should seek to manifest not only our best intentions, but our best effort in our day-to-day Christian lives. An anonymous, yet popular quote in some ways succinctly puts forth the challenge: "Every job is a self-portrait of the person who did it. Autograph your work with excellence." May our daily efforts to bring the presence of Christ to others be so lived and manifested.

Part IV: Teaching and Tradition

Introduction

To properly walk the road with the Lord, to adequately journey with the Lord Jesus, requires much of us. As these reflections have demonstrated, we need to believe in the goodness of God, engage and never run from the various challenges of the Christian life, and meet the needs of our brothers and sisters, and thereby serve the Lord himself, through our active ministry. To minister effectively, however, we need to be literate in our faith. It is unfortunate, but true that far too many Catholics are woefully ignorant of the teachings of the faith. While the post-Vatican II era of the Church has brought many benefits, especially as addressed in Part III of this book with the rise of the laity, so too has this period seen a massive loss in religious literacy. Simply put, many who faithfully come to church every Sunday, as well as those who do not practice the faith, are not conversant with the basic teachings that all who bear the name of Christian should know.

The gaps in our Christian knowledge are found in many avenues. Many have forgotten or never learned some of the basic prayers, such as the Act of Contrition, the Memorare, Hail Holy Queen, or the Prayer to Our Guardian Angel. Too few people understand that Canon of Scripture and why various versions of the Bible separate Protestants from Catholics. Far too many are uninformed about Divine Revelation, especially Sacred Tradition and how this latter idea is so integral to being a practicing Roman Catholic. Christians need to refresh themselves on the various feasts of the Liturgical Year.

While not intended to be a primer to review the entirety of the Catholic faith, Part IV "Teaching and Tradition," presents several essays which describe various doctrines and traditions that unfortunately have become "lost" for many. Understanding how Christians initially worshiped in their own homes, how the Bible was put together in its present form, explaining the lost teaching on purgatory, and describing various feasts celebrated throughout the liturgical year, is vitally important to successfully journey with the Lord. None of us would go to a professional of any stripe, whether that be legal, medical, or business if we were not confident that the individual was competent, and sufficiently knowledgeable to help us. How can we adequately journey with the Lord unless we too have sufficient knowledge to move forward? The challenge of understanding our faith better is one we cannot avoid, but rather something we must fully engage. The challenge is present; our response is awaited.

BUILDING GOD'S KINGDOM TODAY:
CATHOLICISM'S ECUMENICAL CHALLENGE

O
n December 26, 2004, the greatest natural disaster experienced in the world in over a century struck southern Asia. The 9.0 magnitude earthquake with its epicenter some 200 miles southwest of the island of Sumatra generated a tsunami that traveled rapidly in all directions, causing death, destruction, dislocation, and mayhem for literally millions of people in some ten nations that border the northeast regions of the Indian Ocean. Thousands of people, tourists on vacation lying on the pristine white sand beaches in the area, local fisherman and their families plying their trade, children playing in coastal areas, men and women aboard trains traveling to distant locations, were swept away by a tidal surge that came with a ferocity that can only be imagined. Amateur videos of the wave's progress from sea to land can capture neither the fear nor horror that must have run through the minds of many who in literally a few seconds lost everything material and had their lives transformed. Officials say over 250,000 people were killed, millions were left homeless, and destruction ran into the billions of dollars.

The world community responded to the enormous need generated by this disaster in remarkable ways. Governments across the globe pledged money, manpower, and resources to stabilize the situation and prevent further misery from disease. Relief agencies of all stripes, secular and religious, received record contributions. Churches, schools, and other institutions took up collections. Music, television, and film stars staged concerts and other events to raise additional revenue. All these relief initiatives were launched without regard to nation, religion, ethnicity, race or culture. People throughout the world responded because of the obvious need and their desire to help. The world in a significant way demonstrated its solidarity, that we are one, sisters and brothers in the human community.

The world initiative to meet the need after this natural disaster, an example of international cooperation and ecumenical and inter-faith spirit, should be an inspiration to the Christian community to do what it can to cast aside differences, find common ground, and work for unity. Each January since 1908, Christian churches celebrate the Week of Prayer for Christian Unity, an event started through the inspiration of Father Paul Wattson, S.A., founder of the Franciscan Friars of the Atonement. Many other positive ecumenical efforts have occurred, including the prominent Lutheran-Catholic dialogue and its publication of the 1999 document on the Eucharist, but more can and must be done. If the world can come together to aid victims of disaster, the Christian community should be able to make significant strides to find common ground with Jesus, a theme popular in the corpus of St. Paul.

Paul knew the Corinthian people very well, spending considerable time in the city (Acts 18:18). We know he wrote several letters to the Christian community there. We have what is today called First Corinthians, but we also have, as the Scripture scholars tell us, a compilation of several letters which an apostolic-period redactor fashioned into what we today call Second Corinthians. There were several issues that prompted Paul to write his first letter to this nascent Christian community--division, immorality, and abuses in the community, including questions on marriage and divorce and the sanctity of the Lord's supper. Divisions among the people, however, was the first reason he mentions and, thus, it must have been of great significance to him. Paul realized the community was fractured saying that some people claim loyalty to Paul and others to Apollos. This division was problematic for Paul and thus he suggests the solution can be found in Jesus. We read, "The foundation is Jesus Christ." (I Corinthians 3:11b)

The unity that St. Paul seeks for the Corinthians should remind us of our need to find a similar connection with each other. Christianity is one of the great privileges of life. We have the privilege of being members of the community of faith, the Church. We have the privilege of the sacred scripture, which, if we wish, we can read and meditate upon each day. We have the privilege of the sacramental life, special signs from God of the Lord's presence with us. We have the privilege of knowing that God is our Good Shepherd, engaged as British poet Francis Thompson put so powerfully in his epic poem, "The Hound of Heaven," in a relentless and diligent search for our souls. While 99% will receive a grade of A+ in school, that is not satisfactory for God. God will leave the 99 in the desert and search for the one lost sheep. (Matthew 18:12-14, Luke 15:3-7) Yes, we have the privilege of Jesus, the great physician, who is with us every moment and each step of our lives.

The great and multiple privileges of the Christian life come with significant responsibilities as well. Baptism is our common call as Christians to live holy lives. We are called as well to be servants, to aid our brothers and sisters as did Christ, who came to serve, not to be served (Mark 10:45). Christianity calls us to be beacons of light and hope to a world often shrouded in darkness. In short, we are called to build God's kingdom through our united efforts. But, as Paul suggests to the Corinthians and Jesus states directly at the end of his Sermon on the Mount, we must build that kingdom, our spiritual house, on the rock of Christ, the foundation of life. Jesus told his disciples (Matthew 7:24-27):

> Everyone then who hears these words of mine and
> acts on them will be like a wise man who built his house

on rock. The rain fell, the floods came, and the winds blew and beat on that house, but it did not fall, because it had been founded on rock. And everyone who hears these words of mine and does not act on them will be like a foolish man who built his house on sand. The rain fell, and the floods came, and the wind blew and beat against that house, and it fell--and great was its fall.

How can we construct the kingdom centered in Christ in our world? We do so generically by working together, not as individuals, personally or denominationally, but ecumenically as a community of faith. We begin by fostering an attitude of acceptance, working together and not with antagonism. We are all on the same team, which bears the name Christian, as assuredly as the world was on the same team, called humankind, to alleviate the suffering in south Asia.

This shared team mentality is completely consistent with the ideas of Pope St. John XXIII, the genius behind Vatican II. On January 25, 1959, when the Pope astounded the world by calling the Council, he suggested that one of Vatican II's three primary goals was to promote ecumenism, an area where Catholics historically had lagged Protestants. The publication in November 1964 of "The Decree on Ecumenism" *(Unitatis Redintegratio)* synthesized much of what the Council professed on the need for unity among all Christians and even to a larger extent, all people of faith. Stating that the Church's division "openly contradicts the will of Christ," the bishops began the document stating, "The restoration of unity among all Christians is one of the principal concerns of the Second Vatican Council." (*Unitatis*, paragraph 1). While clearly noting that the fullness of truth resides in Catholicism (*Unitatis* paragraph 4), the bishops also stated that other communions "have been by no means deprived of significance and importance in the mystery of salvation." (*Unitatis*, paragraph 3) This is so because many of the most significant elements that give life to the Church, namely Scripture, the life of grace, the interior gifts of

194

the Holy Spirit (as examples), exist outside the visible boundaries of Catholicism. In the "Declaration of the Relation of the Church to Non-Christian Religions," (*Nostra Aetate*) the bishops demonstrate greater inclusion stating, "The Catholic Church rejects nothing of what is true and holy in these religions." (*Nostra Aetate*, paragraph 2) The bishops call for people of faith to form a brotherhood "because all share a common destiny, namely God." (*Nostra Aetate*, paragraph 1) Such a way of thinking was a major shift in the 1960s and so too it may seem for some today. Thus, the bishops challenged the faithful concluding, "There can be no ecumenism worthy of the name without interior conversion." (*Unitatis*, paragraph 7)

Reflecting on Vatican II's call for unity, the Church must take a more inclusive view of its relationship with others, imitating Jesus the master. Scripture is replete with examples of how Christ excluded no one, but rather reached out to all, but in a preferential way, to those whom society had placed on the margins--the poor, sick, stranger and alien, women and those considered sinners. Jesus included all the "lepers" of society, those physically so afflicted and many others who were labeled as outcasts. Too often in history Christians, and more specifically Catholics, have held a pharisaical attitude toward individuals and peoples, leading to their exclusion from dialogue and influence. We must view ourselves, both individuals and faith communities, as belonging to a larger whole, seeking to use our talents toward the common good, not for what I or my specific faith tradition may deem necessary. We must think globally but act locally, building God's kingdom by applying the message of Jesus. Proponents of the Social Gospel in the Progressive Era, people like Walter Rauschenbusch, Washington Gladden, and John Ryan, and more recently in the 1990s college students across the country, had it right when they collectively asked, "What would Jesus do?" Our task of building the kingdom will present many challenges and we will be forced to stand against the tide of contemporary life that seeks, like the tsunami, to drown out our voice. This should be no surprise, however. Paul tells his readers that his efforts in working for Christ will be tested and so too will all others. He also says that the wisdom of God is absurdity to the world. Jesus told his followers, "You will be hated by all because of my name. But the one who endures to the end will be saved." (Matthew 10:22) Thus we must persevere and never lose hope.

Building God's kingdom in our world is not for the faint of heart. It is a task that takes courage, strength, and persistence. But let us never think that if the task is too difficult, we can relax and let others take the lead. No, Jesus the foundation of our faith and the one to whom we will return, demands more from us. As the Lord says, "From everyone to whom much has been given, much will be required; and from the one to whom much has been entrusted, even more will be demanded." (Luke 12:48b) Thus, we need to roll up our sleeves and get to work, in a common unified effort. Let us take up the challenge of building God's kingdom in our world upon Christ the rock foundation. We have a good example of how disaster brought the world together. Let us not wait until disaster strikes the Christian community but let us act now so the Scriptures may be fulfilled, and Jesus' plan can come to full fruition: "That they may all be one. As you, Father, are in me and I am in you, may they also be in us, so that the world may believe that you sent me." (John 17:21) Let us believe, profess, and act the same.

ANGELS: GOD'S MESSENGERS OF HOPE

T he Catholic tradition is replete with stories and celebrations of angels. As with many popular traditions, such as the rosary, Eucharistic adoration, and veneration of the saints, the angels have suffered an eclipse in the contemporary devotion of the faithful. Nevertheless, the teaching and tradition of the Church is strong and secure with respect to the position of angels, God's messengers to our world. Looking at both the history of the Church's understanding of angels and her liturgical celebration of these heavenly beings connects us to our spiritual roots and renews our faith in God's ever-present action in our world.

Angels in the Tradition of the Church

As with all Christian tradition, it is essential to look to Sacred Scripture to establish the basis for our belief concerning angels. Both the Hebrew Scriptures or Old Testament and the New Testament contain numerous references to angels. Angels, understood as God's messengers from the Greek *angelos* and the Hebrew *mal'ak*, have no formal theological definition in the Hebrew Scriptures. Angels are mentioned frequently, however, and overall are understood to be superhuman heavenly beings whose normal habitat is the court of Yahweh (Job 1:6, 2:1). Angels are always subordinate to God (Tobit 12:18, Psalm 102:20-21), although they are normally invisible, unapproachable, and unaffected by human needs. The primary function of angels is to do God's will (Tobit 12:18). Yet, they also intervene in human affairs by exercising power over nature and by communicating God's messages (Genesis 31:11). In the books of Exodus (14:19), II Samuel (14:17) and II Kings (19:35) angels are seen as God's messengers. The New Testament also portrays angels as God's messengers with the Lukan accounts of Gabriel's messages to Zechariah and Mary, the messages to Joseph in Matthew and role of angels in the book of Revelation.

Scripture gives us some insight into the nature of angels. These heavenly beings are spirits. They see, praise, and worship in God's presence. They are stronger than humans and possess intelligence and freedom. With these abilities they have the capacity to reject God. Angels who have rejected God are portrayed in Scripture as in league with Satan (I Corinthians 15:24, Ephesians 2:2).

The tradition of the Church concerning angels has been governed by two main points. First, angels demonstrate that there is more to the created order than we can see, feel, hear, and taste. The existence of angels allows people to believe what seems impossible. Secondly, tradition is clear that angels, like humans, are part of the created order and thus less than God. This second point was made clear by St. Paul in his letter to the Colossians. The Chonae area of Colossae was a place of true worship of angels. St. Paul in his letter to the community (2:18) rejects the heretical teaching offered by some who saw Christ as subservient to the angels. Paul's teaching was confirmed by the Council of Braga in 561.

The spiritual fathers of the Patristic Church made numerous comments relevant to the veneration of angels. St. Justin Martyr (d.165) wrote that the "host of good angels was held in the highest veneration." Eusebius of Caesarea, the father of Church history, distinguished between the veneration rendered to angels and worship paid to God. Pseudo-Dionysius and Augustine promoted the pure spiritual nature of angels. Beginning with St. Benedict in the sixth century and continuing to the time of Bernard of Clairvaux (d.1153), the Western Church maintained a steady tradition of devotion to angels, including Guardian angels for whom Bernard was a great proponent.

The tradition, both Judaic (Tobit 12:15, Enoch 20:2 and the Testament of Levi 3:2-8) and Christian (Romans 8:38, I Corinthians 15:24, Ephesians 1:21 and Colossians 1:16), has shown angels to exist in certain orders. Scripture in total denotes nine categories of angels. Pseudo-Dionysus developed under neo-Platonic influences a hierarchical structure of three triads of angels. This has been accepted in both East and West since the fourth century. Archangels command a leading role. They together with Angels and Principalities form one triad of angels which carries out the decrees of God. Dominations, Virtues, and Powers form a second group who are to rule the world. The third triad, Seraphim, Cherubim, and Thrones are to contemplate God. The Lateran Synod of 745 confirmed these categories and made the additional admonition that no non-Biblical names were to be used for angels.

Official Church pronouncements on angels have been few. The Fourth Lateran Council of 1215 stated, "From the beginning of time [God] made at once out of nothing both orders of creatures, the spiritual and the corporeal, that is the angelic and the earthly." Vatican I (1870) in its document *Dei Filius* published the exact same pronouncement.

Celebrations of Angels

Liturgical celebrations of angels date from the sixth century and are centered in devotion to the archangel Michael. Michael, a name meaning "who is like God." is called by the angel Gabriel in Daniel 10:13 and 21 "one of the chief princes." In Jude 9 Michael is referred to as "the archangel." In Revelation (12:7) Michael appears as the leader of the angels in battle with Satan. Tradition attributes four offices to Michael: (1) to fight against Satan, (2) to rescue the souls of the faithful from the powers of the devil, especially at the hour of death, (3) to be the champion of God's people, and (4) to bring the souls of the faithful to judgment.

The Eastern tradition of the Church is where devotion to St. Michael began. Outside Constantinople in the fourth century Constantine built a church in honor of Michael on the Hestiae headland of the Bosphorus. On the opposite Asiatic shore, the Emperor Justinian (527-565) erected another church to Michael. The historian Du Cange says that there were no fewer than 15 churches and chapels dedicated to St. Michael in and around Constantinople during the Middle Ages. In the sixth century, the districts of Chonae in Colossae and Phrygia were known centers for thecultus of angels, especially devotion to Michael.

Michael was celebrated in the east as the one who cared for the sick. In Constantinople the liturgical celebration for Michael was held on November 8. The Coptic calendar lists no less than six celebrations for Michael, April 7, June 6, August 5, September 9, November 8, and December 8. The Syrian lectionary lists September 6 as the date of Michael's feast.

The Western Church has celebrated Michael for nearly as long as the East. The first church around Rome to honor Michael was located along the Via Salaria at the sixth milestone from Rome. The date of the erection of this edifice is not known, but in the *Liber Pontificalis* of Pope Symmachus (498-514) it states that this church was enlarged and beautified. The oldest sacramentaries of the Western Church, the Gelasian and Leonine, list several Masses for Michael on the dates of September 29 and 30 respectively.

In the sixth century a second festival for St. Michael began to be celebrated in the West in consequence of an apparition near Sipontum on Monte Gargano in southern Italy which took place on May 8, sometime between 520-530. A military victory by the

Lombards at Sipontum on May 8, 663 was attributed to Michael as well. This solidified the May 8 date as an additional celebration for the archangel.

Western churches accepted the Roman date of September 29 to honor St. Michael. In the Medieval period this feast ranked as a holy day of obligation beginning in the eighth century, especially in England where King Ethelred in 1014 stated that the feast should be observed with a vigil and a preparatory fast of three days. Michaelmas, as his feast came to be called, was a special day for all knights who took the angel as their patron.

Many local customs became part of the celebration of St. Michael. The feast was a date in England to settle rents and accounts and was the election day for the Lord Mayor of London. In Normandy Michael became known as the patron of mariners when tradition spoke of the angel's appearance there in 708 to St. Aubert, bishop of Avranche. October 18 became a local Normandy holiday honoring Michael. In Germany the Council of Mainz (813) in its 36th canon established the feast of Michael as a local festival. Similar action was seen in France from the Synod of Tours (858).

Raphael, the companion of Tobiah in the book of Tobit, has also been celebrated in the history of the Church. A Venetian church of the seventh century was dedicated to Raphael. The liturgical feast for Raphael was celebrated locally in different places on October 24 or October 28. Pope Benedict XV in 1921 extended the October 28 feast to the universal Church.

Gabriel, a name meaning hero of God, has been honored by the Church through the centuries as well. He appears in Scripture four times, twice each in Daniel and Luke, the latter being the well-known announcements of the births of John the Baptist and Jesus. A Greek litany of saints of the fifth century mentions Gabriel with precedence over John the Baptist and the Blessed Virgin Mary. Gabriel was celebrated in the Coptic calendar on December 18. The

Syrian lectionary lists the feast as March 26. As with Raphael, a local feast of March 24, associating him with the Annunciation (celebrated March 25), was made universal by Pope Benedict XV in 1921. With the liturgical renewal and consolidation of the Church calendar in 1969, the individual feasts of Michael, Raphael, and Gabriel were combined on September 29 as the celebration of the archangels.

Guardian angels, another tradition in eclipse, has no distinct Scriptural basis, but has been a part of the tradition from the time of the Patristic Church. Devotion to Guardian angels, a development of Catholic theology and piety, was promoted by many of the Church fathers. St. Basil (d.379) stated, "No one denies that each of the faithful has his own guardian angel." Ambrose, the mentor of Augustine, wrote, "We should pray to the angels sent to us as guardians." Augustine himself wrote, "I deem it, O my God, an estimable benefit that thou has granted me an angel to guide me from the moment of my birth to that of my death." Later in the Medieval period St. Anselm commented, "Every human soul is committed to an angel."

Liturgical celebration of the Guardian angels was developed alongside that of the archangels. It was originally part of the commemoration of St. Michael on September 29. In the Middle Ages it became a separate feast, but only local in nature. In the sixteenth century a special feast of Guardian angels was celebrated in Spain on March 1 and in France on the first day not already celebrated after Michaelmas. In 1608 Pope Paul V established the feast on September 27. At the request of the Holy Roman Emperor Ferdinand II, Paul V prescribed the feast's observance throughout the imperial dominions. In 1667 Pope Clement IX placed the feast on the first Sunday in September and provided it with an octave celebration. Pope Clement X in 1670 moved the celebration to its present date of October 2.

Conclusions

Scripture, sacred tradition, and the magisterium have combined to produce an interesting and vivid theology of angels. Scripture and the magisterium have shown us the existence of angels and their efficacy in God's work in the world. Tradition has provided a development in the liturgical celebration of these heavenly bodies. Although people today may not refer much to angels in theological writing or everyday practice of the faith, the tradition keeps these messengers of God before us. Let us remember, as well, that God has sent us as well to be messengers of God's word to our brothers and sisters this day.

THE ANNUNCIATION:
MARY'S "YES" TO GOD

World history is replete with events which have defined the course of human society. When William the Conqueror came from France to England in 1066 it set in motion a series of events that resulted in the formation of the British Empire, which for several centuries dominated the political, economic, and social policies of the world. The expression, "The sun never sets on the British Empire," described the global effect which William's pioneering action so long before had generated. When Christopher Columbus landed on the island of Hispaniola on October 12, 1492, the direction of the world took another major shift. Columbus' courageous voyage set in motion a whole series of events: the voyages of discovery, colonization and evangelization, and the formation of many nations in the Americas. Adolph Hitler's order of a blitzkrieg attack on Poland on September 1, 1939, plunged Europe into World War II which produced the greatest human carnage in history. The war almost wiped out an entire race of people, shifted the map, and was the catalyst behind the development of nuclear weapons, which for time immemorial will keep the world under a veil of fear.

Organized religion has also experienced several events which have defined its course in history. The conversion of Emperor Constantine in 313 to a position favorable to Christianity gave the

Church legal status, allowed it to spread, and changed the course of western civilization. On October 31, 1517, Martin Luther nailed his famous "Ninety-Five Theses" to the door of the castle church in Wittenberg, Germany. This act initiated the Reformation and the division of Christianity, a situation which continues today. For Catholics, in the opinion of the famous twentieth-century German Jesuit Karl Rahner, the start of the Second Vatican Council on October 11, 1962, initiated a new era in the direction and history of the Church.

Most events which have defined the direction of the world, both its secular and religious paths, are well-known by date and place. We read about these events in our history books and are required to know them for examinations. The most important defining moment in all human history, the event which placed into action the culmination of God's plan for the salvation of all people, the Annunciation, cannot be so accurately situated in historical context. We know that it took place but precisely when and where was never recorded. Yet, it is this very event that helped bring to fulfillment God's plan for human salvation.

The Annunciation had been predicted but few probably noticed it. The Prophet Isaiah (7:14) proclaimed, "Therefore the Lord himself will give you this sign: the virgin shall be with child, and bear a son, and shall name him Immanuel." The day of the Annunciation, like most "defining" events, was not so understood when it occurred; its importance was seen only after the great events of Jesus' life and his passion, death, and resurrection. Looking backward it is possible to see not only the event's prediction but more importantly its significance for human history. The Annunciation is celebrated in our churches, but its relevance in leading the world to salvation has transformed society and channeled all our lives in a direction which makes our actions and words tools to build God's kingdom on earth. The Annunciation as an event gave us a reason and purpose for life.

The celebration of this great event today challenges us to understand Mary's great *fiat*, her "yes" to God and our need to imitate her courage. Human beings have been endowed by God with all sorts of wonderful gifts which we use in our daily lives to build the Kingdom. The gifts we possess in many ways define who we are. If we have been given the gift of words we will probably be known as a writer, orator, or preacher. The ability to teach and convey knowledge to others will place us in the classroom. Skill with our hands might define us as a carpenter, mechanic, or artist. Those granted great athleticism find fulfillment on the baseball diamond, the gridiron, or the basketball court. The gifts we possess in many ways define who we are and often dictate the path in life we will follow.

There is one gift, however, which is common to all and defines us as human--it is the gift of free will. No one has more or less free will; it is a special, but general and equal gift of God. How we use our free will, by its very nature, is up to us. It can be used to bring good and further society or, if used with evil intent, can cast our lives and those who know us into darkness. Mary said yes when the Angel Gabriel brought God's invitation that very special day. She had free choice and decided to respond as the author of the Letter to the Hebrews (10:7b) suggests, "I have come to do your will." Mary had no special insight into the future when she said yes. Like all young people she had dreams and hopes, and she knew that this decision would change all her plans. But Mary used the gift which defined her humanity to bring the possibility of salvation to all people for all time. She did not understand this; she had no foreknowledge of God's plan. Mary, however, did possess great faith, which is described in Hebrews 11:2 as, "confident assurance concerning what we hope for, and conviction about things we do not see."

The great gift of free will is the one characteristic which levels us as humans. All of us cannot be great artists, educators, engineers, or athletes, but we can exercise our humanity in such a way that brings greater fulfillment of God's plan for humankind by our free choice to cooperate with God's requests. The philosophy of existentialism tells us that humans must choose. Unlike animals whose instinct produces a predictable response, we can make choices. God never places human free will in a straitjacket; God provides the teaching and the ground rules and then lets us decide.

The Feast of the Annunciation gives us the courage to say yes to God's call and to know that such a decision will be significant in building God's kingdom. The world is filled with choices and options, from clothes, to foods, to channels on cable television. Inspired by Mary's choice for God let us have the courage to choose God. We and the world will not regret it.

THE ASSUMPTION OF MARY: A CELEBRATION OF CHURCH TRADITION

The Sacred Tradition of the Church plays an important role in the daily celebration of our faith. Linked integrally with Scripture and the Magisterium, Sacred Tradition is God's revelation, the source from which our knowledge and practice of the Faith is drawn. The Feast of the Assumption, possibly the oldest celebration of the Virgin, is rooted in the Tradition of Christian practice, supported by magisterial teaching, and defined as one of four Marian dogmas.

The historical evolution of this solemnity demonstrates God's continued revelation to our world.

Historical and Theological Development

Although Scripture makes no direct reference to the bodily ascension of Mary to heaven, several passages speak of the great dignity of her life, lending support to the idea that Jesus desired that his mother would not experience the corruption of the grave, and thus extending to Mary the privilege of the Assumption. In the Hebrew Scriptures the Song of Songs contains passages which some scholars today say are prophetical references to Mary. We read, "Arise, my beloved, my beautiful one, and come!" (2:10) and "The daughters saw her and declared her fortunate, the queens and concubines, and they sang her praises." (6:9b) The New Testament also provides evidence supportive of Mary's special privilege. Gabriel's greeting, "Rejoice, O highly favored daughter! The Lord is with you. Blessed are you among women," (Luke 1:28) and Revelation 12:1, in its description of "a woman clothed with the sun," are illustrative.

The silence of history and Scripture concerning the death of Mary, coupled with the definition at the Council of Ephesus (431) of Mary as the *theotokos* (Mother of God), most probably were the catalysts behind the rise of a wealth of apocryphal literature descriptive of the dormition (falling asleep) of the Virgin. One body of apocrypha from the fourth and fifth centuries, attributed to one Leucius is titled *De transitu Mariae* (The Passing of Mary). *Transitus Beatae Mariae Virginis*, falsely attributed to St. Melito of Sardis, was another popular account of the Virgin's death.

The chief authority for information on Mary's death comes from St. John Damascene (d.750), who used the otherwise unknown scholar Euthymius, for his data. Pulcheria, the wife of Emperor Marcian (450-457), ordered the construction of a church in a suburb of Constantinople called Blachenae to which she wanted brought the earthly remains of Mary. In speaking with Bishop Juvenal of Jerusalem during the Council of Chalcedon (451), the Empress was informed that the Virgin's body was not in Jerusalem. Buried in the Garden of Gethsemane in the presence of the apostles, save Thomas, it was discovered three days later when the apostles came to venerate her body, that the tomb was empty. It was concluded that Jesus had taken his mother to heaven. These apocryphal accounts, although they contain no historical foundation, nevertheless serve an important function in demonstrating what the people believed, which became important for the development of the Tradition of the Church.

As with many Church feasts, the liturgical celebration of the Assumption began its evolution in the East. Church calendars of the ancient Armenian and Ethiopian Churches, as well as the schismatic Nestorian and Monophysite communities, contain a date to commemorate Mary's death, which gives evidence that the feast had deep roots, even before the definition of Mary as Mother of God proclaimed at Ephesus. The first concrete evidence which speaks of a Marian celebration on August 15 is found in a mid-fifth century lectionary in Jerusalem calling the feast "Day of Mary Mother of God." This was transformed into a commemoration of the *dormitio* (falling asleep) which was extended to the entire Byzantine empire by Emperor Maurice in the late sixth century. Additional evidence to the widespread celebration of Mary's dormition is found in the sermons of Modestus, Patriarch of Jerusalem (d.634), Andrew of Crete (d.720), Germanus, Patriarch of Constantinople (d.733), all of whom testify to a feast celebrated to honor Mary's death and her Assumption.

A Gallic liturgy of the mid-sixth century is the first evidence of the celebration of the Assumption in the Western Church. This feast, held on January 18, was called in a seventh century sacramentary the "Feast of Mary's Assumption." St. Gregory of Tours (d.596), in his treatise "On the Glory of the Martyrs," affirms Mary's Assumption: "The Lord bade the sacred body [of Mary] be borne aloft on a cloud and carried to paradise, where, reunited to the soul, and rejoicing with His elect, it enjoys the good things of eternity in unending bliss."

Eastern influence led to the introduction of the Feast at Rome in the mid-seventh century. Proclaimed as *Natale Sanctae Mariae*, this celebration was held, again as in the East, on August 15. Pope Sergius I (687-701), a Syrian who was instrumental in the introduction of many Eastern customs to the Roman Church, made the celebration a principal feast and added a procession to its liturgy. The Gregorian Sacramentary (*Hadrianum*) calls the August 15 feast, "The Assumption of Holy Mary." The first prayer of this Mass says that Mary, "could not be kept in the chains of death." Still later Pope Leo IV in 847 added an octave to the feast as the celebration spread as far west as Spain.

During the Medieval period recognized scholars and leading Church officials continued to promote the celebration of the Assumption. The famous Dominican scholastic St. Thomas Aquinas referenced Psalm 131:8, "Advance, O Lord to your resting place, you and the ark of your majesty," in promoting belief in the Assumption of Mary, the true ark of God. St. Anthony of Padua in a thirteenth century sermon stated, "The Lord arose when he ascended to the right hand of the Father. The Ark which he has sanctified arose when the Virgin Mother was assumed to the Heavenly bridal chamber." Albert the Great, mentor to Aquinas, in commenting upon Luke Chapter 1, wrote, "It is plain that the Most Blessed Mother of God has been assumed in body and soul beyond the choirs of Angels. And this in every way we believe to be true."

The Feast of the Assumption was a major feast of the 1570 Sacramentary published by Pope Pius V during the Counter Reformation. Thus, the Church, in eliminating abuse and defending Catholic teaching and tradition, reaffirmed its belief in this long-standing feast. The final page to the evolution of the Assumption was written on November 1, 1950, when Pope Pius XII in the apostolic constitution *Munificentissimus Deus* stated, "We pronounce, declare, and define it to be a divinely revealed dogma: that the Immaculate Mother of God, the ever-Virgin Mary, having completed the course of her earthly life, was assumed body and soul into heavenly glory."

Contemporary Application

The historical evolution of the Feast of the Assumption is incomplete without some reflection on this celebration's significance for people today. Mary's role as the supreme model to follow in our common vocation to holiness and discipleship finds its ultimate triumph and reward in her Assumption. Our certainty of Mary's return to God, body and soul, prefigures our own resurrection and final union with God. In celebrating Mary's Assumption, we not only celebrate the love that God showed her, but in more general terms the love that God has shown to all his children in granting the possibility of final resurrection to all. Jesus' earthly life brought salvation history to its climax; Mary's Assumption gives us hope that in a constantly changing and ever more complex world God never abandons those who love him, but rather rewards them with eternal life.

Our attitude must emulate the thanksgiving which was the Blessed Mother's constant prayer. In her wisdom the Church uses Mary's Magnificat (Luke 1:46-55) as the Gospel in the Eucharistic celebration of the Assumption. Mary knew that God had done great things for her, and she was grateful. It is our challenge to express equal gratitude to God for what we receive in our daily lives, both the sorrows and the joys. Mary, the Sorrowful Mother, gave thanks to God and received the special privilege of resurrection. So too can all of us find final union with God through lives of thankful praise.

From ancient times the Church has proclaimed *lex orandi lex credendi*, the law of prayer is the law of belief. The Feast of the Assumption, in its evolution from the common belief of the faithful, as represented by the proliferation of apocryphal literature to a dogma of the Church, is a manifestation of this time-honored dictum. Mary's role as the Mother of God and the dignity of her life were rewarded with the privilege of her Assumption. Her life continues to serve as the perfect model of discipleship for all the faithful.

THE BATTLE OF THE BOOKS: ORIGINS OF THE CANON OF SCRIPTURE

*D*ei Verbum, the Dogmatic Constitution on Divine Revelation, published on November 18, 1965, is considered one of the most foundational of the sixteen documents of the Second Vatican Council. Paragraph #10 of this document reads in part, "Sacred tradition and sacred Scripture form one sacred deposit of the word of God, which is committed to the Church." Tradition, formed from apostolic tradition and the teaching Church or magisterium, is unique to Catholicism as a source of divine revelation. Scripture is shared by all Christians as God's word. Even with Scripture, however, there are different understandings of what is considered "canonical" (accepted as part of the Bible) and what is apocryphal (not accepted by all). Roman Catholicism uses a Bible with 46 books of the Old Testament and 27 books in the New Testament. Protestant denominations, however, question the divine inspiration in seven of the Old Testament books, and thus use a Bible with 39 books of Hebrew Scripture. Why is this the case? How and when did the Bible become organized as one compilation of many shorter works? What criteria determined which writings were considered canonical and which were not. These questions and many others can be answered by looking at the origins of the Canon of Scripture, what one might call the "Battle of the Books."

The Old Testament Canon - Hebrew Views

The Hebrew Scriptures, what Christians call the Old Testament, became fixed as canon in three stages. The Torah (Christian Pentateuch) or Law for the Hebrew community was the first sacred writing to be so proclaimed. The Prophets, consisting of the historical books (former prophets) and the major and minor prophets (latter prophets) were next to receive acceptance. The Writings, including (among others) Psalms, Sirach, Wisdom, and Proverbs, were the last to be fixed into the Canon of Scripture.

The Torah, the first five books of the Old Testament, was basic to the Jewish religion. Consensus scholarship today says that the Torah was accepted in the Jewish community as one book with five sections. Uncertainty with respect to the order of the five books was present, but the main historical question concerned the time of acceptance of the Law in the Hebrew community. Most experts today fix the Law as canon at the time of the Samaritan schism and the reign of Alexander the Great in the mid-fourth century BCE. The similarity of the books of law in the Samaritan and Jewish communities is the principal evidence used to fix this date.

With the Torah accepted, the Hebrews began to debate the validity and inspiration of other written sources which described the history of the nation of Israel. The former prophets (Joshua through II Kings) became associated with the Law in the mid-4th century BCE. This fact demonstrated their sacredness. Additionally, these books were thought to be dependent upon Deuteronomy for their origins and general orientation. This enhanced their acceptability as they were seen to serve the religious tradition already laid down in the Torah. The latter prophets, consisting of the major prophets Isaiah, Ezekiel, and Jeremiah and the twelve minor prophets, were written between the eighth and second centuries BCE. The latter date is considered the point of acceptance of all prophetic books.

British scholar John Holland Smith fixes the date as 132 BCE, the thirty-eighth year of the reign of King Euergetes, as stated in the prologue of the book of Sirach, where the Biblical author speaks of the discovery of "our valuable teaching." Additionally, at this time the historical books and prophets began to be used as supplements to the Law in Synagogue services and other Jewish assemblies which added evidence to their acceptability in the community.

The Jewish writings were not as readily accepted as the Law or Prophets. The Hebrew community did not see these books as fundamentally important and thus they received less attention. Some scholars place the Writings in the Jewish canon of Scripture during the Maccabean period (late second century BCE). Others, however, counter this opinion stating that although the Writings were used liturgically before Christ, it does not seem that a collection was complete before the commencement of the Christian era.

Jewish efforts toward the formal adoption of a canon of Divinely inspired literature did not begin until the dawn of Christianity. Josepheus, the famous Jewish historian, writing at the end of the first century CE, in his work *Contra Apion*, stated (in error) that all the inspired books of Hebrew Scripture were written between the time of Moses and Artaxerxes I (d. 42 BCE). He gives as his list of inspired books: five rolls of the Law, four rolls of former prophets (books of Joshua, Judges with I and II Samuel and I and II Kings counting as two), four latter prophets (Isaiah, Jeremiah, Ezekiel, and twelve minor prophets counted as one) and the Kethubim (Writings) which consisted of the scrolls of Psalms, Proverbs, Job, Ruth, Ecclesiastes, Song of Songs, Lamentations, Daniel, Esther, Ezra, Nehemiah and I and II Chronicles.

The work of Josephus raises a long-standing argument on the canonicity of several books not mentioned in his list of inspired works. Scholars have argued for centuries that the books originally composed in Hebrew were found acceptable, while those written in Greek, namely Tobit, Judith, I and II Maccabees, Wisdom, Sirach,

Baruch and sections of Esther and Daniel, were rejected. Recent scholarship, however, challenges this view with historical data which shows Sirach was originally composed in Hebrew and Daniel was probably composed in Aramaic, with later additions in Greek.

It is certain that disputes did exist in the Jewish community during the time of Jesus with the acceptance of several books, including those formerly mentioned, as well as Ruth, Ecclesiastes, Song of Songs, Lamentations and Esther. Different theories are present as to the catalyst that prompted the Jewish people to finalize their canon. Some scholars hypothesize that it was the threat of the Christian "heresy" and the wide diffusion of Christian writings which led Judaism to make decisions with respect to its sacred canon. Another theory says that the rivalry between Greek and Jewish culture prompted the Jews to establish a collection of books which could be accepted as authoritative. The influence of Greek philosophy could be neutralized, it was thought, by a collection of Jewish books. A third opinion states that the Jewish canon was not closed until well into the Christian era. The status of the disputed books, so says the theory, was discussed at the Jewish Council of Jamnia (90 CE), some twenty years after the diaspora and the destruction of the Temple. Jewish teachers of the Law thought it imperative to fix the orthodox traditions before they were forgotten.

The final product of the Hebrew Scriptures contains "canonical" books only. As formerly stated, the long-standing view of canonicity based on the original Hebrew language of composition prevailed. The books of Sirach, I and II Maccabees, Judith, Wisdom, Baruch, Tobit and sections of Esther and Daniel, were classified as deutero-canonical, with the Law and remaining sections of the Prophets and Writings considered the authentic canon.

The Old Testament Canon - Christian Views

In general Christianity accepted the Hebrew Scriptures as the inspired word of God. The birth, ministry, and death of Jesus were predicted in them. Additionally, Jesus used the Hebrew Scriptures to make points on the indissolubility of marriage (Mark 10:6-9 referencing Genesis 1:27), the resurrection of the dead (Mark 12:26-27 referencing Exodus 3:6) and the superiority of the Messiah over David (Mark 12:35-37 referencing Psalm 110:1). Christian writings also spoke of the Hebrew Scriptures as Divinely inspired (II Peter 1:19-21, II Timothy 3:14-17).

The major question for Christians with respect to the Hebrew Scriptures was to accept or reject the deutero-canonical books. The question became acute when Christians began to use the Alexandrian "Bible" as its first canon of Hebrew Scripture. This Greek translation of the Hebrew Scripture, known as the Septuagint, was produced by descendants of Jews who settled in Egypt from the time of the Babylonian captivity in 586 BCE. When the work was begun is not precisely known, but scholars think the books of the Law were translated by 250 BCE with the Prophets and Writings soon thereafter. This version of the Hebrew Scriptures included the deutero-canonical books which created a conflict between the Hellenistic Jews of Egypt and the Palestinian community of Jerusalem.

The consensus of the Western Church favored the Greek text of the Hebrew Scriptures and its use of the deutero-canonical corpus. One detractor was Justin Martyr (d.150), who in his "Dialogue with Trypho" held reservations about the deutero-canonical texts. Jerome (340-420) distinguished between "canonical books" and "ecclesiastical books," the latter being good spiritual reading but not authoritative Scripture. Augustine, however, did not recognize this distinction; he accepted the Septuagint in full. The first Latin translations of the Hebrew Scriptures used the Septuagint as well. The Council of Hippo (393) gives a complete list of the inspired books which included the deutero-canonical corpus. Jerome followed this list in his famous Vulgate Latin translation of the early fifth century.

Controversy in the Hebrew Scripture canon was again raised during the Reformation in the sixteenth century. Protestant reformers accepted the original Jewish canon and thus rejected the deutero-canonical books. The reformers in England accepted the deutero-canonical works as readings but not as a basis for the establishment of points of doctrine. The Roman Church at the Council of Trent, session four (April 8, 1564) declared in *De Canonicis Scripturis* that the tradition from the Fathers of the Church, after long debate, had shown the deutero-canonical books to be of special value to Christians and inspired by the Holy Spirit.

The New Testament Canon

The death of the apostles and those who knew them personally marked the end of the apostolic era. Christians perceived a need to write down their tradition for themselves and especially posterity. In this period the nascent Church recognized three authorities in the development of sacred writings: (1) the Hebrew Scriptures, (2) the spoken words of Christ and (3) the oral testimony of the Apostles. Only later in gradual measure did Jesus' words as recorded by his disciples assume any authority in the community. The waning memories of the early Christians forced their hand to the acceptance of secondhand sources.

The production of its own canon forced the Christian Church to define criteria by which the various writings in circulation could be judged for their authenticity and Divine inspiration. Apostolic origin was the first criterion used. This could be stretched to mean that the book had teachings of apostolic authority, or its author was a close associate of one or more of the apostles (such as the Gospels of Mark and Luke.) The apostles as the "eyewitnesses and ministers of the word" (Luke 1:2) were given final authority on the tradition.

This authority was enhanced by Christian champions of the period. Ignatius of Antioch wrote in his Letter to the Magnesians (13:1) that the people should hold fast to the teachings of the Lord and His apostles. Serapion of Antioch (circa 200) wrote, "We accept Peter and the other apostles as we accept Christ."

Two additional criteria were utilized to determine acceptability of writings. The community addressed was one factor. It was known that apostles had been sent to certain regions and peoples. Thus, letters or writings addressed to these people were viewed more favorably. A third criterion asked the question, did the text of the writing conform to the rule of faith? There could not be any conflict between these new writings and the established authentic words of Jesus, the accepted Hebrew Scriptures, or the oral testimony of the apostles.

The many writings produced in the post-apostolic age were separated into two divisions. The proto-canonical writings, the "first list," consisted of the four Gospels (Luke-Acts considered as one), thirteen Pauline letters (less Hebrews), I John and I Peter. The deutero-canonical books, or "second list" included Hebrews, Revelation, II Peter, II and III John, James, and Jude.

As the Jews found reasons to fix their sacred writings, so the Christian Church found a need to begin an official codification of its canon of Scripture. English historian Gerald Bray states that the need for a Canon became critical after 150 CE with the close of the apostolic age. First-hand knowledge of Jesus and his teachings was no longer available. Bray also states, following the lead of the famous nineteenth century Protestant theologian Adolph Harnack, that the heresy of Marcion (circa 144) provided the catalyst to the establishment of a canon. To separate the Creator from God, Marcion challenged the authority of the Hebrew Scripture and the whole New Testament save Luke and the Pauline corpus.

The Christian canon of Scripture began with the collection of St. Paul's writings. Collections of Paul's letters (thirteen letters less Hebrews) were present by the end of the first century in most Christian communities. II Peter 3:15-16 references the existence of Paul's letters in the community. Scholars differ on the dating of Peter's letter, ranging from 65 (thus seeing the letter as written by the apostle) to 140 CE. If the earlier date is accurate then the process of canon development was present quite early.

Scholars agree that the four Gospels were in existence by the dawn of the second century at the latest. References to these narratives' acceptance in the community are found in several early works. The "Epistle of Barnabas" (circa 100) and the letters of Ignatius of Antioch (115) both refer to Matthew's Gospel. Around the year 150 a Syrian Christian, known to history as Tatian, attempted to harmonize the Gospels in parallel columns in his work the *Diatessaron*, which indicates these works acceptance by the Church.

A survey of the more prominent Patristic writers shows steady progression in the development of the New Testament canon. Polycarp (circa 107-117) references the Pauline corpus as letters "you already know." Clement of Alexandria (d.217) knew of all 27 New Testament books, but showed caution in acceptance of James, II Peter and II John. Additionally, however, Clement considered the "Didache," "Shepherd of Hermas" and "Kerygma of Peter" to "be Divinely inspired." In the year 200 Ireneaus accepted all 27 books save Philemon, though he doubted the Pauline authorship of Hebrews. Origen (185-255) reflected the view of Clement of Alexandria with an acknowledgement of controversy over II Peter, James, Hebrews, II and III John and Jude. Tertullian, the first major Christian theologian to write in Latin, quoted from all the New Testament books, save II Peter and II and III John. Athanasius, in his famous Paschal Letter of 367, presents the complete 27 books. He wrote, "These are the sources of salvation, for the thirsty to drink deeply of the words to be found here. In these alone is the doctrine of piety recorded. Let no one add to them or take away from them."

The historical development of the canon begins with the Muratorian Fragment. Discovered in 1740 in a Milan library, this document is the earliest known authoritative list of the New Testament books, dating from mid-second century Rome. It names all the New Testament books save Hebrews, James, II Peter and II and III John. However, since the document is a fragment, it is not known if books not mentioned were rejected or merely missing from the list.

The authoritative canon continued to develop in decrees of councils and other formal declarations. Eusebius (267-338) in his famous *Ecclesiastical History*, states the Church accepted all the books of today's canon save James, Jude, II Peter and II and III John. The African synods of Hippo (393) and Carthage (397 and 419) accepted all 27 books. In 405 Pope St. Innocent I sent a "complete" canon of Scripture to Toulouse which included all the present 27 books. The Council of Florence (1439) reaffirmed the canon. Finally, as mentioned previously, the Council of Trent finalized the canon in the format we know today.

Reading and praying over God's word in Sacred Scripture is something we regularly do. Yet, when we pick up a Bible few if any of us think about the struggle that ensued to determine which writings were inspired and which were apocryphal. The "Battle of the Books" was waged over a long period of time. Although basically fixed for centuries, it was only in the sixteenth century where the Roman Church clearly defined the canon in response to the Protestant reformers. Learning of the struggles, criteria for acceptance, and theories behind the decisions made in the creation of the Canon of Scripture can give us a greater appreciation of God's word in our daily journey of Christian life.

The "Battle of the Books" produced winners and losers in the establishment of the Canon of Scripture. Although the Canon forms the word of God and its place of honor is secure, the apocrypha is a vast and interesting corpus of literature which provides hidden treasures which have played a positive role in the devotion of God's people.

THE EASTER TRIDUUM: HISTORY AND CELEBRATION

The liturgical year is filled with festivals and celebrations. We celebrate our relationship with God beginning with the events of Advent and Christmas and proceed through the year to the Feast of Christ the King. What we celebrate in our year is the life of Jesus and his time with humankind in the flesh. Although Christmas, especially for children, may be the most popular of all liturgical feasts, it is in the celebration of the Paschal Mystery, the passion, death, and resurrection of Jesus, that our faith finds its full meaning and ultimate hope. As Odo Casel, the well-known liturgical scholar has written, "Easter is ... the sacrament of passage from the world to the life of God, or the entry of the redeemed human race into the kingdom of God and everlasting life with God. In short, Easter is the cultic mystery of the saving work which God accomplished in Christ on behalf of the Church." To better understand this greatest of all feasts, it is important to trace its history and celebration through the centuries.

It seems appropriate that the Easter celebration finds its roots in Judaism, the source of Christian belief. In Exodus 12:1-36 we read the famous story of the Passover, when the angel of death passed over the Israelite homes in Egypt, bringing death to all first born of Egypt. We know from the Gospels that Jesus, a faithful Jew, desired to celebrate the Passover event with his disciples on the night before he died. This celebration of the "Last Supper" of our Lord, became, from early accounts, the beginning of the festival of the Lord's passion. The *Epistula Apostolorum,* a second century apocryphal document, states in an address of the risen Christ to his apostles, "As for you, mark the commemoration of my death, that is, the Passover."

The dating of the events of the Lord's passion, death, and resurrection in the early Church was the source of a major dispute, the Quartodeciman Controversy. Basically, the problem was assigning a date for Christ's death. The testimony of the Synoptic Gospels is clear. The preparation for the festival day is surely 14 Nisan (from the Jewish dating of Passover) and the supper eaten by Jesus and his disciples is the Passover feast. In this chronology, Jesus is thus crucified on 15 Nisan. In John's Gospel, however, the crucifixion itself occurs on 14 Nisan.

Quartodecimans followed the Synoptic tradition quite literally. They believed that the celebration of Pasch (Paschal Mystery) should be on 14 Nisan, the first day of the full moon in the first month of Spring. This was true no matter what day of the week the celebration would fall. This dating for the celebration of our Lord's passion was followed by the Church in Asia Minor and Syria. Quartodecimans emphasized the redemptive death of Christ as related in the Gospel of John.

Non-Quartodecimans followed a similar but modified tradition. Since all the Gospels relate that Jesus rose from the dead on the first day of the week, it was thought that the Sunday Christian tradition should be preserved. Thus, the resurrection should be celebrated on the first Sunday after 14 Nisan. This dating was used in Rome and by most local churches.

The dating of the resurrection was settled at Nicaea in 325 CE. In addition to the council's action against Arius, the bishops ended the Quartodeciman controversy by siding with Rome placing the celebration of Christ's resurrection on the first Sunday following 14 Nisan. This translates to the first Sunday after the full moon after the vernal equinox (March 21). From this contemporary dating all the liturgical calendar is fixed.

Development of Holy Week and the celebration of the Easter Triduum is first seen in the fourth century. Egeria, a fourth century traveler to the Holy Land, left a detailed account of her journey from which we can determine many aspects of Patristic Christian celebrations. Egeria seems to indicate in her writings that the first four days of "Great Week" were very similar to other days in Lent until noon each day. At the ninth hour there was a service of readings that extended to, and most often connected with, the evening office of *Lucernare,* which was celebrated at 7 pm. From fifth century Armenia we learn of a considerable conflation of the services described by Egeria. The hour of the afternoon gathering had been advanced to 4 pm and was no longer a service of readings prior to *Lucernare* but an expanded service of light itself.

The development of the liturgy for Holy (Maudy) Thursday comes from fifth century Armenian documents. This day was distinguished from the other first four days of "Great Week" in that the afternoon service, which normally began at the ninth hour, now commenced an hour earlier and included the Eucharist. This Eucharist was a commemoration of the Passover meal which Jesus celebrated with his disciples the night before he died. As such the Mass took on the flavor of a memorial of the events of that night.

In our contemporary celebration of Holy Thursday, we remember the Last Supper of Jesus, the institution of the Eucharist as well as the washing of feet, which symbolizes the service aspect of love. As the entrance antiphon from the Mass says, "We should glory in the cross of our Lord Jesus Christ, for he is our salvation, our life and our resurrection; through him we are saved and made free." The readings of the Mass, especially the Gospel of John (13:1-15) show that Jesus' purpose is to serve, not dominate others.

The rite of foot washing has an interesting and long history. In the fourth century this practice was part of the rite of baptism, (except in Rome) again with the emphasis on service. Over time this practice died away in baptism but was kept alive in monasteries. The seventeenth Council of Toledo (694) required this solemn action of foot washing on Holy Thursday in all churches in Spain and Gaul. In the Missal of Pope Pius V (1570), the rite was placed at the end of Mass. In the 1955 reordering of Holy Week, the rite was placed after the Gospel and homily where it is today.

The Holy Thursday Eucharist concludes with a procession to the altar of repose. This procession originated in the Middle Ages. During this time the Eucharist began to be held on reserve. Because of the theme on Good Friday, liturgies did not include celebration of the Mass. It was determined, beginning in the Carolingian period, to reserve the Eucharist on Thursday for distribution to the faithful during services on Good Friday. The solemnity of the day led to a procession in silence or chant to a special reservation spot where the faithful could gather for worship.

Fasting has been associated with the Triduum from the earliest times. Irenaeus of Lyon (ca. 200) and the apocryphal Gospel according to the Hebrews state that many people were fasting from Holy Thursday to the celebration of the resurrection as a symbolic gesture to approximate the time Jesus spent in the tomb. Augustine in the fourth century confirms the existence of this practice, stating that the purpose of the fast is to honor the bridegroom who had been taken away. In contemporary practice, the Church asks the faithful to fast on Good Friday only. However, in many circles, fasting from the celebration of the Mass of the Last Supper to the Easter Vigil is still practiced.

Our early knowledge of the celebration of Good Friday also comes from the traveler Egeria. In Jerusalem, according to Egeria, on Good Friday from 8 am until noon the wood of the cross, which Empress Helena discovered in 320 CE, was exhibited and venerated.

This idea still influences liturgical tradition today. In the early afternoon, the people would gather for a liturgy of the word service during which the Passion was read.

We possess a more detailed account of the Good Friday service celebrated in seventh century Rome. The Pope, barefoot, carried the relic of the cross in procession from the Lateran Basilica to the Church of the Holy Cross of Jerusalem. There the relic was venerated not only by clergy but by the whole community. During the veneration two Old Testament passages and the Passion narrative of John were read.

Further developments on the Good Friday liturgy took place during the Middle Ages. The Roman liturgy of the seventh century was taken over by the Franks in the eighth century and developed further along the lines of dramatization. Around the middle of the tenth century some Benedictine Monks of St. Alban's in Mainz recorded a longer celebration of Good Friday in the so-called Romano-German Pontifical, also known as the Mainz Pontifical.

The contemporary practice of receiving pre-consecrated bread on Good Friday originated during the time of Charlemagne. During the medieval period an initially very simple celebration of communion for the faithful was developed into the *Missa Praesanctificatorum* (Mass with previously consecrated gifts). During the Medieval period the faithful rarely received communion and thus many times only the priest communicated on Good Friday. The Tridentine Missal of 1570 turned this custom into a regulation that lasted for almost 400 years.

The new liturgical order of 1955 changed several things about the Good Friday service. The traditional three-fold division of liturgy of the word, veneration of the cross, and the celebration of communion was kept. However, the new order dropped many rites and rubrics. Among those dropped was the prohibition of the faithful from receiving communion. Additionally, the order of 1955 restored the traditional timing of the service. The missal of 1570 had moved all services to the morning hours due to a prohibition of afternoon and evening Masses. After 1955 the Good Friday service was scheduled at 3 pm but could be moved to as late as 6 pm if dictated by pastoral necessity. In 1970 the late limit of 6 pm was eliminated allowing the service to be held at a time when it is most convenient for the faithful to attend.

The contemporary celebration of Good Friday highlights the cross as the tree of salvation. In the Liturgy of the Word, the fourth suffering servant passage from Isaiah, 52:13-53:12 is proclaimed. The Passion according to St. John is used because it sees the ultimate victory of Jesus in his crucifixion. For John, sorrow can be transformed to joy for all humankind. During the veneration of the cross both faithful and clergy come forward. Genuflections and kisses are common means of veneration. After the veneration of the cross the altar is prepared simply, and the Blessed Sacrament is brought forth from the place of reservation. Il present come forward to receive communion. After this the service ends with a concluding prayer.

Holy Saturday and the celebration of the Easter Vigil have had a rather baffling history. In the early Patristic era, Holy Saturday had no liturgy at all; it was a day of grief-inspired fasting. Egeria tells us that in fourth century Jerusalem the Easter Vigil was an all-night affair, beginning after midnight and not concluding until the dawn. Thus, there was no Easter day celebration of the resurrection.

Toward the end of the sixth century, however, it was becoming clear that the timing of the vigil was changing drastically. Documentation shows, that at this time the vigil was ending before midnight and that Easter Sunday now had its own Mass. By the eighth century the vigil Mass was pushed forward to begin with the rising of the first star. The Einsiedeln Ordo, a ninth century liturgical source, names the hour of none (3 pm) as the beginning of the vigil Mass. By the fourteenth century Church law allowed none to be read

(Liturgy of the Hours) in the morning hours with Mass to follow immediately. This pushed the vigil further forward. The Missal of Pius V made this arrangement for the vigil obligatory in agreement with the forbidding of all afternoon and evening Masses through the Bull *Sanctissimus* of 1566.

It was not until the mid-twentieth century that changes were made in the vigil. The Decree of the Congregation of Rites, February 9, 1951, allowed the Vigil service to be celebrated in the night before Easter. This initial one-year experiment became general law in the new Holy Week Order of November 16, 1955. The Roman Catholic liturgy had rediscovered a lost treasure.

The Easter Vigil represents the high point of liturgical celebration. The General Norms for the Liturgical Year state, "During it [the Easter Vigil] the Church keeps watch, awaiting the resurrection of Christ and celebrating the sacraments. The entire celebration of this Vigil should take place at night, beginning after nightfall and ending with dawn." This standard is used in celebrations throughout the Church universal.

The Easter Vigil begins with the service of light. The blessing of the fire seems to come from Frankish origins. The Church used this symbol as a sacramental where the fire replaced the Spring fire of the pagans in honor of Wotan or some other heathen deity. The Easter (paschal) candle itself has its origin from Rome, where the night of Easter was celebrated with numerous candles symbolizing Christ who had been raised up from the night of death. In the fifth century there were two human height candles used but this was reduced to one in the Gallic liturgy of the eighth and ninth centuries. Today the Easter candle is inscribed by the presider. Afterwards the candle is lit from the fire and carried into the church. The Easter proclamation, *Exultet,* is sung in a form which approximates its seventh century Gallic origins.

The Liturgy of the Word comprises the second part of the vigil Mass. The fourth century Jerusalem liturgy used a series of 12 Old Testament readings from the Pentateuch, historical books, and prophets. The theme was the history of salvation. Today there are seven readings from the Old Testament, comprising the history of salvation from the Pentateuch and prophets. Pastoral reasons can eliminate all but two of these readings, but the story of the passage through the Red Sea (Exodus 14:15-15:1) must be read. Additionally, Romans 6:3-11 and the Gospel are read to show our sharing in the life and destiny of Christ by virtue of our baptism.

Since time immemorial Easter has been the preferred time for baptism. Thus, the Easter Vigil has the rite of baptism as an integral part of its service. Today catechumens are baptized and/or received at this celebration. Additionally, confirmations are performed completing the process of initiation. If a faith community has no catechumens or others to be baptized, then a renewal of baptismal promises is made during this part of the service.

The final part of the Easter Vigil is the celebration of the Eucharist. After the Mass of the Last Supper on the previous Thursday evening, the Eucharist is once again celebrated and the faithful participate in the reception of the Lord's body and blood.

As the General Norms of the Liturgical Year (#18) state, "The Easter Triduum of the passion and resurrection of Christ is the culmination of the entire liturgical year." Historically the Easter Triduum has been important in the development of the liturgical practice and renewal of faith. Our contemporary liturgical practice shows the importance of this season. For centuries the Church has taught, *Lex orandi, Lex credendi*, the law of prayer is the law of belief. In our celebration of the Triduum let us pray fervently that the Risen Lord will be present to us and raise our world to a better understanding of life.

THE HOUSE CHURCHES OF ST. PAUL

Travelers are often attracted to the magnificent cathedrals and churches which accent the great cities of Europe. What visitor to London has not stopped at Westminster Abbey or St. Paul's Cathedral? On the continent it is a must to visit Notre Dame in Paris, St. Stephen's in Vienna, and the many famous basilicas and churches in Rome, including St. Peter's and St. John Lateran. The instinct for people today is to see in such great edifices the foundations of Christianity as practiced from antiquity to the present. History and archeology, however, show us that Christians first met as a community to worship in typical homes of the day rather than dedicated churches. Surrounded by a society which did not understand and at times severely persecuted the "new way," Christians gathered in secrecy to carry on the traditions initiated by Jesus and his first followers. Through the Pauline corpus, the Acts of the Apostles, and other relevant texts, a picture can be drawn of the structures of the Church and its worship practices in the apostolic era.

The Concept of Household and Church in Antiquity

How Hellenistic society understood the concept of household is vital to our present knowledge of the "house church." Towns of antiquity were divided in districts based on ethnicity or trades. Thus, for example in the city of Antioch the Kerateion or southeast quadrant of the town was the traditional Jewish quarter. Structured under the level of ethnic districts was the single household which, since the time of Aristotle's *Politics*, had been considered the basic unit of society. The concept of household in Greek antiquity was much broader than what is understood in western society today. The Roman orator Cicero defined the household or *domus* as centered in the parents and children, "and those who look to us alone for support and have no other protection." People of antiquity thus defined the household by a relationship of dependence or subordination rather than kinship. The head of a household was, therefore, responsible for and expected a degree of obedience from not only his immediate family, but slaves, former slaves who were now clients, hired laborers, and sometimes even business associates and tenants.

Christians adopted the prevailing idea of household and adapted it to their gathering for worship. A typical household for a Christian family was composed of the immediate family, servants, and a few close friends who lived in the adjacent area. This idea of *domus* was important for the early Christians because it figured predominantly in the ministry of Jesus and the preaching of St. Paul. Jesus taught in a home (Mark 2:1-3, 7:17-23, Matthew 13:36), acted as a host (Mark 2:15, 6:34-44), and was many times a house guest (Luke 5:29, 7:36-50). Paul used the *domus* in his missionary strategy by converting a whole household (I Corinthians 1:16, Acts 16:15) and then, together with his associates, setting up a house church for purposes of community worship. The house provided an environment that corresponded well with the Christian community's earliest self-understanding. Noted Protestant Scripture historian Robert Banks has written, "Given the family character of the Christian community, the homes of its members provided the most conducive atmosphere in which they could give expression to the bond they had in common." During the first century the private home shaped Christian community life, providing an economic substructure, a platform for missionary work, and a framework for leadership and authority.

The Christian concept of Church was guided by the Resurrection and Pentecost events. Freed from fear the apostles went forth to carry Jesus' message of salvation to all nations. Moving out from Palestine, the formation of Christian communities, and thus house churches, was almost exclusively urban. These earliest communities possessed the conviction that the eschaton was near. This belief (I Thessalonians 4:13-5:22, II Thessalonians 2:1-17) shaped the community's attitudes in prayer, understanding of Christ, and the sharing of material goods.

The challenge of Pentecost and the reality of the diaspora forced Christian groups to adapt their households and house churches to Hellenistic society which generated certain tensions within the community and with outside society as well. The house provided some privacy, a degree of intimacy, and stability of location. However, it also created the potential for the emergence of factions and rival households within the Christian community of a particular urban setting. It may well be the case that the incipient factions of which Paul speaks in I Corinthians 1:10-17 were centered in different households. The concept of *domus* also set the stage for some conflicts, as described by the historian Wayne Meeks in *The First Urban Christians*, in the allocation of power and the understanding of various roles in the community. Society said that the head of the household should exercise authority and have legal responsibility for it; the *domus* was to be hierarchical. Yet, the Christian movement ran in certain ways contrary to this system with egalitarian beliefs and attitudes in conflict with such a formal structure.

The concept of local church as used today was not directly addressed by Paul, but there was some distinction between the individual household and the more universal church. The Greek term *oikos* or household was considered by Paul as the basic cell of the Christian movement. Yet, we know from Paul's letters that the Christian communities to whom he wrote were composed of several households. Paul's use of the Body of Christ metaphor (I

232

Corinthians 12:27 and Romans 12:5) demonstrates that he believed in a unifying factor in the Church. His emphasis on this point shows that he promoted the local city-wide church, and its interaction with other such local churches, over the individual household.

Raymond Brown, the well-known Sulpician Scripture scholar, in his book *The Churches the Apostles Left Behind*, provides a human face to the many Christian communities with which St. Paul had association. Brown cites the city of Corinth as the best example of multiple house churches and their leaders. Titus Justus (Acts 18:7) and Crispus (Acts 18:8), whom Paul baptized, were probable leaders of the Corinthian Church. Stephanas (I Corinthians 1:16), called the first fruits of Achaia, was probably a man of means in Corinth based on his property holdings and the amount he traveled. Gaius (Romans 16:23), based on the number of people in his house, was most probably a person of means as well. Erastus (Romans 16:24) and Phoebe, the deaconess (Romans 16:1), are two additional prospective leaders of house churches. The Pauline Corpus additionally describes four specific house congregations outside Corinth where assembly was held, the home of Prisca and Aquila in Ephesus (I Corinthians 16:19, the letter was written from Ephesus), Prisca and Aquila's home in Rome (Romans 16:5), the house of Philemon in Colossae (Philemon 2), and Nymphas' congregation in Laodicea (Colossians 4:15).

Worship in House Churches

The physical layout of a home generally determined how the Christian community worshipped. Archeological data has shown that most homes that served as house churches took the form of a Roman atrium house, which included a series of rooms facing each other around a central courtyard with a small pool. The courtyard was suitable for instruction and general prayers since it was the largest area and could accommodate the most people. The dining room, usually used by the *paterfamilias* or head of household to entertain guests or clients, was the place set aside for the celebration of the Lord's Supper, in imitation of the upper room used by Jesus and his disciples at the Last Supper. Because large amounts of space were necessary, only wealthy people could provide the necessary accommodations. This is consistent with the Scripture references mentioned above showing the Christian community's assembly in the homes of people of means.

Early Christian worship followed the Jewish customs of the past coupled with the innovations of the new-found belief. Jewish prayers were in evidence, but the community's new-found faith in Jesus and their Pentecost experience of oneness in the Spirit led them to develop their own form of common prayer. Following on the Jewish practice of Sabbath worship, Christians met weekly on the "The Day of the Sun," because, as stated by Justin Martyr, "[I]t is the first day, the day on which God, changing darkness and matter, created the world; and it is the day on which Jesus Christ our Savior rose from the dead." While the Jews centered their worship in the Torah and synagogue, Christians centered their prayer in the assembly. There was no need for a special sanctuary for the assembly itself was the Church.

Christian worship was divided into two separate and distinct services, the sharing of gifts and the Lord's Supper, thus serving as a precursor to the celebration of today's Mass with its liturgies of the word and the Eucharist. The sharing of gifts, described by Tertullian in the late second century as, "united supplications to God, the reading of Scripture and the delivery of exhortations," featured general prayers, a teaching, speaking and interpretation of tongues, and prophecy. Prayers of a spontaneous nature (Acts 4:24-30) were practiced as well as the recitation of the Lord's Prayer, the invocation of Abba (Galatians 4:6 and Romans 8:15), and *glossolalia* (I Corinthians 14:6-19). Teaching, probably a recollection and discussion of some saying of Jesus, as well as reflection and interpretation of the Torah in the light of the events of Jesus' life, death, and resurrection (Acts 17:2-3,11) were also conducted. A "holy kiss" (I Thessalonians 5:26,

Romans 16:16, I Corinthians 16:20) was most probably used as a ritual to mark the end of the sharing of gifts and as a transition to the celebration of the Lord's Supper.

The Lord's Supper, held in the dining room of the house church, most probably celebrated the community's Jewish roots as well as serving to remember Jesus. I Corinthians 11:17-34 gives us our earliest testimony to the celebration of the Lord's Supper. Justin Martyr in the mid-second century, however, gives us the most detailed account of the celebration:

> Having concluded the prayers, we greet one another with a kiss. Then there is brought to the president of the brethren bread and a cup of water and of watered wine; and taking them, he gives praise and glory to the Father of all, through the name of the Son and of the Holy Spirit; and he himself gives thanks at some length in order that these things may be deemed worthy. When the prayers and the thanksgiving are completed, all the people call out their assent saying: "Amen". After the president has given thanks, and all the people have shouted their assent, those whom we call deacons give to each present to partake of the Eucharistic bread and wine and water; and to those who are absent, they carry away a portion. We call this food Eucharist.

Certain questions arise concerning this two-fold Christian worship of antiquity. Scholars disagree on the question if the two assemblies, the sharing of gifts and the Lord's Supper, were held at the same house and combined. Each celebration required different participants. Teachers and prophets (apostles if present) were necessary to share gifts. The Lord's Supper required the patron of the house as the presidential position was based on the hierarchical structure of society. If teachers, prophets, and the patron were all present, then the celebrations could have been combined. The other major question asks, who was invited to the various celebrations? It is the opinion of Catholic scholar Vincent Branick that Paul had no problem welcoming outsiders to the sharing of the gifts (I Corinthians 14:23-25), but he also concludes that the apostle of the gentiles excluded all except the Christian community from the celebration of the Eucharist. The Didache, a treatise written circa 90 CE, gives strength to Branick's argument in its specific exclusion of all but the baptized from the Lord's Supper.

The leadership of house churches was divided into three categories of offices, miraculous functions, and administrators. In writing to the Corinthian Church (12:28) Paul specifies the order for offices as apostles, prophets, and teachers. Apostleship for Paul was broader than the original twelve as he included himself and his associates Silvanus and Timothy (I Thessalonians 2:6) in the category of apostles. For Paul this office was not confined to a local church, but rather as a traveling visitor, an apostle represented a larger, more universal view of the Christian community. Paul sees prophets, who were more stable and less itinerant in their ministry, as "building up the Church" (I Corinthians 14:4). Teachers gave instructions, ethical exhortations, and interpreted Scripture. Miraculous functions of leadership were present in those who possessed "gifts of healing" or the "interpretation of tongues." Church administrators were assistants and patrons in a specific *oikos*. Paul's overarching purpose in describing leadership in the Christian community was to demonstrate the mutual dependence of all members of the Church. All roles are gifts given by the Spirit for the mutual benefit of all (I Corinthians 12:4-11); no function can place itself ahead of the body.

There is no clear evidence as to who served as president for the community Eucharistic celebration. Paul's I Corinthians description of the Lord's Supper strongly suggests that the individual household was the normal environment for this celebration. Although Paul makes no specific mention of who presided, he does show deference to the hierarchy of the household as defined by the prevailing rules of society. Thus, our earlier discussion places the *paterfamilias* or patron of the house as the president. Since men and women were heads of households, it is conceivable that both served as presiders in the house churches. The recognition by Paul of Prisca (short for Priscilla) before her husband Aquila (Romans 16:3-5), is evidence to the apostle's respect for the role of women and the possibility that they presided along with men at the Lord's Supper in their homes.

Following the death of Paul (circa 62 CE) the concept of Church evolved beyond the household. The deutero-Pauline letters of Ephesians, Colossians, and the Pastoral Epistles (I and II Timothy and Titus) show a transition from house churches to a view of Church universal. This shift was necessitated for several reasons. First, poor Christians faced a barrier in worshipping with people of greater means; the Christian concept of egalitarianism necessitated the acceptance of all. More practically, however, with the growth of the Christian community, it became physically impossible to meet in homes in which people lived. The Pastorals see *ekklesia* as local church (I Timothy 3:15) with officers such as bishops mentioned. The heads of households were by the late first century no longer uniquely qualified to serve as presidents of the Christian assembly.

As roles changed and the Christian community grew it became necessary to find a permanent home for worship. Archeological evidence and the reports of Eusebius in his *Ecclesiastical History*, Justin Martyr, and Tertullian show that by the mid-second century private residences had been donated as permanent churches and modified as needed for the assembly. Christians who met in "dedicated" churches possessed a different understanding of themselves and Church. Leadership became concentrated in a clergy while Church activity became ritualized. The edifice rather than the environment became God's temple.

The necessity of secrecy in worship, coupled with a different understanding of Church and few members became a formula for the creation of house churches in the Christian communities of St. Paul. Utilizing the private residence of more wealthy Christians, the community gathered on "The Day of the Sun" to worship God by the sharing of gifts and the celebration of the Lord's Supper. Centering themselves in the Hellenistic concept of household, the Christian house churches spread throughout the urban centers of the Mediterranean world. They served as a first attempt at the formation of Christian community and provided the basic elements of worship which became the Mass as we know it today. The churches the apostles left behind, the house churches of St. Paul, give another view into the fascinating story of Christian history and worship.

Purgatory: The Forgotten Doctrine on Judgment

Question #183 of the 1954 edition of the Baltimore Catechism asks, "What are the rewards or punishments appointed for men after the particular judgment? The answer given is, "The rewards or punishments appointed for men after the particular judgment are heaven, purgatory, or hell." Today when people speak of judgment or Jesus' second coming you will seldom hear purgatory mentioned. The Second Vatican Council does not mention purgatory in its official documents. In fact, the last time the Church officially spoke on the doctrine of purgatory was at Session 25 of the Council of Trent in 1565. In the "Decree on Purgatory" the Council stated, "[T]he Holy Synod enjoins on Bishops that they diligently endeavor that the sound doctrine concerning Purgatory, transmitted by the Holy Fathers and Sacred Councils, be believed, maintained, taught, and everywhere proclaimed by the Faithful of Christ."

What has happened to the doctrine of purgatory? It may seem that this long-standing tradition in the Church is in eclipse, that it is being ignored. True as this may be the doctrine is still part of Church teaching because of its development over the centuries of the Christian era. This evolution of belief encompasses Scripture, Church councils, and the teachings of some of the most learned and well-known theologians who ever graced our world. This evolutionary process had spurts and gaps; it was neither uniform nor inevitable. Yet, it developed and still lives in the minds of many of Christ's faithful people.

Sources for the Doctrine

The first roots to the concept and eventual doctrine of purgatory are found in ancient civilizations of the Near East. Peoples of the ancient world had concepts of the afterlife where those in need of spiritual purification went before their final eternal peace. In India the Hindus called such a belief the passage through fire which led to a cycle of reincarnation. In Iran the Zoroastrian community as well as the ancient Egyptians believed there was a place set aside in the afterlife for those people whose bad actions precisely balanced their good works. Similarly in ancient Babylon, the Gilgamesh epic speaks of a realm in the underworld where people of equal bad and good deeds are judged.

Jewish apocryphal writings give us our next insight into ancient understandings of the realm of the dead. In the Fourth Book of Ezra seven ranks or ordines for the dead are listed. The fifth of these levels is where people, "exult upon seeing that now they have escaped the corruptible [flesh] and are in possession of the bequest to come, still in view of the narrow world of sorrow from which they have been set free and beginning to catch sight of the spacious, blessed, and immortal world they are to receive." Another Jewish apocryphal source, the Book of Enoch, introduces gradations of penalties after death. Here also hell is imaged as a pit or narrow valley where souls go prior to final judgment. This image is continued in Jewish literature written in the common era between the destruction of the second temple (70 AD) and the Revolt of Bar-Kochba (132-135 CE). Treatises describe an intermediate category in Gehenna consisting of souls who are neither entirely good nor entirely bad. Here souls will be punished for a time and then be released to Eden. This idea led later to the idea of an upper Gehenna where temporary punishments were meted out.

Christian accounts of the period also describe ideas which were foundational in the evolution of the doctrine of purgatory. The Apocalypses of Peter and Ezra (2nd century) speak of hell in stages. The image of fire, with bridges spanning the various stages, described how souls could move higher as their earthly sins were purged. The Apocalypse of Paul, a third century account from Egypt which was condemned by Augustine but popular nonetheless, introduced again the Jewish notion of a distinction between upper and lower hell. In the tale, St. Paul comes to "upper hell" where "souls live awaiting the mercy of God." "The Passion of Perpetua and Felicitas" (203 CE) provides another image that contributes to our story. In this account Perpetua has two visions of her dead brother Dinocratus. In the first he is tortured in fire; in the second he is refreshed (*refrigerantem*). This move from fire to bliss again reveals the belief in an intermediate area of temporary punishment where some souls go after death.

Sacred Scripture gives hints but no direct references to a concept of purgatory. In the Hebrew Scriptures Judas Maccabeus exhorts his people to pray for the dead that they might be delivered from sin (II Maccabees 12:41-46). In some ancient manuscripts, Psalm 42:6 refers to a "mountain of torment" where souls climb to their final reward with God. One ancient version of Job 36:12 describes a river over which one must cross to escape Sheol.

New Testament references also hint at some middle ground of judgment after death. Scripture scholar Joseph Kroll in *Gott und Holle. Der Mythos vom Descensuskampfe* has studied the idea of Christ's "descent into hell." Using Matthew 12:40, Acts 2:31 and Romans 10:6-7 as references, Kroll concludes that these passages demonstrate that the writers of the New Testament believed that one's fate was susceptible to amelioration after death.

Three other New Testament passages have been influential in the development of the doctrine of purgatory. In Matthew 12:31-32 there is the indirect implication that sins can be redeemed in the other world. Luke 16:19-26, the story of Lazarus and the rich man, implies that the location of hell must be close to the place where the saved await final judgment since it is possible to see from one place to the other. In Paul's First Letter to the Corinthians (3:11-15) it seems that one's fate in the hereafter depends on the quality of the person. The pericope indicates that there is a relationship between one's merits and demerits in the earthly life and the rewards and punishments to be meted out in the hereafter. Paul also uses the image of fire from which the apocryphal Christian accounts and the martyrdom of Perpetua and Felicitas most probably drew their metaphor.

Doctrinal Development

Doctrinal development of the concept of purgatory truly began with the teachings of the Fathers of the Church. This period of Patristic history produced no consistent pattern of evolution. Rather the great writers of the period presented teachings on various aspects concerning the doctrine of judgment. Using the earlier accounts described above, these theologians produced teachings which by the thirteenth century became the official Church understanding on purgatory.

Although the Greek Church has no concept of purgatory, the two earliest teachings on what became purgatory came from the East, Origen and Clement of Alexandria. Origen (d. 253/54) in his eighth homily on the *Commentary on Leviticus* speaks of the righteous who have a trial by fire after death. During this period the lead that weighs down the soul is melted away, transforming it into pure gold. Clement (d. prior to 215) was the first to distinguish two categories of sinners and two categories of punishments in the life to come. There would be two fires, a "devouring and consuming" one for the incorrigible and one that "satisfies" and "does not consume" for other sinners.

In the Latin Church the Fathers made great strides in their teachings on "purgatory." Tertullian in *Against Marcion* and *On Monogamy* gives detailed accounts of *refrigerium*. Using Luke 16:19-26, he says that ordinary souls, while awaiting resurrection, reside in *refrigerium interim*, the bosom of Abraham. Tertullian's idea is more of a restful state where souls stay in *refrigerium* until the final judgment. Cyprian, bishop of Carthage, in his third century *Letter to Antonian* distinguishes between two types of Christians. He writes, "[I]t is one thing to be relieved and purified of one's sins through a long suffering in fire and another thing to have all one's faults wiped out by martyrdom." St. Jerome, the famous translator of the Vulgate, once wrote concerning salvation, "Christian sinners will be tried and purged in fire mixed with clemency."

Ambrose and Ambrosiaster in the fourth century reached similar conclusions when reflecting upon I Corinthians 3:11-16. Both men divided the dead in three categories, the righteous or saints who go directly to heaven, the wicked and infidels who go directly to hell, and ordinary Christians, seen as a mixture of silver and lead, who go to the purifying fires and then to paradise, because they had faith.

St. Augustine rightly has been labeled the "Father of the Doctrine of Purgatory." Augustine's theology of the afterlife has been thoroughly researched by Joseph Ntediko in his 1966 monograph *Evolution of the Doctrine of Purgatory in Saint Augustine*. In his early Christian life Augustine expressed doubts on any idea of "purgatory" because he found Scripture imprecise and contradictory on the subject. Still, Augustine in his *Confessions*, when speaking about the death of his mother, St. Monica, argues that suffrages for the dead are efficacious. Later in *City of God* (21:24) he again advocates prayers for the dead.

In his theology, Augustine distinguished four categories of the dead: the entirely good, entirely wicked, not entirely wicked (where souls stayed in hell but were afforded some relief), and not entirely good (where souls received purgation for sins, then went to heaven). In his *Commentary on Genesis Against the Manichaeans* (398 CE) Augustine comments on this fourth group and distinguishes between the fires of purgation and damnation. In *On Faith and Works* (413 CE) and *Enchiridion* (421 CE) Augustine goes further in his description of this fourth group. Worthiness he says is determined by generally a good life and the practice of penitence. The famous bishop of Hippo taught that those who had not completed their penance on earth would reach a middle ground between salvation and damnation. Augustine thus became the first theologian to associate penitence with purgatory.

Augustine made two additional contributions to the development of the doctrine of purgatory. First was his notion that the purifying fires were effective only for lesser sins. (At this time, the concept of "venial" sin did not exist.) Augustine also taught that the fire of purgation was present in the interval between death and final resurrection. Like Origen Augustine taught that souls escaped this middle ground once expiation of their sins was complete.

St. Gregory the Great, the famous sixth century pope, added one new idea to the concept of purgatory. In *Moralia in Job* Gregory describes the geography of the afterlife, seeing purgatory, heaven, and hell as places. Relative levels of the afterlife are present. The physically higher realms are closer to the place of God. Souls are placed in levels by God according to the merits of their mortal life. In contrast to Augustine, Gregory taught that no earthly penitence was necessary before death to merit a place in this intermediate place of purgation.

Caesarus of Arles (d.542) in his sermons 167 and 179 confirms the two basic contributions of Augustine and goes one step further. A distinction is made between *crimina capitalia* (capital sins) and lesser sins, *parva* (petty), *quotidiana* (ordinary) and *minuta* (trifling). Caesarus adds that these latter sins are those expiated in the purgatorial fire.

Between the sixth and twelfth centuries little progress was made in the doctrinal development on purgatory. Lack of development, however, did not prevent comment on the concepts of judgment and the afterlife. Three Spanish bishops in the sixth and seventh centuries, Tajon of Sargossa, Isidore of Seville and Julian of Toledo, summarized Augustine and Gregory as they emphasized suffrages for sin. St. Eligius, Bishop of Noyon in Gaul (d.659) taught that the fire of the afterlife would be experienced in different ways by the "godless, the saints and the righteous." Eligius, however, saw this fire at the time of final judgment, which was a regression from the earlier teachings of Ambrose, Ambrosiaster, and Augustine. Venerable Bede in the eighth century mentions purgatorial fire and the possibility of reprieve by means of suffrage.

The Medieval period was filled with visionary writings about purgatory. In the eighth century, for example, St. Boniface wrote about one of his monks in Wenlock who had a vision of being taken by angels and shown a pit of fire where boiling water lapped over a plank bridge which separated the condemned from the purified. These latter, who had been purged of their sins, were escorted to the resplendent walls of the heavenly Jerusalem.

The Medieval period did produce two significant ideas which continued the development of the doctrine of purgatory. Liturgical advances in prayers for the dead led in the eleventh century to the present-day feasts of All Saints and All Souls. The Medieval period also produced an account of a physical location for purgatory. A monk of Saltrey in Ireland wrote of how St. Patrick, when preaching to the recalcitrant Irish, received a vision where Jesus showed him a specific forsaken pit. Patrick was told that if one in a spirit of penitence and faith spent a day and a night in this hole, the person would be purged of sin. Patrick built a church around the pit. The location became known as St. Patrick's purgatory and was believed by many to be the physical location on earth where sins were expiated.

At the dawn of the twelfth century the Church's attitude toward the dead is derivable from documents of clerical origin. In general, the Church understood that after the Last Judgment there would be two groups of souls, the saved and the condemned. The period between death and resurrection was not well defined. Some of the faithful believed that souls occupied a grave or other neutral place. Some believed the dead were "housed" in various dwellings based on their life on earth. Between the saved and the condemned was an intermediate category where the dead, awaiting admission to heaven, would undergo some purgation. This type of purgation was fire; its place was uncertain.

Four major theologians dominate twelfth century teachings on purgatory. Hugh of St. Victor (d.1141) in *De Sacramentis* speaks of how souls emerge from the purgatorial fire stronger as a clay pot is stronger after having been fired. This fire lasts only long enough to purify the soul. Bernard of Clarivaux (d.1153) attempted a spatial description of the afterlife which included an intermediate place of purgation. He also described the future concept of Limbo, where innocent souls rested before judgment. Gratian in his *Decretum* (1140) spoke of how the dead can be delivered by Masses, prayers of the saints, alms of friends, and fasting of relatives. This underscored the need of the Church's mediation in suffrage for the dead. Peter Lombard (d.1159-60) in his *Sententiae* spoke of venial sins which can be consumed by the purgatorial fire. Peter advanced the development of purgatory by separating Augustine's "not entirely bad" souls from hell and moved them (although still a separate group) more toward an intermediate state along with the "not entirely good."

The twelfth century attempted to work out some doctrine on the location of purgatory. It was first necessary to view purgatory as a place rather than refer strictly to purgatorial fire. After 1170 documents begin to speak of *purgatorium* (Latin nominative case) rather than *purgatoriis* (in purgatory fire). Odo of Ourscamp (d.1171) in his writings used this new term. issenting opinions certainly did exist as well. Honorius Augustodunensis in *Scala coeli major* criticized the spatial conception of the afterlife. Souls are bound, he claimed, by time and space. Honorius' view did not win out.

The twelfth century formed the link to scholasticism and the eventual approbation of the doctrine of purgatory. Peter Chanter (d.1197) in *Summa de Sacramentis et Animae Conciliis* spoke of venial sin causing a determinate penalty to be inflicted in purgatory. Simon of Tournai (d.1201) taught that people could win exemption from purgatory through the suffrages of the Church, even to the point of not entering purgatory. Pierre de Portiers (d.1205) in his *Five Books of Judgment* speaks about venial sins, spatial concepts of the afterlife, and purgation based on the degree of sinfulness.

Official Sanctions

The systematization of Scholasticism in the thirteenth century was a precursor to official Church acceptance of the doctrine of purgatory. As with the twelfth century, four chief theologians predominated in their teachings on purgatory. Alexander of Hales, an English Franciscan who taught at the University of Paris, referred to Aristotle's three types of fire, light, flame and coals, and applied them to heaven, purgatory. and hell. Alexander taught that the suffrage of the Church is the merit by which the pain of its members is lessened. St. Bonaventure in his commentary on Peter Lombard's *Sententiae* continued the systematization by physically locating purgatory between heaven and hell. Bonaventure gave no specific location, but he was certain purgatory was a place where good angels acted as guides. Albert Magnus, O.P. was the third great scholastic scholar who produced teachings on purgatory. In *De resurrectione* Albert lists the now traditional three places of the afterlife as heaven, purgatory, and hell. He saw, however, the difference between purgatory and hell, not as one of intensity of punishment, but rather of duration. Albert used scholasticism to show the rationalization of belief in purgatory.

St. Thomas Aquinas, as with most all theological concepts, had much to say about the doctrine of purgatory. Of the scholastic systems on purgatory, the ideas of Aquinas are the fullest and most insightful, but in their intellectualism are the furthest removed from the common thinking of the era. It seems that Aquinas produced teachings on purgatory by default. He was not interested in the concept himself, but the theology of the day necessitated his comments.

Although completed by his students, the Supplement to his famous *Summa Theologica* contains the bulk of Aquinas thought on purgatory. In question 69 on resurrection Aquinas says that souls are assigned to one of four abodes after death, heaven, limbo of children, purgatory, and hell. Thomas has no doubt of purgatory's existence. Its intermediate character, however, is of little concern to Aquinas. Rather its temporality is significant for him. Purgatory is temporal; eternity holds only heaven, limbo, and hell. In question 70 Thomas deals with purgatory directly. He suggests that the site of purgatory is a subterranean place contiguous with hell. Like Albert Magnus, Aquinas taught that the same fire burned in both purgatory and hell. Thomas went out of his way to say there was no quantitative relationship between sins committed and punishment received, although he did say that some souls would be released sooner than others. Suffrages is the topic of question 71. Referring to Augustine's teaching, Aquinas said the dead, especially those in purgatory, benefit from the suffrages of the living.

Conciliar approbation of the doctrine of purgatory was initiated in 1254. In March of that year, Pope Innocent IV, seeking to unite the Greek and Latin Churches, sent a letter to Cardinal Eudes of Chateauroux, his legate to the Greeks in Cyprus. In the letter the name purgatory is used for the first time in a papal document. It is defined as a "temporary fire" where "slight and minor sins are purged."

The attempt to find reconciliation between East and West continued and was one of the primary reasons that the Second Council of Lyons was called in 1274. The purgatory decree issued at Lyons was a compromise statement between Pope Gregory X and Emperor Michael VIII of Constantinople. The statement is an appendix to the constitution *Cum sacrosancta* of November 1, 1274. The decree, although official, is weak. The word *purgatorium* is not used; there is no reference to fire. Historians have attributed this backpedaling to the need for compromise to reconcile the two great Churches. The Council of Trent, Session 6 of 1547, commanded belief in purgatory, "If anyone says that after reception of the grace of justification the guilt is so remitted, and the debt of eternal punishment so blotted out to every repentant sinner, that no debt of temporal punishment remains to be discharged either in this world or in purgatory before the gates of heaven can be opened, let him be anathema."

Conclusion

With conciliar approval in the thirteenth century and reaffirmation by Trent 300 years later, the doctrine of purgatory became a permanent part of Catholic belief. Popular religiosity carried the doctrine through the centuries. Dante's *Divine Comedy*, book two on Purgatory, published in 1319, was a major factor in the spread of the doctrine. Famous saints, such as Teresa of Avila, Magdalen de Pazzi, and Louis Bertrand, wrote accounts of visions they received concerning purgatory. In the pre-Vatican II Church, the doctrine continued to flourish and became the cornerstone in praying for the dead. Today we continue to pray for the dead, but we seldom hear of purgatory. The future evolution of this long held doctrine which has recently suffered an eclipse will be the challenge of the faithful in the twenty-first century.

THE EVOLUTION OF EPIPHANY:
THREE FEASTS IN ONE

During the Christmas season we joyfully sing of the "Twelve Days of Christmas." In today's Church calendar the Christmas season opens with Christmas Day and closes with the Baptism of the Lord. In between these two feasts, at the end of the original festive 12 days, we celebrate the Solemnity of the Epiphany, where Christ was manifest to all people for all time. Today in the Western Church Epiphany celebrates one special event in the life of Jesus, the arrival of the astrologers from the East. This, however, is a recent development in the Church's understanding of this great feast. Looking at the historical development of this very significant celebration tells us something about our roots and why we acknowledge in song the special nature of the twelfth day of the Christmas season.

Historical Derivations

Following the apostolic period, the Eastern Church celebrated the birth of Jesus and the coming of the Magi on the same date. In a celebration of the Winter solstice imitating pagan rites, Christians associated Jesus' birth with the coming of the light. The solstice was originally calculated as December 25. Since the East used the 365-

day Egyptian calendar (instead of the 365 1/4-day Julian calendar), the solstice for these people was celebrated 12 days later or January 6. Thus, January 6 became the date associated with this special feast.

Some evidence exists to suggest that the date and feast of Epiphany have pagan origins. Clement of Alexandria in the third century said that Gnostics celebrated the feast of the baptism of Jesus, which they regarded as the real moment of Christ's birth, on January 6. Recent scholarship by the liturgist Adolf Adam states that the pagans of Alexandria celebrated the night of January 5-6 as the birthday of Aion, the god of time and eternity. It is hypothesized, therefore, that Christians in the East celebrated Epiphany to counter pagan influence.

Celebration of the Epiphany (which included at this time the birth of the Lord) on January 6 became solidified over time. Origen (mid-third century) does not mention a specific date (although he acknowledged the event), but it could not have been long after him that the date was set. It was known in Thrace in 304. John Chrysostom and Gregory Naziansen in the fourth century were well acquainted with the feast. Epiphany was celebrated in Gaul by 361 and in Spain by 380.

The first half of the fourth century saw the separation in the West of the feasts of Christmas and Epiphany. By 336 in Rome the birth of Jesus was being celebrated on December 25. With the establishment of a separate feast of the Nativity, the celebration of the Epiphany began to take on special significance in the West. Not only was it the celebration of the coming of the Magi, but it became the feast celebrating Jesus' manifestation as a public servant and as a miracle worker.

Jesus' role as a miracle worker was seen in a celebration of the miracle at Cana. There seems little doubt that Christians celebrated this event in Jesus' life in response to pagan rites.

Pliny in *Natural History* speaks of water becoming wine in a miraculous flow called *Dios Theodosia* (divine gift of Zeus). This festival was celebrated on January 5. A pagan notion existed that on January 6 many springs yielded wine instead of water. The Christian desire to celebrate the Johannine story of Cana blended in well with the already established pagan festival.

This pagan celebration was carried into Christianity. Antoninus reported each January 6, Christians in sixth century Alexandria drew water from the Nile and used it to sprinkle their boats as a blessing. Two centuries earlier John Chrysostom stated in an Epiphany homily, "Therefore also on this solemnity in the middle of the night all who are gathered, having drawn the water, set the liquid aside in their houses and preserve it throughout the year, for today the waters are sanctified."

The manifestation of Jesus' life as a public servant is seen best in his baptism. Eastern tradition, based loosely on Luke 3:23, celebrated Jesus' baptism on his 30th birthday. Thus, the baptism of the Lord also became part of the January 6th celebration. The placement of Jesus' baptism with the Epiphany is verified by two additional Eastern sources. A fourth century Coptic liturgical calendar expresses the day of Epiphany as *Dies Baptismi Sanctificati* or *Immersio Domini*. In the *Canons of Athanasius* (fourth century) Article 16 reads, "And at the feast of the Lord's Epiphany, which was in [the month] Tubah, that is the [feast of] Baptism, they shall rejoice with them."

The tradition of celebrating the arrival of the "three kings," the more contemporary understanding of Epiphany, has also evolved over time. Scripture says nothing about the arrival of Kings. The Revised Standard Version (RSV) of the Bible speaks of Magi; the New American Bible (NAB) uses the term astrologers. Additionally, Scripture says nothing about there being three magi. Origen in the third century was the first to speak of three, probably based on the three gifts. The term king comes from Caesarius of Arles in the sixth century. The traditional names of Caspar, Melchior, and Baltasar have been used since the ninth century. Archbishop Hildebert of Tours (1133) is the first to call the Magi "Saints." Church authorities did not prohibit the growing cult so that from the twelfth century on Epiphany acquired the popular name "Feast of Three Holy Kings."

As the Patristic era closed the celebration of Epiphany was fixed but manifestations were different in the East and West. The East celebrated December 25 as the Feast of the Nativity and the coming of the Magi. January 6 was the celebration of Jesus' baptism and the miracle at Cana. In the West December 25 was the Christmas celebration alone. January 6, Epiphany, was celebrated as three feasts in one, the coming of the Magi, the Baptism of the Lord, and the miracle at Cana.

Customs and Celebration

In the post-Vatican II Church, we view the Easter season, especially the Easter Vigil, as the most appropriate time for baptism. For close to 1500 years, however, the tradition was to baptize on the Epiphany as it was the celebration of the Lord's baptism. The Church in Constantinople adopted this policy in the mid-fourth century when the Christmas feast was fixed on December 25. The account of the sixth century pilgrim Antoninus of Plaisance attests that baptism was part of the Epiphany rites in the Holy Land. This Eastern custom was celebrated in the West as well in the tripartite Epiphany feast.

The blessing of waters, a practice continued today in the East, was the solemn remembrance of Jesus' blessing of the water made wine at Cana and his baptism. In the rite a priest blessed the waters of a local river, stream, or lake. A crucifix was cast into the water and retrieved by a swimmer to represent the dying and rising of the Lord through baptism. Local people took some of the water as a blessing for their homes and families.

One of the most popular customs celebrated with this feast was a dramatic performance of the Epiphany event. Originated in the Middle Ages, the short play featured three members of the choir who during Mass would come forward and act out the bringing of the gifts to the priest presider, the representative of Christ. Known as the *Officium Stellae* (Office of the Star), this play degenerated over time into a boisterous affair. Herod became part of the play. He was portrayed as a raging maniac who beat clergy and laity alike, creating havoc in the sanctuary and the congregation. Such abuses led to the play's abolishment during Mass. In the early Renaissance period, the play was resurrected as the "Feast of the Star." At this time the drama had no affiliation with the Mass. In the early fourteenth century Franciscan Friars of Milan performed the play as an inspiring religious ceremony.

One popular custom which is still practiced within certain ethnic groups is the blessing of homes on Epiphany. In the blessing rite the letters C, M and B, and the calendar year are traced with chalk on the door of the home. The Roman ritual says that the letters refer to the names of the three kings of tradition, thus favoring the widespread popular explanation. Another interpretation, however, says that the initials come from *Christus mansionem benedicat,* "may Christ bless this dwelling."

More recent developments have changed the structure and emphasis of the Epiphany feast. The recognition by the Magi of Jesus as king made Epiphany the perfect celebration of the kingship of Jesus. In 1925, however, Pope Pius XI, in response to the world situation, established a special Feast of Christ the King. Thus, Epiphany lost this specific emphasis on the kingship of the Lord. Additionally, the religious significance to the custom of the blessing of water became obscured over time. Consequently, the celebration of the miracle at Cana with Epiphany passed into oblivion. Further changes came about because of Vatican II. The 1969 reorganization of the liturgical calendar changed the Christmas season to extend through the newly established separate feast of the Baptism of the Lord. Epiphany, standing at the heart of the Christmas season, thus became the celebration of the coming of the Magi alone. Jesus' manifestation to the world and his own people are now celebrated in separate feasts of the Christmas season.

The liturgical celebration of Epiphany today emphasizes the Messianic presence of Jesus while still referring to the feast's tripartite history. In the Mass for Epiphany Jesus is the Messianic king whose intention is to lead all, even the pagans, to salvation. The coming of the Magi (Matthew 2:1-12) marks the first step in fulfilling the promise of Isaiah (60:1-6), "Rise up in splendor! Your light has come, the glory of the Lord shines upon you. ... Nations shall walk by your light, and kings by your shining radiance." The universality of God's salvation, found in the Church, is expressed in the second reading (Eph 3:2-3a, 5-6), "In Christ Jesus the Gentiles are now co-heirs with the Jews, members of the same body and sharers of the promise through the preaching of the Gospel."

While the Mass concentrates on the event of the Magi's arrival, the Liturgy of the Hours remembers all the three events originally celebrated, the arrival of the Magi, baptism of the Lord, and the miracle at Cana. The antiphon for the Magnificat in Evening Prayer II is most illustrative: "Three mysteries mark this holy day: today the star leads the Magi to the infant Christ; today water is changed into wine for the wedding feast; today Christ wills to be baptized by John in the river Jordan to bring us to salvation."

Epiphany is today properly recognized as the high point of the Christmas season. In differentiating between the two primary feasts of the season Biblical scholar J.A. Jungmann has directed our attention to the importance of the Epiphany feast: "The mystery of the Incarnation is the proper subject of them both; but at Christmas we consider chiefly the coming down of the Son of God who became one of the poor children of men while on the Epiphany we direct our attention to this child's divine dignity which already is beginning to manifest itself in the world."

In the Feast of the Epiphany the Church celebrates Jesus' manifestation to the nations. Today, our primary focus in this feast is the arrival of the astrologers from the East and Jesus' salvation open to all, Jew and Gentile alike. From our tradition, however, we also celebrate other manifestations of Jesus, through his baptism and as a miracle worker turning water into wine. Jesus continues to be manifest to us today in the faces of those we encounter, the wealthy and poor, the powerful and powerless. May the Epiphany message of Jesus' love for all peoples be echoed today through our personal faithfulness and efforts in fostering the reign of God in our world.

DEVOTION TO THE SACRED HEART OF JESUS: CELEBRATING GOD'S LOVE

The celebration of God's love for all men and women most assuredly should be a daily practice through prayer, liturgical celebration, and the way we live out common Christian vocation to holiness. Along with St. Paul, the Church teaches that we show love for God by demonstrating love for one another, since we are brothers and sisters in Christ and members of his Body. The Church in her wisdom provides additional "special" opportunities to celebrate God's love in our lives. The Feast of the Sacred Heart, a celebration rich in tradition and popular devotion, is one such opportunity where veneration of Christ's human heart, as a symbol, shows forth God's love for all people.

Early Beginnings of Devotion

Until the pontificate of Pope Pius XII (1939-1958) it was thought by most scholars that devotion to the Sacred Heart of Jesus found its roots sometime after the first millennium of the common era. More contemporary critical study, however, has brought us a new understanding which sees roots to this devotion beginning with the Hebrew Scriptures. The Book of Psalms contains numerous references to the human heart as the seat of the whole inner person, a symbol for the love which one bears for another. In Psalm 16:9 we read, "Therefore my heart is glad, and my soul rejoices, my body too abides in confidence." In the book of Jeremiah, the reference is more clearly with the heart of the Lord, "The anger of the Lord will not abate until he has done and fulfilled what he has determined in his heart." Scholars today see these passages, and others like them, as a foreshadowing to the human heart of Jesus and the love it will pour forth in Christ's crucifixion.

The primary New Testament passage which figured in the development of the devotion to the Sacred Heart is John 7:37-39 where Jesus tells others to come and drink for, "from within him rivers of living water shall flow." The Patristic understanding of this passage was two-fold. One group led by Augustine, Jerome and Origen saw the living water flowing from the heart of the believer. Another group, however, led by Hippolytus, Irenaeus, Cyprian, and Tertullian, considered the living water as flowing from Christ's heart. Over the course of history, this latter opinion was more influential and paved the way for later public devotion.

The Medieval and Renaissance Church used the flowing waters that proceeded from the heart of Jesus and transformed them into a devotion to the wounds of Christ. Again, reference to St. John's Gospel, 19:31-34, when the soldier pierced the Savior's side with his lance, was used to promote this devotion. Water and blood flowed from Christ's side, symbolizing the unity of God with all people. The wounded heart of Jesus became for those in the eleventh to fourteenth centuries a source of popular devotion. Pope St. Gregory VII (1073-1085) once wrote, "Just as the dove finds nourishment in the hollow places, so the simple soul seeks in the wounds of Christ the food that makes it strong." Devotion to the wounds of Christ is found in the writings and private devotions of many saints through the sixteenth century including St. Francis Borgia (1510-1572), St. Aloysius Gonzaga (1568-1591) and St. Francis de Sales (1567-1622).

Public Devotion to the Sacred Heart

The story of public devotion to the Sacred Heart of Jesus begins with its foreshadowing in the life of St. Gertrude of Helfta (d. 1302). From the tradition we are told that on the Feast of St. John the Evangelist Jesus appeared to St. Gertrude in a vision. She was allowed to place her head near the wound in his side. She listened to the beatings of the divine heart and asked St. John why he had not spoken of what he had heard during the Last Supper when it had been his privilege to rest his head near the heart of the Lord. John answered that the reason for his silence was that this knowledge had been reserved for later ages, when the love of humankind for God would have grown cold, so that it might be rekindled.

The person initially responsible for bringing to light a special devotion to the Sacred Heart was St. John Eudes. Living in the post-Reformation Church (1601-1680), St. John reawakened in the faithful the special love of God, a love which, as foretold to St. Gertrude, had fallen cold. Although he has been overshadowed through popular devotion by his famous successor, St. Margaret Mary Alacoque (1647-1690), St. John Eudes has rightly been called by Pope St. Pius X, "the father, the doctor and the apostle" of devotion to the Sacred Heart.

St. John was important because he moved the devotion to the wounds of Christ forward to a celebration of the immense and ineffable love of Jesus in all aspects. In his book *Le Coeur Admirable de la Tres Sacree Mere de Dieu,* Eudes outlines his theology of devotion to the Sacred Heart. First, he describes why celebration is appropriate by outlining four categories of devotion. First, he says devotion is appropriate to adore the Sacred Heart of Jesus. Next, St. John says that humanity has a need to praise, bless, glorify, and thank Christ for his love. Devotion is also necessary to ask pardon for our offenses against his great love and to make reparation for such sins. Finally, celebration is needed to demonstrate love to Christ in return for all his love and to beg him to establish within our hearts the reign of his love.

St. John also synthesized the object of our devotion in this celebration. For Eudes the Sacred Heart of Jesus is a unity of the divine uncreated love of Christ, the human love of Jesus proceeding through his human will, and the sensible, emotional love of Jesus symbolized by the heart of flesh. To designate this three-fold unity, St. John distinguished three hearts in Jesus: his divine heart, his spiritual heart, and his corporeal heart. For Eudes the divine heart is the soul, the life, and the heart of both the spiritual and corporeal hearts.

Beyond theology, St. John Eudes is significant as well in the development of devotion to the Sacred Heart in its liturgical celebration. Although accounts differ as to dates, it is certain that St. John was the first to receive permission to celebrate an office and Mass in honor of the Sacred Heart. Scholars claim the Feast of the Sacred Heart was first celebrated at the Seminary of Rennes on August 31, 1670, by Eudes' own communities, the Congregation of Jesus and Mary (Eudist Fathers) and the Order of Our Lady of Charity. In a more contemporary study, the liturgist, Adolph Adam states that the first celebration was on October 20, 1672. The prayers of both the office and Mass in this early stage of devotional development referred more to the Immaculate Heart of Mary than to the Sacred Heart of Jesus (Eudes was famous for both devotions).

St. John Eudes was the initiator of devotion to the Sacred Heart, but it was the revelations between 1673-1675 of Jesus to St. Margaret Mary Alacoque, a 26-year-old Visitation sister of the convent at Paray-le-monial in France, and their popularization which brought the devotion into public prominence. The revelations began quite undramatically on December 27, 1673. On that day, as was her custom, St. Margaret was praying before the Blessed Sacrament in her convent chapel. As she prayed Jesus appeared to her. He referred to her as "the beloved disciple of the Sacred Heart." In this first revelation Jesus took the heart of St. Margaret and joined it to his own. Her heart was then placed back in her body. From then on, however, on each first Friday, she experienced pain in her side from where Jesus had temporarily removed her heart to be joined with his. About this first revelation St. Margaret later wrote, "His Sacred Heart was shown to me as a brilliant sun of blinding light, where burning rays filled directly my heart, which immediately felt as though kindled by such an intense fire that it seemed it would reduce me to ashes. And it was especially at this time that my Divine Master would teach me what He wanted of me and revealed the secret of His loving heart."

St. Margaret's three remaining revelations were received on first Fridays. In her second vision, early in 1674, Jesus revealed himself to her as a heart surrounded by a crown of thorns with a cross above it. The bleeding heart would thus become the symbol of Christ's burning love for humankind. In her third revelation, June 1674, St. Margaret was told to receive the Eucharist as much as her vow of obedience would allow, especially on first Fridays. Additionally, she was told to spend one hour on Thursday evening preceding the first Friday in prayer where special instructions would be given to her. Finally, the Lord told her to spend one hour per week in prayer before the Blessed Sacrament. The final revelation of Jesus to St. Margaret took place between June 13-20, 1675. It was during this revelation that Jesus asked that the first Friday after the octave of Corpus Christi be dedicated to a special feast in honor of the Sacred Heart. (Remember that St. John Eudes had begun such a devotion before St. Margaret's revelations.)

The popular devotion which the contemporary Church celebrates in honor of the Sacred Heart developed from the time of St. Margaret. After her third revelation she revealed the secrets of her visions to Mother Saumaise, superior of the convent. Mother Saumaise suggested that Margaret should share her revelations with others who were more versed than she in such matters. Thus, St. Margaret spoke with Father (now Saint) Claude de La Colombiere,

SJ, the new superior of Paray-le-monial. Father Colombiere listened and became a believer in the revelations. He immediately began to promote the cause for devotion to the Sacred Heart.

The public cultus of devotion to the Sacred Heart was introduced by Charles Francois de Lomenie, Bishop of Coutances, the diocese of Paray-le-monial. Because of St. Margaret's revelations and with the encouragement of Father Colombiere, the Bishop consecrated a chapel in honor of the Sacred Heart in his seminary in 1688 and erected a confraternity under the same title. Other dioceses in France furthered the devotion. Peter de Grammant, Bishop of Besancon, in 1692 ordered a special Mass with the title *Cordis Jesu* to be printed in the missal of his diocese for the Friday after the octave of Corpus Christi. In the diocese of Langies the Mass of Bishop Grammant was also adopted. In 1718 the Archbishop of Lyons and primate of the area ordered the feast to be kept by all churches under his jurisdiction.

Official approbation from Rome for the Feast of the Sacred Heart was an evolutionary process. In 1693 Pope Innocent XII extended the feast to all Visitation monasteries worldwide. In 1765 Clement XIII allowed the Polish bishops and the Roman Confraternity of the Sacred Heart to celebrate the Feast. In 1854 Blessed Pope Pius IX approved, after the work of Henri Ramiere and the Apostleship of Prayer, that groups, families, and communities could consecrate themselves to the Sacred Heart. In 1856 Pius IX extended the feast to the universal Church. In 1899 Pope Leo XIII in his encyclical *Annum sacrum* furthered the efforts of Pius IX and decreed the consecration of the whole world to the Sacred Heart of Jesus.

Contemporary Devotion and Practice

Contemporary devotion to the Sacred Heart has organized and synthesized the thought and practice which have evolved since the time of John Eudes and Margaret Mary Alacoque. The tradition was unclear as to the precise nature of the devotion. Was the heart to be taken as physical, metaphorical, or symbolic; was the love of Christ which we honored human or divine? Following Pope Pius XII and his encyclical *Haurietis Aquas* ("On Devotion to the Sacred Heart"), issued on the centennial anniversary of the Feast's universal recognition, it is generally agreed that both the physical heart and the total love of Christ are included in the devotion. Pius XII wrote, "We can most correctly consider and venerate the heart of the divine Redeemer as the significant image of His love, the proof of our redemption, and the mystical ladder by which we climb to the embrace of 'God our Savior.'"

Devotion to the Sacred Heart has continued and been promoted in the post-Vatican II Church as well. Common belief has incorrectly credited Vatican II with invalidating many popular devotions present in the Church. To the contrary, *Sacrosanctum Concilium* ("Constitution on the Sacred Liturgy," #13) stated, "Popular devotions of the Christian people, provided they conform to the laws and norms of the Church, are to be highly recommended, especially when they are ordered by the Apostolic See." As we have seen, devotion to the Sacred Heart has been closely linked to the Office of the Pope and thus is to be promoted under the Vatican II guidelines.

Post-Vatican II theology has associated the Sacred Heart with Jesus' wounded side and with the Eucharist. Neither *Sacrosanctum Concilium* nor *Lumen Gentium* ("Dogmatic Constitution on the Church") speak of the Sacred Heart directly, but rather, see the wounded side of Jesus as the source from which flows the divine and human love of Christ. Pope St. Paul VI in *Investigabiles Divitias Christi* (February 1965) proclaimed devotion to the Sacred Heart as an excellent form of piety which is intimately connected with the Eucharist. Pope Paul wrote, "We especially desire ... a greater devotion to be given to the Sacred Heart of Jesus, whose outstanding gift is the Eucharist."

Pope St. Paul VI expressed the desire to renew devotion to the Sacred Heart. In a compendium letter to his encyclical *Investigabiles* he wrote, "It is absolutely necessary that the faithful venerate and honor this [Sacred] Heart." When addressing the General Congregation of the Society of Jesus in 1966 he commented, "The cult rendered to the Sacred Heart is the most efficacious means to contribute to that spiritual and moral renewal of the world called for by the Second Vatican Council."

Pope St. John Paul II continued the tradition of his predecessors in promoting devotion to the Sacred Heart. Along with Paul VI he saw an intimate connection between the Eucharist and the Sacred Heart. Additionally, Pope St. John Paul viewed devotion to the Sacred Heart as integral to the life of the Church. He wrote in his encyclical *Dives in Misericordia*, "The Church seems in a particular way to profess the mercy of God and to venerate it when she directs herself to the Heart of Christ."

Today popular devotional practice to the Sacred Heart of Jesus is seen in First Friday and holy hour devotions. The famous "Promises of the Sacred Heart" given to St. Margaret in a private revelation continue to speak to many of the faithful. Jesus told St. Margaret, "I promise you, in the excessive mercy of my heart, that my all-powerful love will grant to all who receive Holy Communion on the First Friday of the month for nine consecutive months, the grace of final penitence; they shall not die in disgrace and without receiving the sacraments. My divine heart shall be their refuge in their last moment." Holy hours, including exposition of the Blessed Sacrament and benediction are still celebrated in many parishes.

The contemporary Mass and liturgical office for the Feast of the Sacred Heart are based on the thoughts of Pope Pius XI (in collaboration with the Benedictine abbot H. Quentin) who wrote his own celebrations in 1928. Pius emphasized expiation in his writings. For example, the original introit prayer asked that we may "offer Him [Jesus] worship by love-filled service to our brothers and sisters."

The present-day celebration of the Sacred Heart, celebrated on the Friday after *Corpus Christi*, emphasizes the love of God for all people. In the prayers of the Mass we hear, "[W]e rejoice in the gifts of love we have received from the heart of Jesus" and "Father, we honor the heart of your Son broken by man's cruelty yet symbol of love's triumph." The preface synthesizes the ideas of Jesus' wounded heart and ever faithful love. "Lifted high on the Cross, Christ gave his life for us, so much did he love us. From his wounded side flowed blood and water, the fountain of sacramental life in the Church. To his open heart the Savior invites all men, to draw water in joy from the springs of salvation."

The readings of the Mass continue the theme of Jesus' love for us. Over the three cycles of readings, we read Matthew 11:25-30 that challenges us to seek and find rest in the heart of Jesus. I John 4:7-16 says, "God is love and he who abides in love abides in God and God in him." In Ephesians 3:8-12, 14-19 we hear of Jesus' love, "which surpasses all knowledge." In Luke 15:3-7 we hear Jesus described as the Good Shepherd, so great is his love for us.

Popular devotion, although not as strong today as in earlier periods of the Church, continues to be a significant part of Roman Catholic practice. Reading the daily newspaper, one will find many "thank you" messages to St. Jude and to the Sacred Heart for favors rendered. Devotion to the Sacred Heart celebrates the undying love which Jesus showed for us on Calvary, a love which continues to manifest itself each day in magnificent and subtle ways. Confident of God's love let our celebration of the Feast of the Sacred Heart renew in us the desire to seek a greater love of God and all God's people.

Part V: Saints: Past and Present

Introduction

T radition holds that St. Francis once said, "Preach the gospel and when necessary, use words." We all remember the dictum, "Actions speak louder than words." In more contemporary parlance we hear people say, "One must not only talk the talk, but must walk the walk." The words of the famous saint from Assisi and the two more contemporary expressions clearly state that our actions are very important. As we have seen, our journey with Jesus requires us to appreciate the goodness of God, engage the challenges of contemporary life, and minister to God's people, utilizing the time, talent, resources, and opportunities provided for us. We have also learned that it is essential that we refresh the tools we possess by renewing our knowledge of the doctrines and tradition of our faith. If we are to stay on the road, however, to continue the journey with Jesus, we need examples of men and women, both past and present, who have met the challenges of their day, persevered, and in the end, by their words and actions, provided the Christian faithful with a pattern of life which we can emulate.

When considering people who are saints, quite naturally we think of the famous people of the past who have been so recognized by the Church for their heroic lives. These men and women are celebrated throughout the liturgical year. Some, like the apostles, are remembered with great fanfare in solemnities and feasts; others are remembered through memorials, both obligatory and optional. Many have a favorite saint, whether that be their patron, a name taken at the time of confirmation, or one, for whatever reason, who has been inspirational. Some saints, such as St. Anthony of Padua and St. Jude are rather universally celebrated because the tradition associates them with the person to whom one should pray for lost items or hopeless causes respectively. Others, like St. Francis, have gained great rapport due to a universal love of nature and a general appreciation of simplicity. Still others, such as St. Augustine, St. Thomas Aquinas, St. Bonaventure, or St. Teresa of Avila have been recognized for their intellectual prowess.

These great men and women of faith are certainly wonderful examples but there are others who are saints, who while not recognized in an official capacity by the Church, have provided great example. Notable individuals in this category would include the great social activist Dorothy Day, the rosary priest Patrick Peyton, CSC, and Navy Chaplain, Father Vincent Capodanno, M. M. We badly need examples of people who have journeyed with Jesus, and, we are confident, now rest with the Lord in eternal life. The "saints" presented herein, both canonized and on the sainthood track, provide the examples we need to maintain ourselves on the road so that we will one day join us with Jesus in the abode of heaven.

St. Athanasius - Defender
of the Faith

Throughout Christian history the Church has struggled against the forces which have threatened the integrity of the Faith. The battle which has pitted orthodoxy against heterodoxy has seen the heroism of many martyrs and the publication of many polemical tracts and treatises. Catholicism has also seen many who have bravely defended Church teachings against incalculable odds. One great champion of the Faith was St. Athanasius, bishop of Alexandria, who in the fourth century stood firm as the leader of an orthodox minority which continued to preach against the heretical opinions which pervaded society. History records the expression, Athanasius *contra mundum*--Athanasius against the world--as an accurate description of the fourth century Church. The life of Athanasius, one of the greatest "defenders of the Faith," is inspirational to all who live in the many times unchristian environment of the twenty-first century.

Athanasius was born to a Christian family in 295 in Alexandria, a leading city in North Africa. He received a classical education followed by a solid formation in Scripture and theology. At an early age he came to the attention of Alexander, bishop of Alexandria, who was impressed with the young Athanasius and took him into his home to further his educational experience. In 318 Athanasius was ordained a deacon and entered Alexander's service as his secretary, traveling extensively with his bishop, including a trip to Nicaea in 325 to attend the first ecumenical council, an event which would have great ramifications on the young man's future life as bishop.

According to Athanasius' first Festal Letter (an annual announcement concerning Lent and the date for Easter), Alexander died on 22 Parmuthi (April 17) 328. Although Alexander had designated his secretary as his successor, the transition of episcopal power would not be smooth. Rival factions placed their candidates before the faithful for election. The Melitians nominated Theonas; the Arians, who would be Athanasius' great nemesis, put forth Achillas. Eventually on 14 Pauni (June 8) 328 Athanasius was elected and assumed the episcopal office in Alexandria.

The Melitians and Arians made Athanasius' episcopal administration a difficult experience from the outset. Melitius, bishop of Lycopolis, championed a heretical group which originated during the persecution of the emperor Diocletian (303-305). Like the Donatists who plagued St. Augustine in the latter portion of the fourth century, Melitius believed that any Christians who had apostatized should be readmitted only with great precaution and under severe penance. Peter, bishop of Alexander during the persecution, took a more lenient view. Melitius, rejecting Peter's opinion, began to ordain bishops and presbyters to replace the *lapsi*. For his action Melitius was excommunicated. During the time of Athanasius, the Melitians continued their campaign in a righteous and dogmatic manner which forced the bishop to make every effort to rid Egypt of Melitian sympathizers.

Arianism dominated the Eastern Church in the fourth century pushing orthodox belief into a minority status. St. Jerome's famous comment, "The world awoke and groaned to find itself Arian," accurately portrays the situation. In response to the request of Alexander, Arius, a presbyter in Alexandria, made comments on Proverbs 8:22 which reads, "The Lord begot me, the firstborn of his ways, the forerunner of his prodigies of long ago." Arius taught that the *Logos*, Jesus, was, "merely called son, he too by adoption, as a creature." Jesus was thus higher than any human, but subordinate to God. Arius went further and declared in a letter to Eusebius, bishop of Caesarea, "Before he [Jesus] was begotten or created or appointed or established, he did not exist, for he was not unbegotten." Colossians 1:15, "[Jesus] the firstborn of all creatures," gave Arius more fuel for the fire he generated in his promotion of the *Logos* as a subordinate creature, a theology which today scholars say was based on the philosophy of Aristotle and the need to assure the oneness and unity of God.

Reaction against Arius' teaching was swift and strong. Alexander called a local council of 100 bishops from Egypt and Libya which anathematized the errors of Arius and excommunicated him along with many of his partisans, including two bishops from western Egypt. Arius quickly sought support from the Eusebius in Caesarea, an apologist for Origen (who had in the third century supported a subordinationist view of Christ) and was his theological heir.

The spread of Arianism, which was swift and extensive, forced Emperor Constantine to call the Council of Nicaea in 325 to unify the Church and stem the tide of heresy. Three hundred eighteen bishops attended the council, almost all from the East. At that time, the Arian debate was not an issue in the West. Additionally, the difficulty of traveling long distances kept Western bishops at home. The Council produced the Nicene Creed as a confession of faith. This formula declared that Father and Son were *homoousious*, of one nature. Additionally, the council issued an anathema against any who professed the beliefs held by the Arians. Arius and two other bishops refused to sign the credal statement and were excommunicated.

Despite the creation of a profession of faith and the condemnation of Arius, the Arian heresy only grew to greater heights after Nicaea. Between 325 and 381 orthodox and heterodox forces clashed severely over the Arian position. Athanasius many times stood alone as the defender of the true faith.

Athanasius based his whole theology on a defense of the Church which he saw under attack. His unceasing battle with heretics explains the polemical nature of his dogmatic writings, his biased selection of documents in his historical compositions, and the lack of serenity in his argumentation. Athanasius' doctrine is eminently traditional. He created no new synthesis of his own, but rather clarified and defended the central mysteries of the Trinity and the Incarnation by means of revealed concepts instead of the philosophical constructions used by the Arians. His theological thought is centered around the dogma of redemption. Athanasius saw the *Logos* as the mediator of divine salvation. Thus, Jesus' divinity was essential for human salvation and redemption. In *On the Incarnation of the Logos of God* Athanasius argued that redemption was only possible by God's active presence. Thus, the Incarnation required the full and true presence of God.

Athanasius' *Orations* against the Arians represent his greatest theological defense of the faith. These tracts contain a summary of Arian doctrine, a defense of the Nicene confession and a comprehensive Scriptural argument supporting the orthodox position. In the *Orations* Athanasius argued against adoptionism (the idea that Jesus merely "adopted" a human body, and thus was not fully human) and docetism (the concept that Jesus only appeared to have a human body). He wrote, "If the works of the *Logos'* Godhead had not been done by means of the body, humanity would not have been divinized."

Athanasius' Trinitarian theology focused on the life of the Spirit. His "Four Letters to Serapion" (359-360) set forth his understanding of the divinity and the procession of the Holy Spirit. He used the Nicean term *homoousious* to speak of the relation between the Son and the Spirit, which with the formula at Nicaea, links the Trinity as one.

The Post-Nicene period saw four groups, each with a different theological understanding, vie for power. To the far left, the *Anomoeans*, Arian position, saw the Father and Son as dissimilar. Two groups represented the middle ground, the *Homoean* and the *Homoiousians* (both semi-Arian). They held that the Father and Son were of like and similar substance (consubstantial) respectively. The orthodox side was the *Homoousious* group which defended the Nicene confession. Working within the political structure of the Empire, these groups battled to gain adherents. The East supported the Arian position; the West, when it showed interest, supported the orthodox position of Nicaea, championed by Athanasius.

The Post-Nicene period saw Athanasius in a continual battle with heterodox forces to maintain his episcopal see. Between 335 and 366 Athanasius was exiled from Alexandria five times for a total of more than 17 years. Since the Arians dominated this period in the East, Athanasius, with his defense of the true faith, became a marked man. Athanasius' problems began shortly after Nicaea adjourned when Constantine abruptly shifted to the Arian position and received Arius back into the communion of the Church. The emperor ordered Athanasius also to receive Arius, but the bishop refused on two occasions. Moreover, Athanasius made every effort to have Arius physically removed from Alexandria.

In 335 Athanasius was called to a council at Tyre which was organized against him. The Council Fathers, supporters of Arius, denounced the bishop. Athanasius appealed to the Emperor in Constantinople, but to no avail. Worried again about the unity of the Church and the threat of Athanasius to delay critical grain shipments from Alexandria to the Eastern capital, Constantine exiled the bishop of Alexandria to Treves in northern Gaul in 336. The next year, however, Constantine died, and Athanasius was allowed to return to his see.

Athanasius' stay in Egypt was brief. Constantine's death brought his two sons, Constans and Constantius to power in the West and East respectively. Constantius, persuaded by the opponents of Athanasius, pressured Pope Liberius to condemn the bishop of Alexandria. Athanasius was forced in 339 to go to Rome to exonerate his name. Not until 342 at the Council of Sardica was Athanasius able to clear himself of all accusations. He did not return to Alexandria, however, for three more years, arriving in October 346. During this second exile Athanasius had found favor in the West with the support of Pope Julius I and Emperor Constans.

The murder of Constans in 350 allowed his brother Constantius to unify the empire, politically and religiously. As a supporter of the Arian position Constantius pushed for the elimination of orthodoxy. Bishops at the Councils at Arles (353), Milan (355) and Beziers (356) aligned themselves with the Arians. In 356 a military force was sent to Alexandria to flush Athanasius from his see. Escaping with his life, the bishop fled to the Egyptian desert where he remained, moving for six years among the desert monks, including Pachomius and St. Antony. During this third exile Athanasius produced some of his most important writings including his *Life of Antony, Apology Against the Arians, Apology to Constantius* (important for its doctrine on Church-State relations), and *History of the Arians*, the latter written at the request of the monks.

In 361 Constantius died in battle against Julian (the Apostate) who ascended the imperial throne. Julian granted toleration to all parties which provided the vehicle for Athanasius' return to Alexandria in February 362. Again, Athanasius' stay was brief. Power struggles caused by the death of Julian and the rise to power of Valens again forced the bishop to flee, from October 362 to September 363 and October 365 to January 366.

The remainder of Athanasius episcopal career was dedicated to efforts to unify the Church. After his return from his fifth and final exile, the bishop gathered into some sort of doctrinal harmony those who sympathized with him over the Arian question. This was aided by imperial leaders, such as Valens, who formed a neo-orthodox party which merged with the supporters of Nicaea. Among the party's members were the great Cappadocian Fathers, Basil of Caesarea, his brother Gregory of Nyssa and their mutual friend Gregory of Nazianzus. Athanasius was able to consolidate his ecclesiastical authority primarily because of his tenacity and the fact that he outlived his opponents. Athanasius spent his last seven years in relative peace. He died on May 3, 373, after naming a faithful companion, Peter, to be his successor and to carry on the orthodox faith.

Athanasius' efforts as a defender of the Faith were crowned after his death. During the reign of Valens (364-378) the Cappadocians began their great work to define doctrine pertinent to the Holy Spirit. Their efforts led in 380 to the Edict of Thessalonica where the emperor Theodosius imposed Catholic orthodoxy on all subjects. In 381 an ecumenical council was called for Constantinople to unify the empire under orthodoxy. The Nicene-Constantinopolitan Creed, produced at this Council, reestablished orthodoxy in its definition of the relationship of Father, Son, and Spirit in the Trinity.

St. Athanasius truly was the great defender of the faith. The scholar, Paul T. Fuhrmann has written, "While many faltered, and many doubted, Athanasius stood firm; and if the faith of Nicaea won the day at last, it was largely due to him." In the complex and often unchristian world in which we live today, Athanasius can be a model of faithfulness for all to follow.

St. Ignatius of Antioch:
His Life and Letters

C hristians throughout the world are quite familiar with St. Paul, both his life and writings. The conversion of Paul on the road to Damascus is one of the most familiar stories of the New Testament. Equally well known and loved is the Pauline Corpus, numbering from seven to thirteen letters, depending on the school of Scriptural exegesis to which one prescribes. Living only about one generation after Paul was Ignatius of Antioch, bishop, martyr, and writer of epistles. Ignatius' contribution to the theology given us by the Apostolic Fathers was significant. An exploration of the life and theology of this saint reveals many of the needs and difficulties of the second century Church as expressed by one whose martyrdom was a source of inspiration for all Christians of Asia Minor.

Ignatius' Life and Journey to Rome

Historians know very little about the life of Ignatius. The principal sources in the ancient Church from which we receive information about him are Eusebius, the Father of Church history, who dedicates several pages of his fourth century masterwork *Ecclesiastical History* in discussion of Ignatius and Irenaeus, Bishop of Lyons, in his second century treatise, *Against Heresies*. His writings, like those of St. Paul, also give us information about his life.

Most probably Ignatius came from Syria, being born about the time of Jesus' death in 30 CE. In his letters Ignatius refers to himself as Theophorus meaning God-borne or God-bearing. Some in recent scholarship have conjectured that this refers to the passage in Mark 9:36-37 where Jesus places a little child amid the apostles and extolls the virtues of being childlike. Proponents of this school see Ignatius as a Christian from childhood. Most scholars, however, refer to the passage in Ignatius' Letter to the Romans, chapter 9, where he refers to himself as "one born out of due time," suggesting that he was probably a convert from paganism. Eusebius tells us that Ignatius was the third bishop of Antioch.

Ignatius' prominence in history and theology stems from his arrest and ultimate martyrdom. Pliny in the second century tells us of a limited persecution of Christians conducted by the Roman Emperor Trajan in the year 111. Most likely Ignatius was arrested in Antioch under this imperial edict. Eusebius says that Ignatius was condemned to die in Rome to become "food for wild beasts on account of his testimony to Christ."

From Ignatius' writings we are given a general itinerary of his journey to Rome. Most probably he went by ship from Antioch to some port on the southern coast of Asia Minor. Then the expedition, which was accompanied by ten Roman guards, set out by land bound for Ephesus. From this city, which had a lively Christian community, Ignatius and his captors went north by way of the juncture of the Lycus and Maeander Rivers to the town of Philadelphia. From here the party went on to Smyrna, where Polycarp was bishop. In Smyrna Ignatius received visitors from Ephesus, Magnesia, and Tralles. While there he wrote his first four letters, initially to the Ephesians, Magnesians, and Trallians; later he wrote to the Christian community at Rome. Leaving Smyrna, the expedition proceeded to Troas where Ignatius wrote his last three epistles, to the Philadelphians, Smyrnaeans, and a personal letter to Bishop Polycarp, who would also suffer the glory of martyrdom. From Troas the party headed to Neapolis, the seaport of Philippi. From this point the trail is cloudy. Presumably the expedition traveled the Egnatian Way to Dyrrhachium. The group then boarded a vessel and sailed to Rome. It seems that Ignatius was martyred in Rome shortly after his arrival. The only confirming source we have on this fact is Polycarp.

Ignatius saw his journey to Rome as a march of triumph. In his writings he asks Christians to grasp the mythic proportions of the journey. Ignatius sought martyrdom, a common desire of the period, and did not want anyone to interfere in the glory that would be his. This is most graphically explained to the Romans when he instructs them to use no political means to secure his release. He wrote, "May it be for my good that the wild animals are ready for me: I pray that I may find them promptly. ... May nothing seen or unseen grudge my attaining Jesus Christ! Let fire and cross, encounters with wild animals, tearing apart of bones, hacking of limbs, crushing of the whole body, tortures of the devil come upon me, if only I may attain to Jesus Christ."

The Letters and Theology of Ignatius

As previously mentioned, Ignatius wrote his famous letters on his journey toward Rome and martyrdom. Polycarp was the first person to mention a collection of letters written by Ignatius. In his *Against Heresies*, Irenaeus quotes from Ignatius' Letter to the Romans. Eusebius was the first to indicate there were seven letters in the Ignatian corpus, Ephesians, Magnesians, Trallians, Romans, Philadelphians, Smyraeans, and Polycarp.

What was the motivation behind Ignatius' writings? The scripture scholar Cyril Richardson has given two principal reasons for the letters. First, Ignatius wanted to warn his fellow Christians to avoid certain heresies (discussed below). Secondly, the Bishop of Antioch wanted to impress upon his readers the importance of Church unity as expressed through obedience to ecclesiastical officials, namely the bishop, presbyters, and deacons. Scripture scholar William Schoedel has suggested a more generic reason for the letters. He states that Ignatius wrote to reaffirm the value of his ministry and as witness value to the Christian community

The Ignatian corpus, again like that of Paul, is contested as to its authenticity. Ignatius' writings have been handed down in three different recensions, traditionally labeled as short, middle, and long. The short recension, preserved only in Syriac, is an abridgement of the letters to Polycarp, Ephesians, and Romans with a paragraph from Trallians. The middle recension is most associated with an eleventh century Greek text which contains all the letters, save Romans. At some time, these became detached and incorporated into an account of the saint's martyrdom. Versions and fragments of the middle recension exist in Latin, Syriac, Armenian, Coptic, and Arabic. The long recension is contained in several Greek manuscripts. This version contains expanded texts of the traditional seven letters, plus six additional letters, one to Ignatius from a certain Mary of Cassobola, the others from Ignatius to this same Mary, the Tarsians, Antiochenes, Hero, and Philippians.

Traditional study of the Ignatian corpus has concentrated on the middle recension. In the late nineteenth century, the work of J.B. Lightfoot and Theodore Zahn labeled the middle recension as the most authentic. In more recent scholarship Professor Reinoud Weijenborg views the middle recension as a shortened version of the long recension, where he places greater authenticity. J. Ruis-Camps agrees that historically the middle recension appeared before the long recension but claims that it is forgery. Along with Weijenborg, Ruis-Camps opts for the authenticity of the long recension. These recent exegetical efforts have not swung most opinion which still lies with the theory of Lightfoot.

The influences upon Ignatius in his writing style and theology are predictable. Although the references are limited to three, Ignatius uses the Hebrew Scriptures in his writings. The tone of the letters also speaks to some familiarity with the Gospel of Matthew, although there is no direct reference or evidence that Ignatius had a copy of the Gospel to consult. Ignatius style, as might be expected in highly Hellenistic, especially in the way he places relationships between words and deeds in the actions of humankind.

The influence of St. Paul is predominant in the letters of Ignatius of Antioch. Paul, the evangelizer of the gentiles, is mentioned in Ignatius' letters to the Ephesians (12:2) and Romans where he is described as an apostle and saint. Several reminiscences to I Corinthians are found in the Ignatian corpus (Ephesians, Romans, and Philadelphians), but there is no direct quotations. In Ephesians, Ignatius recognizes that Paul has written several letters, including one to this same Christian community at Ephesus. Some scholars have made attempts to show reminiscences to Paul's letters to the Ephesians and II Corinthians, although the evidence is not well substantiated. Since Ignatius and Paul were relative contemporaries, the Hellenistic letter style which they both used contains similarities in format and method.

The letters of Ignatius can also be compared with Paul in their theological perspectives. Both men concentrated on the centrality of Christ to Christian faith. The death and resurrection of Christ is the cornerstone to God's plan for bringing eternal life to all believers. This plan is carried out in the Church with the Eucharist as its binding force. Differences in the understanding of Paul and Ignatius are also present. Nowhere in Ignatius' writings is the concept of the indwelling Spirit found, especially as a means of moral renewal as seen in Paul. Also, Ignatius shows no understanding of humankind's dying and rising with Christ as part of the paschal mystery.

The long recension of Ignatius' letters contains material that seems to show the influence of St. John the Evangelist. Ignatius stresses the pre-existence of Christ, access to God the Father through Christ, and eternal life as a present possession as well as a future hope. Richardson points out, however, that the above ideas, which certainly are contained in John, are also present in Paul. He argues that Ignatius most probably had no access to John's Gospel. Contemporary scholarship would verify this idea since it is probable that the Johannine writings had not been written before Ignatius' martyrdom. Ignatius was much more a disciple of Paul than John.

St. Ignatius plays an important role in the history of doctrine, not as an original thinker, but as one who reflected the ideas of his day. Unity of the Church was very important for Ignatius, a concept vital to an institution under attack from the prevailing Roman government. Like Paul, Ignatius sees the Christian community as the body of Christ. Unity for Ignatius is best expressed in fealty to episcopal authority and general Church leadership. Ignatius sees a hierarchical Church where the power of the clergy is derived from God. He wrote in Magnesians, chapter 6, "I exhort you to be careful to do all things in the harmony of God, the bishop having primacy after the model of God and the priests after the model of the Apostles, and the deacons having entrusted to them the ministry of Jesus Christ." Despite the horizontal structure of his concept of Church, Ignatius mentions nothing about "Apostolic Succession." The bishop receives authority by the will of God; presbyters and deacons are confirmed and strengthened in their office by the Holy Spirit.

Ignatius concept of God presents a somewhat contradictory picture. God is seen in Ignatius' thought as a personal agent who resists the proud (Ephesians) and is concerned about humans (Magnesians). Yet, he goes further than all New Testament writers in stressing the transcendence of God. This latter notion reflects the influence of Hellenism in his thinking. The attainment of God for Ignatius is not taken for granted, but rather is seen as the goal of Christian existence in this life.

Ignatius' Christology also reflects the thinking of his day. Some scholars today see both "subordinationist" (the idea that Jesus is God but lesser than the Father) and "adoptionist" (that Jesus the human being was adopted by Christ the divine sometime after the former's physical birth from Mary) tendencies in his theology. Others, however, say that such technical language falsifies the picture which Ignatius tries to present in his letters. Ignatius does stress the unity of flesh and spirit in Jesus as he proclaims him to be, "son of Mary and Son of God." (Ephesians 7:2) This theological concept foreshadowed the great Christological debates of the Patristic period and the dogmatic definition of the two natures in one person of Jesus Christ defined at Chalcedon in 451.

Ignatius sees the Eucharist as the central act of Christian worship. The Eucharist functions as the premier sign of God's love for humanity as well as being the "medicine of immortality and the antidote against death" (Ephesians 20:2) for all who believe. Again, in union with St. Paul, Ignatius sees the Eucharist as another visible sign of Christian unity where all come to be one in thought and belief (Philadelphians 4:1). Only in Smyraeans, chapter 6, does Ignatius state that the Eucharist is the Body and Blood of Christ. Scholars feel that the passage is sufficiently impressive, however, as to suggest that the sacrament was taken for granted as central to Christian worship.

Faith and love are used by Ignatius as expressions of true Christian life. From these virtues all others flow. Faith and love are linked with the most desirable state of affairs; they show the unity and good order of the Christian faithful. Faith for Ignatius is implicit trust in God and absolute obedience to divine rule. Love is more the practical aspect of Christian life. In Ephesians Ignatius uses images of faith as the guide and love as the road that leads to God.

As mentioned earlier, experts today see the combating of heresy as one of the primary reasons for Ignatius' writings. In all his letters except Romans, Ignatius speaks out against the heresy of docetism, the belief common in this era that denied the humanity of Christ.

Against this belief Ignatius emphasizes the reality of Christ's human suffering, the Real Presence of Christ in the Eucharist and Jesus' resurrection in the flesh. Richardson has also seen in the letters to the Magnesians and Philadelphians references against Judaizers, a group of Judeo-Christians who viewed adherence to the Mosaic law as necessary for salvation.

Conclusion

Although we know relatively little of the details of his life, the writings of St. Ignatius of Antioch, bishop and martyr, are a treasure rarely appreciated by other than a few learned scholars and theologians. Ignatius speaks as a representative of his time to problems and questions of the day. He stressed unity in the Church, through the hierarchy, the Eucharist and the virtues of faith and love. Influenced by St. Paul, Ignatius' theology speaks of the centrality of the Incarnation and our participation with Jesus in the mission of salvation. United as Church, we are richer today because of his contribution.

Our Lady of Sorrows: The Spiritual Martyrdom of Mary

The Blessed Virgin Mary plays an integral role in Roman Catholic theology and liturgical practice. Sprinkled throughout the liturgical calendar, Marian feasts remind us of the important role the Blessed Mother played in the salvation of humankind and how she continues to intercede for us at God's right hand. The "Memorial to Our Lady of Sorrows," celebrated on September 15, commemorates the role played by Mary in living out the prophecy of Simeon at the time of the Presentation of Jesus in the Temple: "[Y]ou yourself shall be pierced with a sword." The theology and historical development of this feast accurately demonstrates the spiritual martyrdom which was the life of the Blessed Mother.

Devotion to the Sorrowful Mother finds its earliest roots in the Patristic Church. Except for St. Ambrose, the Latin Fathers concluded that the New Testament texts which speak of Mary's trials and the events on Calvary should be interpreted in terms of Mary's sorrows. This theme carried over to the East as evidenced by the mid-sixth century liturgical poetry of St. Romanus Melodus, that described the faith of Mary during her time of sorrow.

In the late Medieval period, the Church began to commemorate the sorrows of Mary during the season of Lent. This devotion was especially strong in the Rhine area of Germany. In a Provincial Synod of 1423 at Cologne, devotion to the sorrows of Mary led to a feast celebrated on the third Sunday before Easter. Various dioceses and religious communities incorporated the feast in their liturgical calendars under the title of *Lamentatio Mariae* (Wailing of Mary). In 1482 Pope Sixtus IV composed the first Mass to commemorate Mary's sorrows. In 1721 Pope Benedict XIII extended the feast to the universal Church to be celebrated on the Friday preceding Palm Sunday.

While a feast commemorating Mary's sorrow was developing in the Western Church, a second similar feast was instituted in parallel under the auspices of the Order of Servants of Mary, the Servites. In 1607 Pope Paul V granted the Servites the exclusive rights to form confraternities based on the sorrows of Mary. This devotion was promoted throughout Europe, especially in the Low countries by Servite priest John of Coudenberg. In 1668 Pope Innocent XI granted the Servites a special feast based on Mary's sorrows, to be celebrated on the third Sunday of September. Around this same time the seven sorrows that we know today became fixed: (1) the prophecy of Simeon, (2) flight to Egypt, (3) loss of the 12-year-old Jesus, (4) Mary meets Jesus on the Via Dolorosa, (5) the hours spent beneath the cross, (6) resting of the slain Jesus in his mother's arms and (7) laying of Jesus in the tomb. The Servite feast was universalized by Pope Pius VII in 1814. In 1913 St. Pius X transferred the feast to September 15, placing it on the octave of Mary's birth and following the Feast of the Triumph of the Cross on September 14.

Thus, at the dawn of the Vatican II Council there existed two feasts honoring Mary as our Sorrowful Mother. Through the 1960 Code of Rubrics the Lenten feast was reduced to a commemoration. In the 1969 reorganization of the liturgical calendar the Lenten feast was dropped altogether, and the September 15 feast was given its present name of the "Memorial of Our Lady of Sorrows."

The theology presented in this special feast of Mary stands in stark contrast to the Triumph of the Cross, celebrated the previous day. The mood of the feast is a somber reminder to us of Mary's pain and suffering. This motif seems consistent with the ascetic piety of the Order of the Servites, the religious community, as we have seen, that developed the feast. The contemporary theology of this day is reminiscent of the Lenten themes present in the feast's Western Church development.

The spiritual martyrdom of Mary is clearly celebrated in Our Lady of Sorrows. Speaking of the feast, St. Bernard (d.1153) wrote, "The martyrdom of the Virgin is set before us, not only by the prophecy of Simeon, but also in the story itself of the Lord's passion." The concept of martyrdom is found in both the prayers and readings of the Mass. In the opening prayer we hear, "We reverently recall her sufferings and sorrow. Mercifully grant us the fruits of your [Jesus'] own sufferings." The prayer over the gifts is even more illustrative, "May we who commemorate the piercing of the soul of Blessed Mary, your mother, share the reward of the saints through her loving and constant intercession." The most graphic depiction of Mary's martyrdom is seen in the Gospel acclamation where we proclaim, "Happy are you, O Blessed Virgin Mary; without dying you won the martyr's crown beside the cross of the Lord."

Father Basil Moreau, founder of the Congregation of Holy Cross, possessed a special devotion to Our Lady of Sorrows. He wrote of Mary's martyrdom in his meditations: "What was the mind of the Church in calling upon you [people] to honor the memory of this long martyrdom. Her intention was to make you share in the suffering of the Mother of God."

Father Moreau's comment hints at the second major theme of Our Lady of Sorrows, the need for all people to share in the sufferings of Mary and Jesus. This idea is brought out strongly in the liturgy of the word for this feast. The optional sequence of the Mass manifests this theme most clearly. Composed by Jacoponi da Todi, OFM (d.1306) or possibly St. Bonaventure (d.1274), this sequence, known as the *Stabat Mater*, is a personalized expression of the great asceticism which existed during the scholastic period. This hymn, based on John 19:35, Luke 2:35, Ezekiel 13:6, II Corinthians 4:10 and Galatians 4:17, is written in both prose and poetic style. In the prose version we read, "Holy Mother, do this for me. Pierce my heart once and forever with the wounds of your crucified Son. Let me share with you the pain of your Son's wounds, for he thought it right to bear such suffering for me." Again, we read, "Grant that ... I may feel the pains of my crucified Lord." The 20-stanza poetic version contains a similar message:

> "O Sweet Mother, font of love
> Touch my spirit from above
> Make my heart with your accord."

We also hear:

> "Let me share with you his pain,
> Who for all our sins was slain.
> Who for me in torments died."

The other readings of the Mass continue the theme of sharing in Jesus and Mary's pain. The first reading, Hebrews 5:7-9, tells us that by Jesus' perfect suffering he became for us the source of eternal salvation. As we share in Christ's suffering so we shall share in his glory. The alternative Gospel reading, John 19:25-27, allows us to suffer with Mary as she waits beneath the cross.

The Memorial of Our Lady of Sorrows is a feast rich in history and theology. Through the combination of two feasts commemorating the sorrows of our Blessed Mother this celebration became fixed on September 15 only in the early twentieth century. With its roots in the Lenten season and its Biblical base in the passion narratives, it is quite understandable that a somber state and a theme of suffering accompanies the celebration. The spiritual martyrdom of Mary together with our need to share in her sufferings and those of her son dominates the liturgy of the feast. In contrast to the exaltation of the previous day's celebration of the Triumph of the Cross, the Memorial of Our Lady of Sorrows is a special reminder to us that suffering will accompany us along the road that leads to salvation. The author of II Timothy (2:11-12) has put it well, "You can depend on this: If we have died with him, we shall also live with him; if we hold out to the end, we shall with him." The theological challenge of this Marian celebration awaits our response.

St. John Eudes: Church Reformer and Spiritual Leader

The name John Eudes does not normally evoke significant reaction from the average Catholic. When thinking about French saints of the post-Tridentine period the names of Francis de Sales, Vincent de Paul, or Margaret Mary Alacoque may come to mind. The contribution of St. John Eudes, however, to the spiritual renewal of the French Church, as a reformer, writer, and founder of religious congregations, equaled his more famous contemporaries and raised to new heights the religious sensibilities of clergy and laity.

The early life of John Eudes (1601-1680) was formulative for his future ministry. He was born in the small village of Ri in the district of Normandy and was educated by a local priest, James Blanette, until he was 14. Eudes was then sent to Caen where he matriculated at a newly opened Jesuit college. After completion of his philosophical studies, St. John made the decision to become a priest, against the wishes of his father. In 1621 Eudes received tonsure and minor orders. Two years later he entered the Oratory of Jesus where Pierre de Berulle became his mentor. St. John was ordained on December 20, 1625.

After ordination Eudes began to prepare himself for a preaching career under the direction of the Father Charles de Condren. Sidetracked for a few years by local plagues which required his ministerial assistance, Eudes began to preach parish missions in 1633. His gifts as a speaker were abundant which enhanced his work. The missions he preached were highly successful and earned him a reputation for fervor and eloquence. During his life Eudes preached over 100 parish missions, most of which lasted at least six weeks with some extending for several months. His mission field was primarily his native Normandy, but he did minister in Brittany, Bourgogne, and Ile-de-France as well.

The dawn of the seventeenth century revealed the poor state of preparedness in the French clergy. Ecclesiastical discipline had all but collapsed in the French Church. The clergy were ill prepared, both spiritually and intellectually, for their work as preachers, educators, and pastors. Eudes realized the great need for spiritual renewal which existed. Beginning in 1641 St. John gave many conferences aimed at renewing the interior life of the French secular clergy. More fundamental changes in the formation of the clergy, however, were necessary. This realization led Eudes to suggest the need for new seminaries to renew the clerical life of the nation. The Superior General of the Oratorians, Charles de Condren, supported Eudes' plans. Condren's successor, however, was not open to his suggestions.

The opposition which Eudes found to his plans for renewal forced him to strike out on his own. With the support of Cardinal Armand-Jean Duc de Richelieu, Eudes withdrew from the Oratorians and began his own community. In 1643 he founded a new society of secular priests (without vows) under the title the Congregation of Jesus and Mary (Eudists). The community was dedicated to the formation of a well-trained and spiritually mature clergy. The congregation saw its two-fold purpose as: (1) to provide seminaries for the formation of the clergy according to the Tridentine decrees and

(2) to preach missions. In Eudes' life the Congregation founded six seminaries at Caen, Coutances, Lisieux, Rouen, Evreux, and Rennes. These seminaries (today we would call them retreat houses) provided intensive training of a few months' duration to clerical candidates under the supervision of Eudes and his fellow Eudists.

John Eudes also acted as a reformer and founder to aid women. In 1641 he assisted in the establishment at Caen of a religious society of women. Called the Congregation of Our Lady of Charity, the new community was established to provide refuge for women of ill repute who wished to do penance. The Congregation was approved by the Bishop of Bayeux in February 1651 and by Pope Alexander VII in January 1666. Eudes was responsible for the foundation of four convents in this community.

The contribution of John Eudes in the realm of spiritual renewal was significant. He based his personal spirituality on the principle which saw Jesus as the source of all sanctity and Mary as the model of Christian life. Using this idea, Eudes contributed many noteworthy books including *La Vie et le Royaume de Jesus dans les Ames Chretiennes* (1637), *Le Contrat de l'Homme avec Dieu par le Saint Bapteme* (1654), *Le Bon Confesseur* (1666) and *Le Memorial de la Vie Ecclesiastique* (1681).

John Eudes' most famous, yet unheralded contribution to the spiritual life and popular religiosity, was his promotion of devotion to the Sacred Heart of Jesus. Popular religion today attributes the genesis of this devotion to St. Margaret Mary Alacoque and her apparitions between 1673-1675 at the convent at Paray-le-Monial in Paris. While St. Margaret Mary popularized devotion to the Sacred Heart, it was John Eudes who initiated it. He was honored by Pope St. Pius X with the titles of the "Author of the Liturgical Worship of the Sacred Hearts of Jesus and Mary" and "The Father, The Doctor and The Apostle" of this devotion.

St. John's work was important in propelling devotion to the Sacred Heart into its modern context. The sixteenth century Jesuit saints, Francis Borgia (1510-1572) and Aloysius Gonzaga (1568-1591), promoted devotion to the five wounds of Christ. Eudes carried this further to a general celebration of the immense and ineffable love of Jesus in all aspects. In his book *Le Coeur Admirable de la Tres Sacree Mere de Dieu* Eudes describes his theology of devotion to the Sacred Heart.

St. John outlines why celebration is appropriate by outlining four categories of devotion. First, he says devotion is appropriate to adore the Sacred Heart of Jesus. Next, St. John says that humanity has a need to praise, bless, glorify, and thank God for his love. Devotion is also necessary to ask pardon for our offenses against his great love and to make reparation for such sins. Lastly, celebration is needed to demonstrate love to Christ in return for all his love and to beg him to establish within our hearts the reign of his love.

St. John also synthesized the object of our devotion in this celebration. For Eudes the Sacred Heart of Jesus is a unity of the divine uncreated love of Christ, the human love of Jesus proceeding through his human will, and the sensible, emotional love of Jesus symbolized by the heart of flesh. To designate this three-fold unity, St. John distinguished three hearts in Jesus: the divine heart, the spiritual heart, and the corporeal heart. For Eudes the divine heart is the soul, the life and heart of both the spiritual and corporeal hearts.

Beyond theology, St. John Eudes' work is significant as well in the development of devotion to the Sacred Heart in its liturgical celebration. Although accounts differ as to dates, it is certain that Eudes was the first to receive permission to celebrate an office and Mass in honor of the Sacred Heart. One source claims that the Feast of the Sacred Heart was first celebrated at the Seminary of Rennes, one of the institutions of Eudes' Congregation of Jesus and Mary, on August 31, 1670. In a more recent study, however, the liturgist, Adolf Adam, states that the first celebration was held on October 20,

1672. Eudes composed Divine Offices for the Immaculate Heart of Mary in 1648 and the Sacred Heart of Jesus in 1672.

The life and work of St. John Eudes was crowned in the twentieth century. In 1909 he was beatified by Pope St. Pius X. On May 31, 1925, he was canonized by Pope Pius XI. As a preacher of missions and promoter of spiritual renewal and popular devotion, St. John Eudes was one who embodied the Gospel edict of discipleship. In understanding his contribution to the Faith, we can see better our own call to ministry in our Church, as baptized sons and daughters in the Lord.

KATHARINE DREXEL'S MISSION TO AMERICA

C atholicism's mission to the peoples of color in the United States has an inglorious history. As chronicled by historians Cyprian Davis, OSB and Stephen J. Ochs, Black Catholics have fought prejudice and misunderstanding in their drive for acceptance in the Church. Native American Catholics have been frustrated by the inability to establish the institutional Church within their community. The life and work of St. Katharine Drexel and her Sisters of the Blessed Sacrament paints a positive picture in a tapestry laced with negatives. Born into a family of wealth and privilege, Drexel focused her life's work through outreach to Catholics who had for the most part been forgotten. The story of her community is one of the triumph of hope over distrust, faith over fear.

Katharine's road to a life of ministry was atypical for her day. She was born in 1858 the second of three children of millionaire banker Francis A. Drexel. Katharine and her two sisters, Elizabeth and Louise, were raised in an environment of family prayer and Catholic precepts. Upon the death of their father in 1885, the three Drexel sisters inherited approximately $14 million. Such wealth would cause most to shy away from the difficult decisions of life; such was not the case with Katharine Drexel.

The Drexel sisters were true philanthropists. Many associations and foundations, including the endowment of a chair of moral theology at The Catholic University of America, benefited from their contributions. It was the Native American missions, however, which captured their attention. The "Peace Policy" of President Ulysses Grant, an effort to bring education to Indians, was by 1882 an avowed failure. Bishop Martin Marty of the Dakota territory and Father Joseph Stephan, Director of the Bureau of Catholic Indian Affairs, asked the Drexel sisters for economic assistance for the Indian missions.

In September 1887 the three sisters visited the Dakota territory and experienced there the work of the Sisters of Mercy. This visit prompted the Drexel sisters to act. By 1907 Katharine, Elizabeth, and Louise Drexel had contributed over $1.5 million to the Indian missions. This work was quietly accomplished; few people knew of their generosity.

Katharine Drexel desired a more personal involvement with the Native American missions. She corresponded throughout the 1880s with Father (later Bishop of Omaha) James O'Connor, who served as an important spiritual guide for her. She wrote to her mentor, "I want [to establish] a missionary order for Indians and Colored people." O'Connor cautioned her to be patient – "think, pray, wait" was his advice to her. Katharine pressed her desire, however, and thus in December 1888 the bishop recommended Katharine to the Sisters of Mercy who, he felt, could provide the most helpful novitiate experience for her future needs. He further recommended that her proposed order serve both Negroes and Indians (the terms of the day), "as a much more direct and economical use of your money than an Indian bureau alone."

Katharine became a postulant for the Sisters of Mercy in May 1889. Her associates were unexpectedly struck with the spirit of poverty which this millionaire heiress possessed. Six months later, on November 7, 1889, Katharine formally received the habit and, after the completion of her canonical year as a novice, made her profession as the first Sister of the Blessed Sacrament for Indians and Colored People (today Sisters of the Blessed Sacrament) on February 12, 1891.

Katharine had three principal goals in her new life as a religious. First, she wanted to experience personal growth in the love of God. Second, she sought to deepen her understanding of religious life as practiced in the Church. Lastly, she planned to aid the Native and African American people of America by disbursement of her inherited fortune. Katharine Drexel combined these concerns in her lived experience as a religious and missionary.

The Blessed Sacrament Sisters began with thirteen members who followed Katharine from the Mercy Sisters' novitiate. Archbishop Patrick Ryan of Philadelphia, who served as a second spiritual father to Katharine after the death of Bishop O'Connor in 1890, authorized a new habit for the community which included the Benedictine scapular and the Franciscan cord. The community was based temporarily in the Drexel country manor in Torresdale, Pennsylvania until a permanent motherhouse could be constructed at Cornwells Heights.

Mother Katharine lost no time in putting her plans into action. As mentioned above she had economically supported the American Indian community prior to the foundation of her community. Her monetary contribution was responsible for the construction of St. Catherine's School for the Pueblo Indians of the New Mexico territory. With the blessing of Archbishop Ryan, Drexel began her first mission when she sent nine sisters to St. Catherine's in June 1894. Katharine visited this mission in September and was pleased with the initial results.

In July 1894 plans for the second mission of the Blessed Sacrament Sisters were started. Katharine purchased a 600-acre former plantation in Rock Castle, Virginia. There St. Francis de Sales

School was built and made ready for students in 1899. Started as an industrial and normal school, it emerged in the early twentieth century as a fully accredited high school for girls.

As the twentieth century dawned the Congregation's mission to the Indian population of America continued to expand. In 1902 Mother Katharine offered to staff St. Michael's School which served the Navajo nation in Arizona. Twelve Sisters were sent in October. The charm of the sisters created a feeling of confident assurance among the Indians. Within a short amount of time the maximum complement of 150 students was enrolled.

The Congregation's ministry to America's Black Catholic community began in 1904. Bishop Thomas Byrne of Nashville asked Mother Katharine to open a school for Blacks in his diocese. Initially Drexel offered money for the construction of a school with hopes that another community could staff it. Bishop Byrne, however, persisted in his request and in the end, Katharine agreed to help. Much agitation was present when the local citizens of Nashville learned that a school for Black girls was planned. Nevertheless, Drexel went forward with her plans. The school, Immaculate Mother, opened on September 5, 1905, with 28 students. By the end of the first academic year the enrollment had swelled to over one hundred.

Outreach to the Black community expanded greatly in the next decade. Invitations were extended to start schools in Columbus, Ohio, New York, and Chicago. In 1912 Mother Katharine, in her usual thorough style, supervised the establishment of institutions in all three cities. In 1913 the community established a school in Boston at the invitation of Cardinal William O'Connell.

The arrival of the Congregation in Louisiana in 1915 proved to be, in the opinion of Drexel's biographer, Sr. Consuela Duffy, "the crowning point of all endeavors of the Sisters of the Blessed Sacrament." The catalyst which brought the sisters to New Orleans was the possibility of opening a school of higher education for Black

Catholics. Mother Katharine purchased the land and buildings in the city when Southern University vacated the premises and moved outside of Baton Rouge. The existing facility was reopened as Xavier University. Initially planned as a school for grades 7-10, an 11th grade was quickly added. By 1925 Xavier had been established as a college of liberal arts and sciences. In addition to Xavier, the 1920s saw the establishment of many rural schools for Blacks throughout the state, all funded by Mother Katharine.

As the work of the community expanded so too the energy needed to control community affairs grew. Mother Katharine, who normally maintained a tortuous schedule, was forced in 1937 to yield control to others. A series of minor heart attacks forced her to retire to the Motherhouse. In a reversal of roles Mother Mercedes was elected the new Superior General of the Community and Katharine was elected her vicar.

Katharine Drexel spent almost twenty years in retirement before she returned to God. During this period, she spent long hours in prayer with special devotion to the Blessed Sacrament, a tradition that had been part of her faith practice since she was a child. In 1941 the community celebrated its golden jubilee. Mother Katharine was honored at that time with the first honorary doctorate ever awarded to a woman by The Catholic University of America. After a long life of service to God and God's people, Katharine Drexel died on March 3, 1955. The *Catholic Standard and Times* of Philadelphia described her as "one of the most remarkable women in the history of America." Recognition of Katharine Drexel's contribution and holiness was made when she was beatified by Pope John Paul II on November 20, 1988. She was canonized by Pope St. John Paul II on October 1, 2000. The Church celebrates her life on the anniversary of her death.

The work and dreams of St. Katharine Drexel continue today. More than 300 professed Sisters of the Blessed Sacrament minister in 14 dioceses in the United States and in Haiti. The community still operates St. Catherine's in Santa Fe, St. Michael's in Arizona, and Xavier Prep in New Orleans. The Congregation's dedication to the intellectual and moral preparation of Native Americans and Blacks continues as its primary apostolate. St. Katharine Drexel's charism and model continues to serve as an example for all who minister for the betterment and equality of all God's children.

Radical and Conservative: The Paradox of Dorothy Day

Christianity speaks of the paradox of the cross. How could Jesus find life for us through his own death? Paradoxes are discovered in some of the most unexpected places. Such an example exists in the life of Dorothy Day, social radical and conservative Catholic. How was it possible for the founder of the Catholic Worker Movement, described by the historian Mel Piehl as, "the first major expression of radical social criticism in American Catholicism," to be at the same time unmoved by progressive thought in liturgy, doctrine and ecclesiology? The answers are found in the paradox of Dorothy Day, a woman many claim to be the premier twentieth century American saint.

Dorothy Day's early life could be described as time in isolation. She was born on November 8, 1897, into a Brooklyn family of modest means. Her father's occupation as a newspaper sportswriter caused the family to move frequently. Eventually, the Day family settled in Chicago; she matured during the Progressive Era. Although middle class, she witnessed the pain of poverty around her and read about same in the novels of Upton Sinclair. Her social awareness grew as she read and became familiar with the sermons of John Wesley and Jonathan Edwards and the writings of St. Augustine.

From childhood, Day was an avid reader and a gifted writer. Her talent was rewarded by the Hearst newspaper chain with a scholarship to the University of Illinois. She spent two years in school. While there she worked service-related jobs, refusing better paying and less menial tasks. She wrote for the school newspaper, contributing editorials supporting the efforts of social progressives and radicals. At Illinois, she remained aloof from most, associating with a few avant-garde literary types. She began to question Christianity (she had been raised in a house indifferent to religion), seeing religion in general as a sign of weakness that seemed inconsistent with the problems she saw all around her. However, classes and the academic routine became lifeless and inimical to Day.

Departing the University after her sophomore year, Day moved to New York City and quickly blended in with the pre-World War I radical element. New York radicals rejected bourgeois society while advocating an experimental approach to life expressing freedom and the wholeness of human existence. Consistent with her beliefs and skills she found work as a reporter for the *New York Call* (a Socialist daily) and later *The Masses*, another radical periodical. In her job Day covered strikes, the peace movement, and numerous anarchist groups. She was able to meet many well-known radicals of her day. As World War I approached, she began to work in the non-conscription league. All these positions left her with a vivid mental picture of the dark side of life.

The 1920s for Dorothy Day ran opposite to the euphoria of the period. She moved from job to job and from relationship to another. Day continued to write for radical papers which brought her in contact with many journalists. She began a steamy love affair with one, Lionel Moise. She became pregnant and in 1919 obtained an abortion. In 1920 she married Barkeley Tober, a literary promoter. The union was annulled in the summer of 1921. Later she moved to Chicago to rekindle her relationship with Moise, but nothing materialized.

In 1923 Day found regular work in New Orleans. While there an autobiographical novel she had written, *The Eleventh Virgin,* was published. Royalties from the book and eventual movie rights provided her with the resources to move back to New York. In 1926, she bought a cottage on Staten Island and began a common law marriage with Forster Batterham. On March 3, 1927, a daughter, Tamar Teresa, was born.

The birth of her only child provided the catalyst Day needed to find conversion in her life. She had her daughter baptized into the Catholic faith in July 1927. This bold move so greatly angered Batterham that he abandoned both mother and daughter. The story of Day's conversion is complicated. One cannot adequately explain her mindset without a detailed analysis. Her autobiography, *The Long Loneliness*, fully describes this significant step in her life. It can be said that Day had discarded both her earlier notion of Christianity's weakness and the socialist idea of religion's placebo effect on society. Dorothy Day followed her daughter and was baptized on December 28, 1927. She had produced family and discovered faith, only a cause remained to make her life complete.

As fate would have it her cause, her life's work, was not far off. After a series of jobs which required her to move to Los Angeles and then Mexico City, Day again found herself living in New York as a reporter. While in Washington, D.C. covering a political march, she went to the Shrine of the Immaculate Conception. She prayed that some way would open for her to use her God-given talents for fellow workers and the poor. The answer she sought was awaiting her return to New York.

In December 1932, only days after Dorothy's visit to the Shrine, she received a visitor to her apartment. Michael Williams and George Shuster, associated with *Commonweal*, sent Peter Maurin, a Frenchman who embodied personal poverty and radical ideas, to Day's residence. Dorothy was impressed with Maurin and his ideas. The team became the foundation of the Catholic Worker Movement. Maurin supplied the ideas; Day brought the energy, know-how, and organization.

Maurin proposed a three-point plan or program of action to serve the hungering masses. Round table discussions to find solutions for today's problems were necessary. Houses of hospitality were required to provide shelter and food for those in need. Farming communes needed to be established to return society to the land. These three ideas together with the publication of the *Catholic Worker* monthly became the Catholic Worker Movement. Dorothy Day spent her final 47 years in service to this radical Gospel call.

The precepts and lived experience of the Catholic Worker Movement were a radical response to Jesus' message of discipleship, service, and love. In 1936, with the nation mired in the depths of the Great Depression, the houses of hospitality began on Mott Street in New York. This facility and many that followed offered shelter, food, and used clothing to all that could be accommodated. By 1941, 32 houses in 27 cities had been established. The farming communes, as envisioned by Maurin, operated on the concept of subsistence, not profit.Manual work was required of all, but only four hours per day; the rest of the day was spent in reading and discussion. The first farm opened near Easton, Pennsylvania in 1936. Others followed but all eventually failed, victims to internal dissension and societal pressures.

The most visible and definable characteristic of the Catholic Worker Movement and its founders, Day and Maurin, was voluntary poverty. Peter Maurin once wrote, "It is inconceivable that one can truly be 'religious' and not embrace voluntary poverty." Workers at the houses of hospitality lived spartan lives, sacrificing some of their meager possessions so that others could have something.

The Catholic Worker Movement and the efforts of Dorothy Day are known to most through the *Catholic Worker* newspaper. The first issue, published on a shoe-string budget (as it always seemingly was), hit the streets of New York on May 1, 1933. It was published, "For those who are sitting on park benches in the warm spring sunlight. For those who are huddling in shelters trying to escape the rain. For those who are walking the streets in all but futile search for work. For those who think that there is no hope for the future, no recognition of their plight." Day designed the paper to appeal to a diverse constituency including the alienated poor, religious leaders, and lay Catholics interested in social change.

The *Catholic Worker*, which was published for analysis and advocacy over news, increased in circulation rapidly. The first issue printed 2,500 copies. By 1935 circulation was up to 65,000; by 1940 185,000 copies were being printed. Day sent courtesy copies to editors, bishops, and influential clerics to expand the paper's popularity and distribution.

Day's importance to the *Catholic Worker* was primarily as an editor and journalist. During the 1930s she personally edited each issue, except when traveling. In the 1940s and thereafter she relied on a series of managing editors, but she never relinquished control. This is evidenced by her rejection of an editorial in 1952 which supported Adlai Stevenson for president, in violation of her editorial policy against political endorsements. Day's popular column, "Day by Day," later changed to "On Pilgrimage," was a highlight of each issue. In these columns Day was highly influenced by the French periodical *L'Esprit* and the novels of Fyodor Dostoyevsky.

Dorothy Day possessed a complex personality. She was a visionary, public dissenter, spiritual writer, and conservative Catholic; Dorothy Day was a paradox. In her expression of Christianity, Day found Catholicism mystical, liturgical, sacramental, and ecclesiastical. Her approach to practicing her faith was unswervingly orthodox. Within the confines of Catholic belief and practice Day found her vocation in challenging the State, through legislation, and the Church, through social action, to become more radical in the service of society.

Dorothy Day's spirituality was consistent with her radical and socialist background. She sought to integrate her Catholicism and her Americanism on the level of the individual. She stressed, in contrast to the great social advocate John A. Ryan, the convergence, not the separation (common theological understanding) between nature (the world) and grace (the Catholic faith). Day labored unceasingly in her practice of love through a combination of uncompromising Catholicism and equally strong advocacy of social reform. She found models of a similar spiritual approach in the lives of Saints Teresa of Avila and Therese of Lisieux.

Dorothy Day, although a progressive for social action saw no merit in progressive theological thought. The stirrings for change as advocated by Virgil Michel in liturgy and John Courtney Murray in Church/State relations did not interest Day. She found the changes of Vatican II difficult to integrate into her understanding of the Church. Throughout her lifetime, Day paid deference to the hierarchy. [She was once quoted as saying, "[I]f Cardinal Spellman ordered me to close down the *Catholic Worker* tomorrow, I would." Such submission coupled with such active advocacy demonstrates the complex personality Day possessed.

Dorothy Day's spiritual journey was highly influenced by John Hugo. From 1941-1976 she attended numerous retreats that Hugo directed. The Hugo retreat consisted of a week of absolute silence, meditation, and spiritual exercises. This was a liberating spiritual experience for Day. It was an encounter with the radically inward Christianity she had only previously experienced in books. These opportunities for reflection gave Dorothy greater perspective on sanctity and social radicalism. Those who knew Dorothy Day best said the Hugo retreats provided the great social activist with her spiritual *metanoia*.

The radical Gospel which Dorothy Day preached was manifest most strongly in her absolute pacifism. While on the lecture circuit in the 1930s she encouraged people to "work and pray for peace." Her views were Scripturally based referencing Matthew 5:38-39 and Luke 6:27-29. The first major test for Day's pacifist stand was the Civil War, 1936-1939. She and the *Catholic Worker* refused to take sides in the affair. Day's belief was simply stated, "We must stand opposed to the use of force. ... There is the 'better way' - the way of the Saints - the way of love."

Day's refusal to modify her pacifist belief created friction and eventually losses in the Movement. In several houses of hospitality, the staff refused to fall in line with Day's 1940 edict asserting the centrality of pacifism to the Catholic Worker charism. In Chicago, John Cogley broke with Day over this issue. His exodus precipitated others. By the end of 1942 only 16 houses of hospitality remained. By 1945 only 10 houses were in operation. *Catholic Worker* subscriptions declined by 100,000. Certainly, other factors contributed to this reduction in Catholic Worker presence, but the pacifism issue, especially in the highly charged and emotional period of World War II, was a major catalyst to the decline.

The pacifism issue lay dormant for some 15 years until the onset of the Vietnam War. In the 1960s Day again began to become vocal in her pacifist stance. She joined forces with A.J. Muste, the leading American figure in twentieth century pacifism, in opposition to the war and to armed resistance. In this decade Day was granted a greater hearing as society in general questioned the morality of America's presence in Southeast Asia. Catholic Worker presence was small numerically on the protest line, but Mel Piel has stated, "Day and her followers exercised an influence far out of proportion to their numbers or political importance." Dorothy Day did what she felt was necessary and did not worry about the consequences.

Paradoxes exist to confuse the mind and amaze the unbeliever. At first glance one might conclude that Dorothy Day exercised a radicalism which was unchecked in its forcefulness. There is no doubt that Day and the Catholic Worker Movement, which she guided for 47 years, advocated a radical understanding of the Gospel dictate to love. A deeper view of this contemporary saint, however, reveals the paradox of a women with unswerving devotion and loyalty to Roman Catholicism, its doctrine, ecclesiology, sacramentality, and spirituality. God sends the world people who challenge us to look beyond our present state, asking what could be. Dorothy Day was sent to challenge our world to love more deeply and fully. May we be worthy of our call.